# THE MUSIC OF SOUTH ASIA

An Institutionally Appropriate
Approach to the Classical Music of India,
Bangladesh, and Pakistan

# THE MUSIC OF SOUTH ASIA

An Institutionally Appropriate Approach to the Classical Music of India, Bangladesh, and Pakistan

First Edition

by

David Courtney

and

Chandrakantha Courtney

Houston, TX

2015

ISBN  978-1-893644-10-6
      (1-893644-10-3)

© 2015 David & Chandra Courtney

Sur Sangeet Services, Houston, TX

David and Chandrakantha
11130 Cedarhurst Dr.
Houston, TX 77096

# CONTENTS

| | |
|---|---|
| Preface | vii |
| Ch. 1. Introduction | 1 |
| Ch. 2. Melodic Fundamentals | 7 |
| Ch. 3. Fundamentals of Tal | 19 |
| Ch. 4. Instrumental Music & Dance | 27 |
| Ch. 5. Vocal Styles | 59 |
| Ch. 6. Language | 67 |
| Ch. 7. Bilawal That | 79 |
| Ch. 8. Kalyan That | 89 |
| Ch. 9. Khammaj That | 105 |
| Ch. 10. Kafi That | 115 |
| Ch. 11. Asawari That | 131 |
| Ch. 12. Bhairav That | 145 |
| Ch. 13. Bhairavi That | 159 |
| Ch. 14. Purvi That | 173 |
| Ch. 15. Marwa That | 185 |
| Ch. 16. Todi That | 195 |
| Ch. 17. Conclusion | 207 |

| | |
|---|---|
| Appendix 1. Common Thats in the Key of C | 211 |
| Appendix 2. Common Thats in the Key of C# | 215 |
| Appendix 3. Common Thats in the Key of D | 219 |
| Appendix 4. Common Thats in the Key of D# | 223 |
| Appendix 5. Common Thats in the Key of E | 227 |
| Appendix 6. Common Thats in the Key of F | 231 |
| Appendix 7. Common Thats in the Key of F# | 235 |
| Appendix 8. Common Thats in the Key of G | 239 |
| Appendix 9. Common Thats in the Key of G# | 243 |
| Appendix 10. Common Thats in the Key of A | 247 |
| Appendix 11. Common Thats in the Key of A# | 251 |
| Appendix 12. Common Thats in the Key of B | 255 |
| Appendix 13. Sample Questions | 259 |
| Glossary | 273 |
| Bibliography | 299 |
| Index | 305 |

# PREFACE

This book is about *Hindustani Sangeet*. This is the system of classical music which is found throughout Northern India, Pakistan, Bangladesh, Nepal, and even into Afghanistan. This book is a greatly edited version of *Elementary North Indian Vocal*.

Why?

OK, it's time to address the elephant standing in the room. We are in the middle of a cultural war, and the schools are on the front lines of this war. As public school educator, you know this. There is pressure to teach American history with material that seems to be derived from old John Wayne movies. Biology classes are supposed to give equal time to nonsensical "theories" as to the origins of life, and general education is being replaced with test coaching.

But you are desperately trying to educate within this hostile environment. This means opening your student's minds to things that are beyond their daily experience, and beyond the narrow dictates of mandated curricula.

You are holding this book in your hand because you wish to expose your students to the music of South Asia. You may have looked at all of the other material and found that so much of it had a strong religious orientation. This is the nature of the subcontinent and its art forms. But are you willing to be taken before the school board to have to explain it to them? Probably not.

This book follows a strongly secularly approach to the subject. It does not dwell upon Ram, Krishna, Allah, Ali, or any other religious figure.

Furthermore, there are no maps in this book. The intensity of feelings concerning disputed territories is great. It would be very difficult to include a map and not have angry parents reproaching you.

Do these things distort the the subject? That is hard to say. Everything in this book is correct, but it is arguable that the color has changed due to the omissions.

But this is material that you can give to your students, and not have to worry about irritate parents lodging formal complaints. It is politically safe, yet it does not get bogged down in the morass of American lysenkoism.

The theoretical foundation for this work is based upon Bhatkhande's system. This is a nearly universal convention. However, for a variety of musical and pedagogical reasons we may deviate from a strictly Bhatkhandean approach. We do not feel it necessary to note every deviation.

Peace

David Courtney

July 2, 2015

# CHAPTER 1.
# INTRODUCTION

The North Indian system of classical music is called *Hindustani Sangeet*. It is the classical system of Northern India, Pakistan, Bangladesh, and even much of Afghanistan. It is a vast and complex system of music.

We can begin our discussion with the concept of *sangeet*. This is generally considered to be synonymous with "classical music"; however, it is actually the threefold art form of vocal music, instrumental music, and dance. Since classical dance is also a component, *sangeet* is not strictly synonymous to the Western term "music". In this work, we will concentrate only upon the musical aspect and say very little about dance.

# HISTORY

There are many milestones in the evolution of South Asian music. These milestones give an indication of the development of musical concepts from its inception to the present day.

The early prehistory may be explained by the Indo-European theory. According to this theory, there was a culture, or group of cultures, who were so successful that they spread throughout Europe and parts of Asia. Although no one knows where they came from, present thought tends to place their origins somewhere in Eurasia, either north of the Black Sea or north of the Caspian (Mallory 1989). The classical music of India is said to have its roots in this culture.

The connection between Indo-European expansion and Indian music may be seen in mythology. Myths refer to music being brought to the people of India from a place of celestial beings. This mythical land (*Gandharva Desh*) is usually equated with heaven. However, some are of the opinion that this mythical land could actually be Kandahar in what is the modern Afghanistan. Therefore, the myths of music being given to the world by celestial beings (*gandharva*) may actually represent a cultural connection with this ancient homeland.

Further evidence may be seen in musical structure. In the first few centuries B.C.E., South Asian music was based upon seven modes (scales). It is probably no coincidence that Greek music was also based upon seven modes. Furthermore, the South Asian scales follow the same process of modulation (*murchana*) that is found in ancient Greek music.

The link to Sanskrit is another strong indication of Indo-European roots. Many of the earliest texts were written in Sanskrit. It is also generally believed that classical music is derived from the Samveda. However, this belief is difficult to justify because intermediate forms have never been found.

In the final analysis, the roots of classical music being Indo-European are a reflection of modern paradigms concerning ancient Indian history. Although supporting evidence may be slim, conflicting evidence is absence. Until we are faced with significant conflicting evidence we should accept the Indo-European theory.

The nature of music in prehistoric South Asia may be obscure, but the picture begins to become clear in the first few centuries B.C.E. Bharata's *Natya-Shastra* (circa 200 B.C.E.), provides a detailed account of stagecraft in that period. Here we find mention of seven *shuddha jati* (pure modes) and eleven mixed *jatis* (modal forms not produced by simple modulation). There is also a very detailed discussion of the musical instruments.

The *Brihaddeshi* written by Matanga (circa 700 C.E.) is another major milestone in the development of Indian music. It is in this work that we first find the word "*rag*" mentioned. However, there is some doubt whether the concept is the same as it is today.

The *Sangeet Ratnakar* by Sharangdev is another treatise on Indian music. This work, written around the thirteenth century C.E., gives extensive commentaries about numerous musical styles that existed at that time.

Perhaps one of the most significant milestones in the development of Indian music was the life of Amir Khusru (Bhatkhande 1934). Although the extent of his contribution to Indian music is more legendary than factual, he nevertheless symbolizes a crucial turning point in the development of Indian music. Amir Khusru is an icon representing a growing Persian influence on the music. This influence was felt to a greater extent in the North than in the South. The consequence of this differing degree of influence ultimately resulted in the bifurcation of South Asian music into two distinct systems; the *Hindustani sangeet* of the North and the *Carnatic sangeet* of the South.

The musical career of Tansen is another landmark in the development of Indian Music (Mital 1960). He is significant because he symbolizes the maturing of the Hindustani system as a distinct entity from south Indian music.

The early part of the 20th century brings the most recent innovations to north Indian music. This is due to the work of two people: V. N. Bhatkhande and V. D, Paluskar. These two men revolutionized the concept of Indian music. Paluskar is responsible for the introduction of the first music colleges while Bhatkhande is responsible for the introduction of an organized system which reflects current performance practice.

## PRESENT MUSICAL SYSTEMS

Today, there are two systems of South Asian music. One system is found in Northern India, Pakistan, and Bangladesh. This system is called *Hindustani sangeet*. The second system is found in Southern India. This system is called *Carnatic sangeet*. These two systems are both based upon similar concepts of *rag* and *tal* (rhythm). They both are said to be derived from the *Vedic* tradition. However, they differ in terms of theory, nomenclature, and performance.

The *Hindustani* (Northern) system may be thought of as a mixture of traditional Hindu musical concepts and Persian performance practice. The advent of Islamic rule over Northern India caused the musicians to seek patronage in the courts of the new rulers. These rulers, often of foreign extraction, had strong cultural and religious sentiments focused outside of India. Yet they lived in, and administered kingdoms which retained their traditional Hindu culture. Several centuries of this arrangement caused the Hindu music to absorb a Persian character. The *Carnatic* (Southern) system was relatively immune to the cultural impact of the Islamic invaders. South Indian musicians still enjoyed the patronage of the temples and Hindu rulers. Therefore, the south Indian system evolved along different lines from its northern counterpart. In some ways the south Indian system is closer to the older forms.

It is helpful for us to summarize the important points of this chapter. We have seen that there are differences between the Northern and the Southern systems of music. The Northern system evolved under cultural pressure from Persia and eventually acquired a different character from the Southern system.

There are numerous aspects of theory and practice in South Asian music. We have seen in this chapter that it is part of one of the oldest musical traditions in the world. As such, it is inextricably linked to the ancient stagecraft. Therefore, the traditional word for music does not restrict itself to melodic forms, but also encompasses the classical dance. The three aspects of *sangeet* will be discussed in greater detail in the coming chapters.

## WORKS CITED

Bhatkhande, Vishnu Narayan
1934 *A Short History of the Music of Upper India*. Bombay, India: (reprinted in 1974 by Indian Musicological Society, Baroda).

Courtney, D.R.
1980 *Introduction to Tabla*. Hyderabad, India: Anand Power Press.

Garg, Lakshminarayan
1984 *Hamare Sangeet-Ratna*. Hathras, India: Sangeet Press.

Mallory, J.P.
1989 *In Search of the Indo-Europeans; Language Archaeology and Myth*. London: Thames and Hudson Ltd.

Mital, Prabhudayal
1960 *Sangeet Samrat: Tansen: Jivani aur Rachanaen*. Mathura, India: Sahitya Samsthan

Rangacharya Adya
1966 *Introduction to Bharata's Natya-Sastra*. Bombay, India: Popular Prakashan.

Shankar, Ravi
1968 *Ravi Shankar: My Music, My Life*. New Delhi, India: Vikas Publishing House Pvt. Ltd.

# CHAPTER 2.
# MELODIC FUNDAMENTALS

There are certain melodic fundamentals which we must mastered. There are definite structures and rules. We must understand these rules so we can form a proper conceptual framework.

# SWAR

The *swar* is a convenient place to begin. *Swar* is nothing more than the seven notes of the South Asian musical scale. At a fundamental level they are similar to the *sol-fa* of Western music. These are shown in Table 2.1.

Table 2.1. The Seven Swar

| | |
|---|---|
| Shadaj | Sa |
| Rishabh | Re |
| Gandhar | Ga |
| Madhyam | Ma |
| Pancham | Pa |
| Dhaivat | Dha |
| Nishad | Ni |

Two of these *swar* are noteworthy in that they are immutably fixed. These two notes are *shadaj* (Sa) and *pancham* (Pa), and are referred to as *achalla swar*. These two *swar* form the tonic foundation for all Indian classical music.

The other notes are not fixed, for they have alternate forms. The notes; *rishabh* (*Re*), *gandhar* (*Ga*), *dhaivat* (*Dha*), and *nishad* (*Ni*), may be either natural (*shuddha*) or flattened (*komal*). *Madhyam* (*Ma*) is unique in that its alternate form is augmented or sharp. This note is called *tivra madhyam*. Therefore, we find that we are actually dealing with 12 *swar*. This extended concept is shown in Table 2.2.

### Table 2.2 Extended Scale

| Shadaj | Sa |
| Komal Rishabh | R̲e̲ |
| Shuddha Rishabh | Re |
| Komal Gandhar | G̲a̲ |
| Shuddha Gandhar | Ga |
| Shuddha Madhyam | Ma |
| Tivra Madhyam | M'a |
| Pancham | Pa |
| Komal Dhaivat | D̲h̲a̲ |
| Shuddha Dhaivat | Dha |
| Komal Nishad | N̲i̲ |
| Shuddha Nishad | Ni |

These are roughly comparable to the keys on a harmonium, or piano (chromatic scale).

This brings us to the topic of musical notation. One may have noticed that the natural notes (*shuddha swar*) do not have any marks while the alternate notes do. The *komal* notes (i.e., *Re, Ga, Dha, Ni*) are denoted by a line underneath. The *tivra ma* (augmented fourth) is denoted by a vertical line over it. This is a convenient, intuitive approach to the notation.

# THAT

The concept of *that* is essentially the same as the Western concept of mode. It has already been pointed out that several of the *swars* have alternate forms. The permutations of these various forms give rise to numerous scales with vastly differing intervals. A simple mathematical approach tells us that there are 32 seven-note combinations of the *swar*. However, only ten are conventionally accepted as *thats* (Jairazhhoy 1971).

The ten *thats* are:

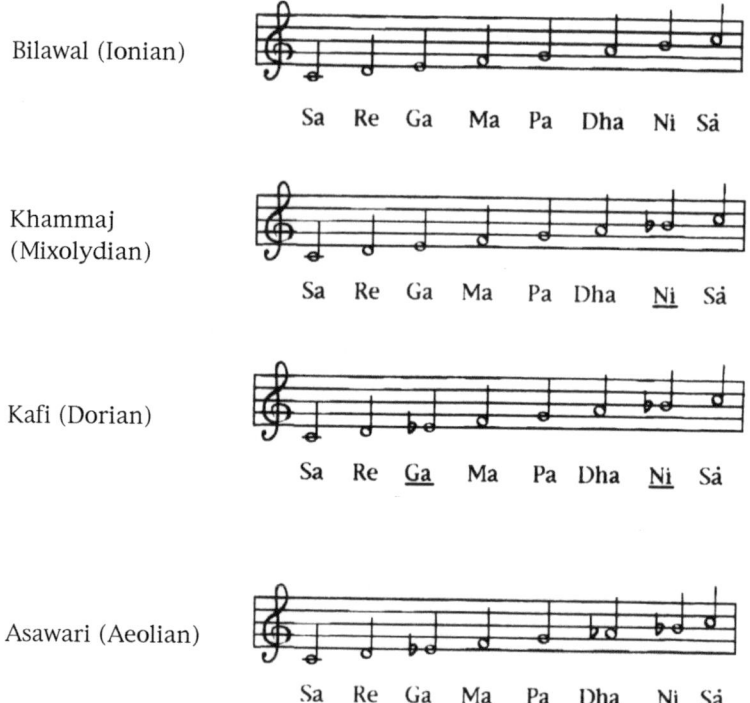

Bilawal (Ionian)

Sa  Re  Ga  Ma  Pa  Dha  Ni  Sá

Khammaj (Mixolydian)

Sa  Re  Ga  Ma  Pa  Dha  <u>Ni</u>  Sá

Kafi (Dorian)

Sa  Re  <u>Ga</u>  Ma  Pa  Dha  <u>Ni</u>  Sá

Asawari (Aeolian)

Sa  Re  <u>Ga</u>  Ma  Pa  <u>Dha</u>  <u>Ni</u>  Sá

Problems arise when one is talking about the number of *thats*. Historically, only 10 were acknowledged; 20 are in common usage; and 32 are possible given present concepts of scale construction. This has created a certain amount of confusion in north Indian pedagogy.

# SAPTAK

The *saptak* may be directly translated to mean octave; as such it has two common definitions. The most fundamental definition is of the South Asian gamut (i.e., the seven *swar*) (Shankar 1968). This is shown in expressions such as *shuddha swar saptak* (natural scale).

However, a more common definition is the register (Table 2.3). The middle register is referred to as *madhya saptak*; the upper register is referred to as *tar saptak*; and the lower register is referred to as *mandra saptak*. Additionally, two octaves above the middle is called *ati-tar saptak*; three octaves is called *ati-ati-tar saptak*, etc. In a similar manner, two octaves below is called *ati-mandra saptak*, three octaves below is called *ati-ati-mandra saptak*, etc.

Table 2.3 The South Asian Registers

| | |
|---|---|
| Ati-ati-tar-saptak | Three octaves above middle |
| Ati-tar-saptak | Two octaves above middle |
| Tar-saptak | Upper octave |
| Madhya-saptak | Middle octave |
| Mandra-saptak | Lower octave |
| Ati-mandra-saptak | Two octaves below middle |
| Ati-ati-mandra-saptak | Three octaves below middle |

The register is indicated by a dot. The dot over a *swar* indicates that it is *tar saptak*, and two dots over the *swar* indicate that it is *ati-tar saptak*. Conversely, a dot below indicates that it is *mandra saptak*, and two dots below indicate that the *swar* is *ati-mandra saptak*, etc.

# RAG

The *rag* is the most important concept that any student of music should understand. Unfortunately, it is not easy to describe what a *rag* actually is. It is not a tune, melody, scale, mode, or any concept for which an English word exists. It is instead a combination of different characteristics.

One of the sources of confusion is that the *rag* may be defined at different levels. There are cases where a *that* has only a single *rag* in it. In such cases the modality is sufficient to define the *rag*. However, most *thats* have several *rags* in them; therefore, we must look to increasingly subtle levels to make the distinctions.

JATI - The *jati* is one such level. *Jati* is the number of notes in the *rag*; for not every one uses all seven notes. Normally, a *rag* will consist of either five, six, or a full seven notes. A five-note *rag* is said to be an *audav jati*; a six note *rag* is said to be *shadav jati*; and one of seven notes is said to be *sampurna jati*. Furthermore, *rags* may have different *jatis* for the ascending and the descending structures. For instance, a *rag* which has only five notes in the ascending, but all seven notes in the descending would be called *audav-sampurna*.

We now have two levels that may be used to define the *rag*. We have the *jati* and the *that*. These two characteristics are sufficient to define a few *rags*. Yet, this is not sufficient to define them all, we need a further level of distinction.

AROHANA / AVAROHANA - *Arohana* and *avarohana* are further levels of definition. The *arohana*, also called *aroh*, is the pattern in which a *rag* ascends the scale. The *avarohan*, also called *avaroh*, describes the way that the *rag* descends the scale.

Both the *arohana* and *avarohana* may use certain characteristic twists and turns. Such prescribed twists are referred to as *vakra*. Furthermore, notes may have different levels of significance. Notes may be strong or weak.

**VADI / SAMAVADI** - The fact that the notes may have a different level of significance is very important. The note which is strongly emphasized is referred to as the *vadi*. Another note which is strong but only slightly less so, is the *samavadi*. A note which is neither emphasized nor deemphasised is called *anuvadi*. Notes which are deemphasised are referred to as being *durbal*, while notes which are excluded are called *vivadi*[1].

The concept of *vadi* and *samavadi* are particularly problematic for the music student. Although certain notes clearly show importance, the "official" *vadi* and *samavadi* are sometimes different. In many cases, this reflects the fact that the theory was laid down quite a few years ago, while the performance of the *rags* continued to evolve. In other cases it reflects Bhatkhande's failed efforts to develop a cohesive time theory about the structure of *rags*.

**PAKAD** - Implicit in the *arohana/ avarohana* is the *pakad*. This is a defining phrase or a characteristic pattern for a *rag*. Not every *rag* has a clear *pakad*, but a large number require one to distinguish them from related ones. Pakad is sometimes called swarup.

When we examine all of these points, these are the characteristics which make the *rag*. Collectively, the *vadi, samavadi, that, jati, pakad*, etc., define a *rag*.

**OTHER CONCEPTS** - There are a few other characteristics which should be mentioned. Although these do not have the same level of importance they still should be kept in mind.

The *samay* or time is one such quality. Tradition ascribes certain *rags* to particular times of the day, seasons, or holidays. It is said that appropriate performance may bring harmony, while playing at different times may bring disharmony. Stories are even told of musicians who were able to create rain by singing a monsoon *rag*.

There is not a universal agreement as to the correctness of *samay*. There are some musicians who argue that a *rag* must be performed at the time of day that it is assigned; conversely, other musicians argue that one may play a *rag* at anytime if one wishes to evoke the mood of that time. For instance, if one simply wished to evoke the mood of a monsoon day, one could perform *Megh Malhar*, even in the middle of summer. The concept of *samay* is complicated by the fact that there are a number of *rags* that have different times ascribed by different musical traditions. This question is further complicated by an absence of any scientific process to determine *samay*. The great musicologist Bhatkhande attempted to develop a theory of *samay* which could be explained in terms of the structure. Unfortunately, his system must be considered a failure.

If one is disposed to follow the system of *samay*, one can only accept that it is merely a question of tradition. Attempts to justify the concept by looking at the internal structure of the *rag* have failed.

The concept of time is further weakened by the influx of *rags* from South India. Many years ago, Carnatic musicians and musicologists abandoned the concept of *samay*. It seems that it did not fit into their rational, scientific system. The result is that when Carnatic *rags* enter the *Hindustani* system, they come stripped of any conventionally accepted timings.

The concept of "families" of *rags* is another characteristic worthy of note. It was briefly mentioned that *rags* were ascribed to certain demigods. A natural consequence of such anthropomorphism is that there should be a familial relationship between them. Therefore in the past few centuries, there arose a complicated system of *rags* (male *rags*), *raginis* (female *rags*), *putra rags* (sons of *rags*), etc. (Kripalvanand 1972). This was the basis for a system of classification before the advent of modern musicology. Although this may have been a great inspiration to the painters of the old *ragmala* tradition, it proved to be worthless as a means of taxonomy. The obvious problem was that there was no way to accommodate the new *rags* that were coming into existence.

Ornamentation is essential to proper performance. When one hears Indian music, it is the ornaments which first make an impression. However, this is often a confusing subject. The concept of an ornament implies a technique which is used for artistic reason yet not necessarily of theoretical importance. This is usually the case; however, there are many instances where such ornamentation is a defining characteristic of the *rag*.

Here are some common ornaments. *Meend* is the the most common; it is a slide or *glissando*. *Andolan* is another common ornament; this may be described as a slow vibrato. *Krantan* is a purely instrumental ornament; this may be described as a hammering action of the left hand. *Krantan* is often used on the *sarod* or *sitar*. Notes may also be sharpened or flattened by only a few cents (microtones). *Rags* such as *Todi* or *Darbari Kanada* use lower forms of some notes as part of their definition. In many other cases these are mere ornaments and have no theoretical significance.

We have tried to cover in some detail the nature of *rag*. Any music student should understand these principles. Concepts such as *that* (the mode), *vadi* (important note), *samavadi* (consonant of the *vadi*), etc., must be mastered if the student is to have a firm background.


# AESTHETICS

*Rag* is very important because it conveys certain aesthetic qualities. According to the ancient South Asian system of aesthetics, there are nine principal moods. Just as primary colors may be mixed to produce any hue, so too the nine principal moods may be combined to produce any human feeling.

Table 2.4 The Nine Moods

| | |
|---|---|
| Shringar | Love |
| Hasya | Comic |
| Karuna | Sadness |
| Raudra | Furious |
| Veera | Heroic |
| Bhayanaka | Terrible / Frightful |
| Vibhatsa | Disgusting |
| Adbhuta | Wonderment |
| Shanti | Peace |

# ENDNOTE

[1] *Vadi* and *samavadi* play a crucial role in Bhatkhande's system of time theory of *rags*. In many cases he declared that certain notes were *vadi/samavadi*, not because of their usage, but rather to come up with a system which would describe the timings by an internal structure. This was unfortunate for two reasons. Firstly, it failed to develop a functional time theory; secondly, it muddled the theory of *vadi* and samavadi.

# WORKS CITED

Jairazbhoy, N. A.
1971 *The Rags of North Indian Music.* Middletown, CT. Wesleyan University Press.

Kripalvanand, Swami
1972 "Purush Rag, Stri Rag Aur Putra Rag", *Rag-Ragini Ank.* Hathras: Sangeet Karyalaya; pp. 7-51.

Shankar, Ravi
1968 *Ravi Shankar, My Music, My Life.* New Delhi: Vikas Publishing House.

# CHAPTER 3.
# FUNDAMENTALS OF TAL

Many suggest that rhythm is fundamental to the creation of any musical system. Certainly from a historical standpoint rhythm existed many centuries before the word *rag* was ever used. Given this historical preeminence, it is not surprising that rhythm occupies an important position in the Indian system of music.

# BASIC TERMS

There are a number of terms used in the Indian science of rhythm. The first of which is *tal*. *Tal* literally means "clap" (Kapoor - no date). Today, the *tabla* has replace the clap in the performance, but the term still reflects the origin. The basic concepts of *tal* are: *tali, khali, vibhag* or *ang, matra, bol, theka, laya,* and *avartan*. We will now discuss these terms in greater detail.

**TALI** - This is the pattern of clapping. Each *tal* is characterized by a particular pattern and number of claps.

**KHALI** - In addition to the claps, there are also a number of "waves". These have a characteristic relationship to the claps.

**VIBHAG (ANG)** - Each clap or wave specifies a particular section or measure. These measures may be of any number of beats, yet most commonly 2, 3, 4, or 5 beats are used.

**MATRA** - This is the beat. It may be subdivided if required.

**BOL** - This is the mnemonic system where each stroke of the drum has a syllable attached to it. These syllables are known as *bol*. It is common to consider the *bol* to be synonymous to the stroke itself.

**THEKA** - This is a conventionally established pattern of *bols* and *vibhag* (*tali, khali*) which define the *tal*. This is very important, yet we will postpone our discussion until later.

**LAYA** - This is the tempo. The tempo may be either slow (*vilambit*), medium (*madhya*), or fast (*drut*). Additionally, ultra-slow may be referred to as *ati-vilambit* and ultra-fast may be referred to as *ati-drut*.

**AVARTAN** - This is the basic cycle. It has been stated that the *tal* revolves around an established number of beats. This number of beats represents one cycle. Therefore, one *avartan* (cycle) of *Tintal* will be 16 beats; one *avartan* of *Ektal* will have 12 beats, etc.

**SAM** - The first beat of the cycle is referred to as *sam*. It is important because it marks a point of convergence between the vocalist, instrumentalist and percussionist.

These are the most common terms used in the Indian science of rhythm. They are dealt with in much greater detail in other sources (Courtney 1994). Let us now look more closely at the accompaniment forms.

## THEKA

The basic concepts behind *tal* are much easier to comprehend than to implement. It is very difficult for beginner to sing with the *tabla*. It is usually difficult because the student has not bothered to memorize the *thekas* that the *tablist* plays. The memorization of basic *thekas* is absolutely crucial to the musical development of the vocal student.

Here is a list of common thekas:

**TINTAL**- This is the most common *tal* in North Indian classical music. It is a 16 beat *tal* composed of 4 measures (*vibhag*) of four beats (*matra*) each. It has the clapping arrangement of clap, clap, wave clap.

| Dhaa Dhin Dhin Dhaa | Dhaa Dhin Dhin Dhaa |
| X | 2 |

| Dhaa Tin Tin Naa | Naa Dhin Dhin Dhaa |
| 0 | 3 |

> Internet Resource
>
> "Bollywood Film Songs in Tintal and Punjabi Theka"
>
> http://chandrakantha.com/tala_taal/bollywood_songs/tintal_film_songs.html

JHAPTAL - This *tal* is declining in popularity. Today. it is used primarily in *Rabindra sangeet*, and for a few older *kheyals*. It is a 10-beat *tal* composed of four *vibhags*. The number of *matras* per *vibhag* is two, three, two, and three *matras*, respectively. It has the clapping arrangement of clap, clap, wave, clap.

| Dhin Naa | Dhin Dhin Naa | Tin Naa | Dhin Dhin Naa |
| --- | --- | --- | --- |
| X | 2 | 0 | 3 |

> Internet Resource
>
> "Bollywood Film Songs in Jhaptal"
>
> http://chandrakantha.com/tala_taal/bollywood_songs/jhaptal_film_songs.shtml

RUPAK TAL - *Rupak tal* is unique among the *tals* in that the *sam* is *khali*. Therefore, the first clap has no major significance. It is also interesting to note that it is asymmetric. For the last few centuries it has been usual for *tals* to be an even number of beats with a strong sense of symmetry. *Rupak tal* has seven *matras* arranged into three *vibhags*. The number of *matras* is three, two, two. It has the clapping arrangement of wave, clap, clap. This *tal* is quite common in a broad variety of styles, including *ghazal*, classical instrumental, classical vocal, and even film songs.

| Tin Tin Naa | Dhin Naa | Dhin Naa |
| --- | --- | --- |
| 0 | 1 | 2 |

> Internet Resources
>
> "Bollywood Film Songs in Rupaktal and Pashtu" (A-L)
>
> http://chandrakantha.com/tala_taal/bollywood_songs/rupak_film_songsA.shtml
>
> "Bollywood Film Songs in Rupaktal and Pashtu" (M-Z)
>
> http://chandrakantha.com/tala_taal/bollywood_songs/rupak_film_songsM.shtml

**EKTAL** – Ektal is very common in a style of vocal known as *kheyal*. This *tal* is 12 *matras* divided into six *vibhags* of two *matras* each. It has the clapping arrangement of clap, wave, clap, wave, clap, clap. Although the medium tempo *theka* is shown here, *ektal* is usually found in either very fast or very slow tempo.

| Dhin Dhin | DhaaGe  TiRiKiTa | Tun Naa |
|---|---|---|
| X | 0 | 2 |

| Kat Taa | DhaaGe  TiRiKiTa | Dhin Naa |
|---|---|---|
| 0 | 3 | 4 |

> Internet Resource
>
> "Bollywood Film Songs in Ektal"
>
> http://chandrakantha.com/tala_taal/bollywood_songs/ektal_film_songs.shtml

**DADRA TAL** – This *tal* is very common in the semiclassical styles. It is used extensively in *ghazal, bhajan, Rabindra sangeet*, and film songs. It is six *matras* divided into two *vibhags*. Each *vibhag* is of three *matras*. It has the clapping arrangement of clap, wave.

| Dhaa Dhin Naa | Dhaa Tin Naa |
|---|---|
| X | 0 |

> Internet Resource
>
> "Bollywood Film Songs in Dadra Tal and Khempta"
>
> http://chandrakantha.com/tala_taal/bollywood_songs/dadra_film_songs.html

**KAHERAVA TAL** (standard) – This is a very common *tal* for light, and semiclassical music. It is eight *matras* divided into two *vibhags* of four *matras* each. It has the clapping arrangement of clap, wave.

| Dhaa Ge Naa Ti | Naa Ka Dhin Naa |
|---|---|
| X | 0 |

> Internet Resource
>
> "Bollywood Film Songs in Kaherava Tal"
>
> http://chandrakantha.com/tala_taal/bollywood_songs/kaherava_film_songs.html

**KAHERAVA** (*Bhajan-ka-Theka*) – This is a variety of *kaherava* which is used extensively in *bhajans*. It is normally considered to be an eight-beat *tal*. However, it is often easier to conceive as a fast 16-beat *tal*.

| Dhin - Naa Dhin - Dhin Naa Ga | Tin - Naa Tin - Tin Naa Ga |
| X | 0 |

> **Internet Resource**
> see again "Bollywood Film Songs in Kaherava Tal"
> http://chandrakantha.com/tala_taal/bollywood_songs/kaherava_film_songs.html

**CHAUTAL** - This is a very ancient *tal* which was much used in the *dhrupad* style of singing. It is composed of 12 *matras* divided into four *vibhags*, of four, four, two, and two *matras*, respectively. It has claps for all of the *vibhags*. There are some interpretations which divide *chautal* into six *vibhags* in a manner similar to *ektal*; however, this interpretation is probably of recent origins.

| Dhaa Dhaa Din Taa | ⌒TiTa⌒ Dhaa Din Taa |
| X | 2 |

| ⌒TiTa⌒KaTa⌒ | ⌒GaDi⌒GeNaa⌒ |
| 3 | 4 |

> **Internet Resource**
> "Bollywood Film Songs in Chautal"
> http://chandrakantha.com/tala_taal/bollywood_songs/chautal_film_songs.shtml

We have covered the basic rhythmic material that a beginner should know. These were the basic concepts (*bhari*, *khali*, *vibhag*, etc). Furthermore, we have presented a list of common *thekas* that the student should know.

## WORKS CITED

Courtney, David R.
1994 *Fundamentals of Tabla*. Houston, TX; Sur Sangeet Services.

Kapoor, RK.
no date *Kamal's Advanced Illustrated Oxford Dictionary of Hindi-English*.
    Delhi, India: Verma Book Depot.

# CHAPTER 4.
# INSTRUMENTAL MUSIC AND DANCE

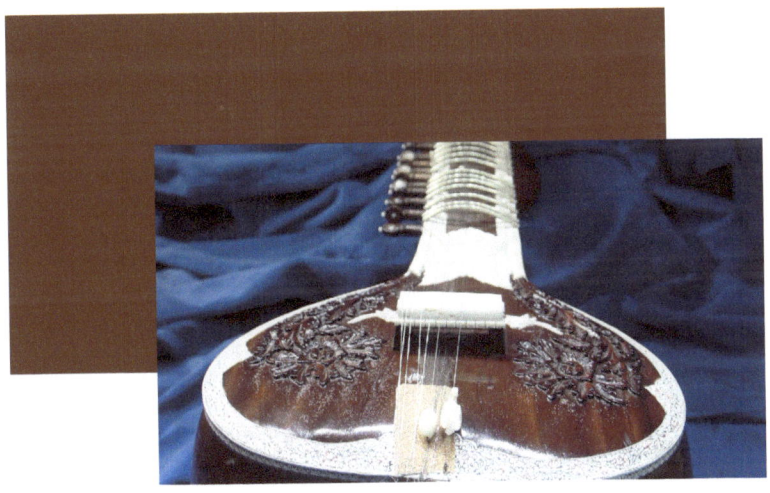

One cannot learn vocal music without an understanding of the related disciplines of instrumental music and dance. It takes all three components to make up the field of *sangeet*. Let us begin with a study of instrumental music.

# INSTRUMENTAL MUSIC

Instrumental music has the closest conceptual similarity to vocal music. In Bharat's time it was part of the overall tradition of stagecraft (Rangacharya 1966), but today it is a fully developed artform in its own right.

> Internet Resource
>
> "Indian Instruments"
>
> http://chandrakantha.com/articles/indian_music/instruments.html

There is a traditional system for the classification of instruments. This system is based upon non-membranous percussion, membranous percussion (*avanaddh*), wind blown (*sushir*), plucked string (*tat*), and bowed string (*vitat*).[1]

The classes and their respective instruments are as follows:

## NON-MEMBRANOUS PERCUSSIVE (GHAN)

This is one of the oldest classes of instruments in India. This class is based upon percussive instruments which do not have membranes, specifically those which have solid resonators. These may be either melodic instruments or instruments to keep *tal*.

**KASHT TARANG** - *Kasht tarang* is a type of xylophone. It is characterized by the use of wooden resonating bars.

**JAL-TARANG** - *Jal tarang* is a set of china bowls that are filled with water. Each bowl is struck with a light wooden mallet to cause it to ring.

**MANJIRA** - *Manjira* is a set of small cymbals. It is a ubiquitous component of dance music and bhajans.

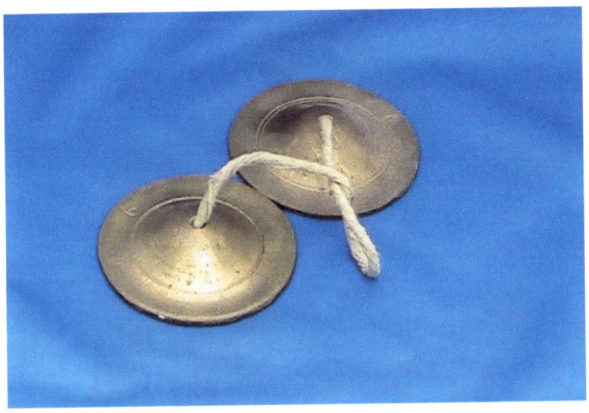

Figure 4.2 - Manjira

**GHATAM** - *Ghatam* is nothing more than a large clay pot. It is very commonly played in south Indian classical performances. There are two actions of resonance. The primary one is the ringing of the pot caused by striking. A very low resonance is also produced by the cavity. This pitch is raised or lowered by opening or closing the hole with the stomach.

**MURCHANG** - *Murchang* is a Jew's harp. It is commonly played in south Indian performances.

**CABAS** - *Cabas* is an instrument imported into India. It is usually constructed by weaving beads upon a coconut shell. It produces a rasping sound which is appropriate for light music.

Figure 4.3 - Cabas

**GHUNGHURU** - *Ghunghuru* are the "tinklebells" or "jingle bells" which are used to adorn the feet of dancers. When tied to the feet, it is played by the act of dancing. It may also be played by hand. This instrument evolved from the tinkling of the *payal*, which are traditional anklets worn by women in India.

Figure 4.4 - Ghunghuru

**KARTAL** - *Kartal* are a pair of wooden blocks or frames with small metal jingles mounted in them. They are simply beaten together to provide rhythmic support for *bhajans, kirtan*, folk, and other light music.

Figure 4.5 - Kartal

## BLOWN AIR (SUSHIR)

This class of instruments is characterized by the use of air to excite the various resonators.

**BANSURI** - *Bansuri* and *venu* are common Indian flutes. They are typically made of bamboo or reed. There are two varieties, transverse and fipple. The transverse variety is nothing more than a length of bamboo with holes cut into it. This is the preferred flute for classical music because the embouchure gives added flexibility and control. The fipple variety is found in the folk and *filmi* styles, but seldom used for serious music. Because the absence of an embouchure limits the flexibility of the instrument, the fipple variety is usually considered a toy.

Figure 4.6 - Venu and Bansuri

The flute may be called many things in India: *bansi, bansuri, murali, venu,* and many more. Although names may vary across India, there are two main types: *bansuri* and *venu*. The *bansuri* is found in the North. It typically has six holes; however, there has been a tendency in recent years to use a seventh hole for added flexibility and correctness of pitch. It was previously associated only with folk music, but today it is found in classical, *filmi*, and numerous other genre. *Venu* is a south Indian flute. It typically has eight holes. The *venu* is very popular in South Indian styles.

Internet Resource

"Bansuri and Venu"

http://chandrakantha.com/articles/indian_music/bansuri.html

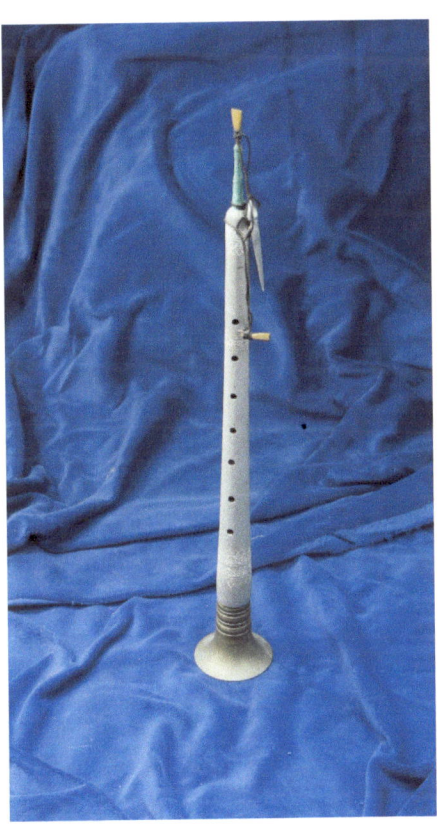

Figure 4.7 - Shehnai

**SHEHNAI** - *Shehnai* may be thought of as a north Indian oboe. Although it is referred to as a double-reeded instrument, it is actually a quadruple-reed instrument. This is because it has two upper reeds and two lower reeds. The instrument has a wooden body with a brass bell. The reed is attached to a brass tube which is wrapped in string. The shehnai has eight holes, but it is common to find some of the holes partially or completely occluded with wax.

The sound of the *shehnai* is considered particularly auspicious. For this reason, it is found in temples and is an indispensable component of any north Indian wedding. In the past, *shehnai* was part of the *naubat*, or traditional ensembles of nine instruments found at royal courts.

**PUNGI or BIN** - *Pungi* is a snake charmer's instrument. The word "*pungi*" is a generic term for many reeded noisemakers. The term "*bin*" is really a misnomer. The word *bin* is a typical Indian corruption of *vina*. The term *vina* implies a stringed instrument so it could not be applied to a reeded instrument.

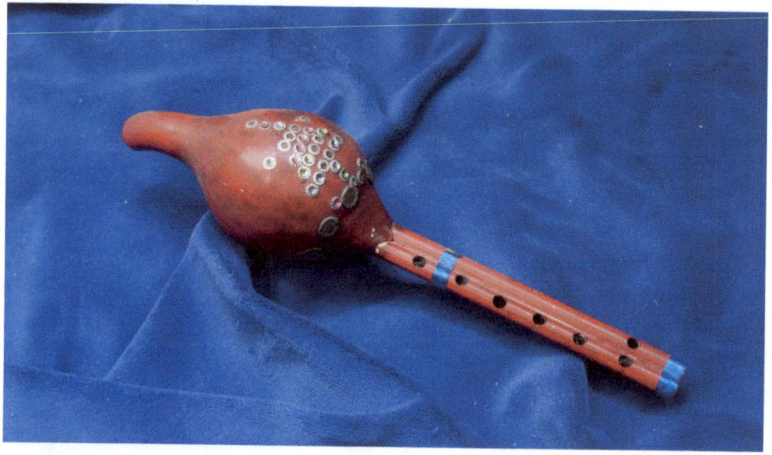

Figure 4.8 - Pungi (a.k.a. Bin)

**HARMONIUM** - The harmonium is not a native Indian instrument. It is a European instrument which was imported in the last few centuries. It is a reed organ with hand pumped bellows. Although it is a relatively recent introduction, it has spread throughout the subcontinent. Today, it is used in virtually every musical genre except the south Indian classical.

Although the harmonium is a European invention, it evolved into a truly bicultural instrument. The keyboard is European, but it has a number of drone reeds which are particularly Indian. European models came in both hand-pumped and foot-pumped models. The foot-pumped models disappeared in South Asia many years ago. This is because the foot pedals required one to sit in a chair (something which is unusual for an South Asian musician.) Furthermore, the only advantage of the foot model was that it freed both hands so that both melody and chords could be played. Indian music has no chords, so this was no advantage. Although the hand pumped models required one hand to pump, they were more comfortable when played on the floor.

Figure 4.9 - Harmonium

**SHANKH** - *Shankh* is a conch shell. This instrument has a strong association with the Hindu religion. It is said that when it is blown it announces the victory of good over evil. This instrument has limited musical applications.

4.10 - Shankh

**NADASWARAM** – *Nadaswaram* is a South Indian version of the *shehnai*. It is substantially larger than the *shehnai* and has a simple double reed rather than the more complex quadruple reed. It is considered a very auspicious instrument and is found at temples and at weddings.

Figure 4.11 Nadaswaram

# PLUCKED STRINGED INSTRUMENTS (TAT)

This class of instruments is characterized by plucked strings. In ancient times, virtually all instruments of this class were referred to as *vina*.

**SITAR** - Sitar is perhaps the most well known of the South Asian instruments. Artists such as Ravi Shankar have popularized this instrument around the world. Sitar is a long necked instrument with an interesting construction. It has a varying number of strings, but seventeen is usual. It has three to four playing strings, and three to four drone strings. These strings are plucked with a wire finger plectrum called *mizrab*. There are also a series of sympathetic strings lying under the frets. Although these strings are almost never played, they vibrate whenever the corresponding note is sounded. The frets are metal rods which have been bent into crescents. The main resonator is usually made of a gourd. Sometimes there is an additional resonator attached to the neck.

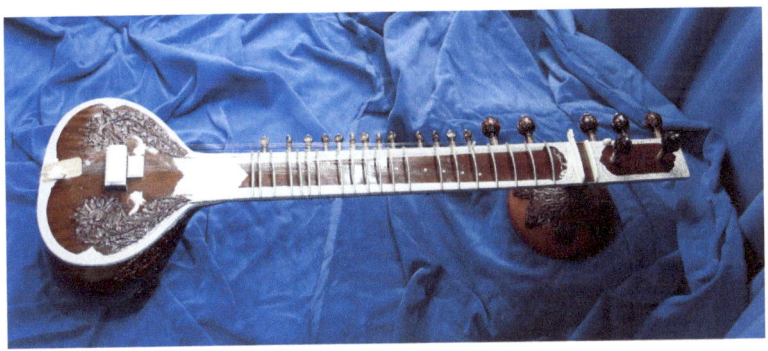

Figure 4.12 - Sitar

Internet Resource ▯ "The Sitar: An Overview"

http://chandrakantha.com/articles/indian_music/sitar.html

**RABAB** - *Rabab* is a very ancient instrument found primarily in Kashmir, Pakistan, and Afghanistan. It is a hollowed-out body of wood with a membrane stretched over the opening. Combinations of gut (or nylon) and metal strings pass over a bridge which rests on the taut membrane. The *rabab* is mentioned quite frequently in old texts. However, it appears that this was actually a different *rabab* from what is common today.

**VINA** - *Vina* is an instrument associated with Saraswati, the goddess of learning and the arts. It is made of wood and has frets which consist of brass bars set into wax. Unlike Northern instruments, the *vina* has no sympathetic strings. It has only playing strings and drone strings (*thalam*). It is played with wire plectra on the fingers. This instrument is common in Southern India.

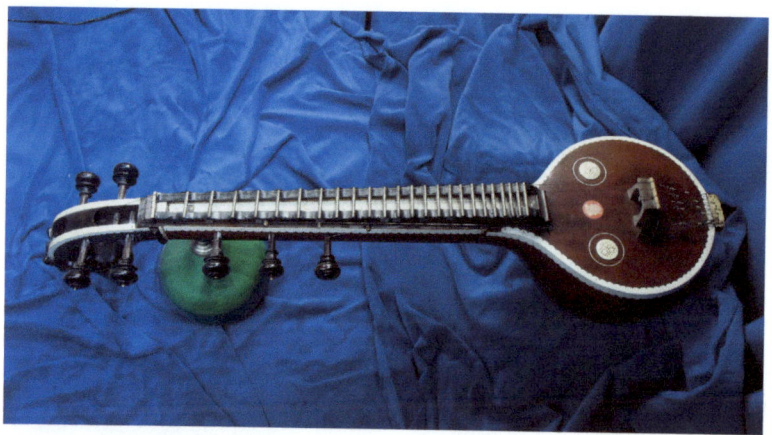

Figure 4.13 - Vina

Many ascribe this instrument to the *vina* which is mentioned in t h e *Vedas*. However, if iconography from stone carvings is examined, it can be deduced that instruments of the lute class (i.e., stringed instruments where the neck and resonator are integrated) did not show up in South Asia until long after the *Vedic* period. It appears that the *vina* of the *Vedas* was probably a stringed instrument of the stick zither class or possibly of the harp class.

**SAROD** - *Sarod* is an instrument which is derived from the *rabab*. It is not an ancient instrument and it is probably no more than 150 to 200 years. It is essentially a bass *rabab*. It has a metal fingerboard with no frets. The bridge rests on a taut membrane which covers the resonator. The *sarod* has numerous strings which are either drone, played, or sympathetic. It is played with a coconut shell pick.

**SURBAHAR** - *Surbahar* is essentially a bass sitar. It is substantially larger, and is tuned anywhere from four steps to an octave lower than a regular sitar. Its technique is similar enough to sitar so that musicians have no trouble going from one instrument to another. The *surbahar* has an advantage over sitar in that it has a longer sustain and an ability to *meend* (glissando) up to an octave in a single fret. Therefore, it is possible to play complex melodies without using more than a single fret. This instrument is very well suited to long slow *alaps*. The instrument's main weakness is that its long sustain causes a fast *jhala* to become indistinct and muddy. It is for this reason that some artists prefer to play the *alap* with *surbahar*, but shift to sitar for *gat* and *jhala*.

**GOTUVADYAM** - *Gotuvadyam* is similar to the *vina* except it has no frets. Furthermore, many versions have sympathetic strings. It is played with a slide in a manner somewhat like a Hawaiian guitar. This instrument is common in Southern India.

**RUDRA VINA** - *Rudra vina* appears to be the oldest style of *vina*. Such evidence is readily seen in elements of its construction, and from its depiction on the walls of ancient temples. This instrument is basically a bamboo stick with two gourds attached.  It has frets which are set into wax.  This instrument is quite rare nowadays.


**VICHITRA VINA** – *Vichitra vina* is an instrument similar to the *rudra vina* except it has no frets.  It is played with a slide like a Hawaiian guitar.


**TANPURA** – This is a drone instrument.  It resembles a sitar except it has no frets.  It is composed of a resonator made of a gourd and a long neck.  The usual number of strings is four, but one occasionally finds five and six string models.  This instrument is also called *tambura* in the South.

Figure 4.14 - Tanpura

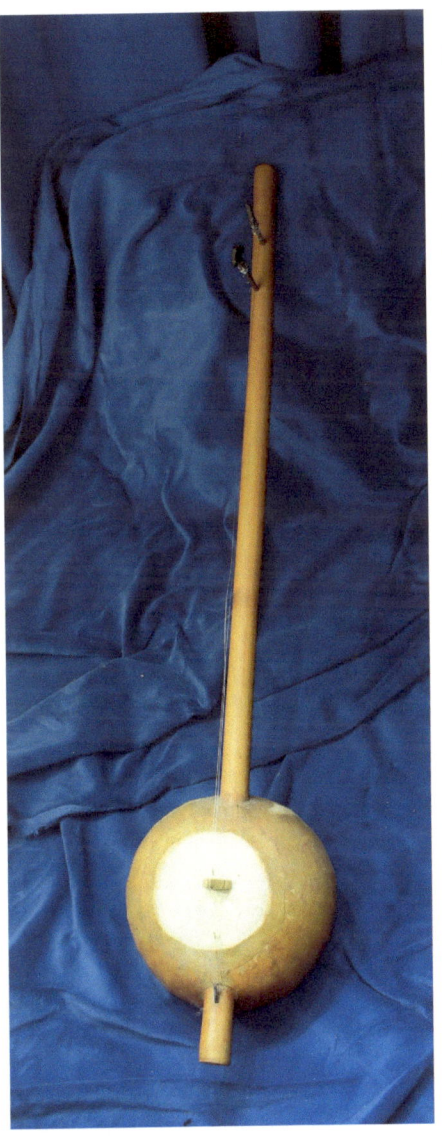

**DOTAR** – This is a two stringed version of the *ektar*. However in Bengal, there is an unrelated instrument which is also called *dotar*. This is very similar to the *Afghani rabab*.

Figure 4.15 - Dotar

SANTUR - This is an instrument indigenous to Kashmir, but nowadays played throughout the North. It is a hammered dulcimer which is struck with light wooden mallets. The number of strings may be as few as 24 or more than 100. A typical *santur* will have around 80 strings. It has a vibrant tone and has become very popular in the last 40 years.

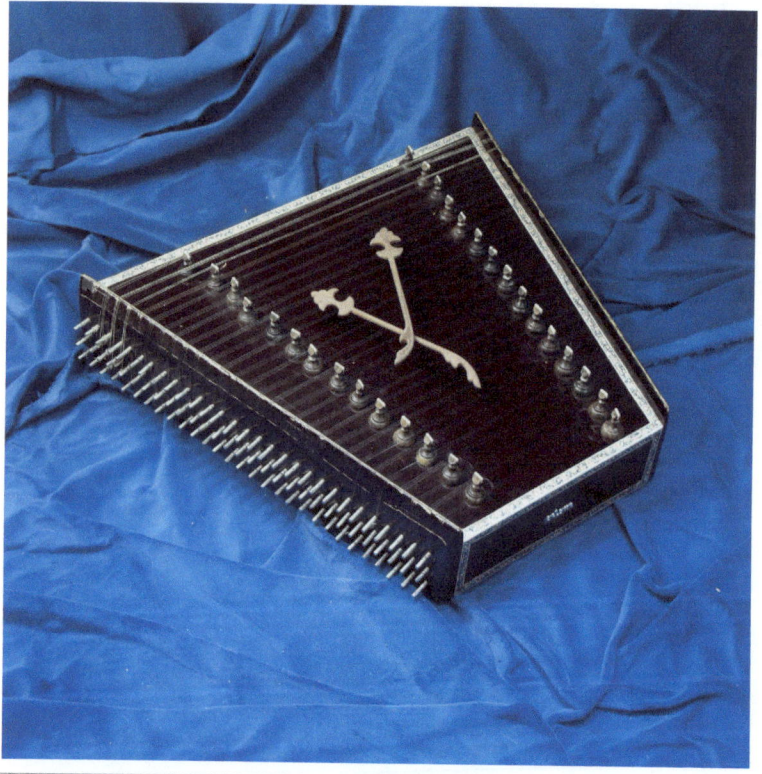

Figure 4.16 - Santur

EKTAR - *Ektar* is a simple folk instrument. It may be the oldest stringed instrument in the Indian subcontinent. In its simplest form, it is nothing more than a gourd which has been penetrated by a stick of bamboo. Another piece of bamboo forms the tuning peg. The bridge is nothing more than a coin, piece of coconut, plastic, or similar object. *Ektars* such as this are common in the South. In the North, their construction is a little more complicated. A membrane is stretched over an opening in the gourd, and the bridge is placed over the membrane.

**SURMANDAL** - *Surmandal* is a small harp. It is generally used for the accompaniment of vocalists. Although it is considered a minor instrument, the harp class is very old.

Figure 4.17 - Surmandal

# BOWED-STRINGED INSTRUMENTS (VITAT)

This is a class of stringed instruments which are bowed. This class appears to be old, yet these instruments did not occupy a place in classical music until the last few centuries (Bor 1987).

This class of instruments acquired a stigma at the turn of the 20th century. In the case of folk instruments, it was considered to be very low class to play such an instrument. However, its most popular classical form, the *sarangi*, acquired a stigma due to its association with dancing girls. Even today, only the Western violin is free of this stigma.

**SARANGI** - *Sarangi* is a common representative of *vitat*. It has three main playing strings, one drone, and approximately sixty sympathetic strings. The instrument has no frets or fingerboard. The playing strings float in the air. Pitch is determined by sliding the fingernail against the string laterally rather than pressing it against a fingerboard. This instrument has traditionally been associated with the *kathak* dance and the vocal styles of *thumri*, *dadra*, and *kheyal*. The *sarangi* saw a steady decline in popularity from the end of the 19th century. In the period just following independence, it was almost extinct, but in the last two decades, there has been a resurgence in its interest.

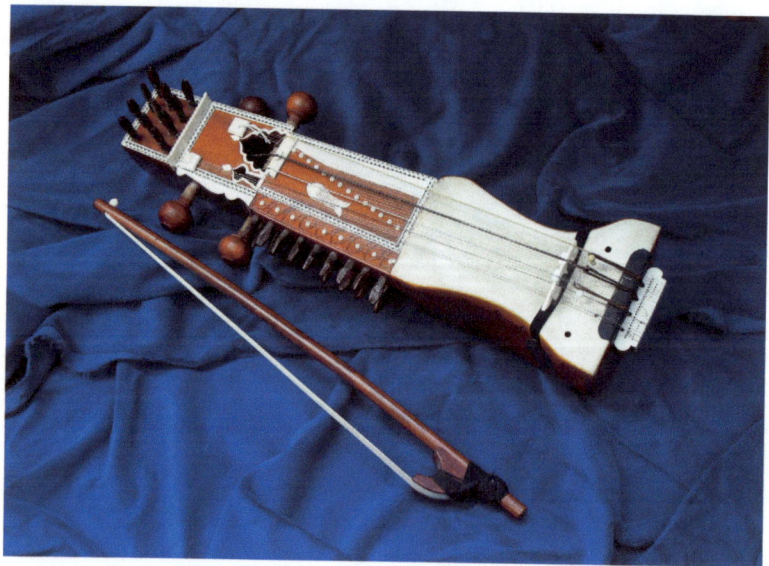

Figure 4.18 - Sarangi

> Internet Resource
> "Sarangi: An Overview"
> http://chandrakantha.com/articles/indian_music/sarangi.html

**ESRAJ** – *Esraj* is a combination between *saringda* and sitar. The base of the instrument is like *saringda*, while the neck and strings are like sitar. It gives a sound very much like *sarangi* without being as difficult to play.

Figure 4.19 - Esraj

Internet Resource
"Esraj"
http://chandrakantha.com/articles/indian_music/esraj.html

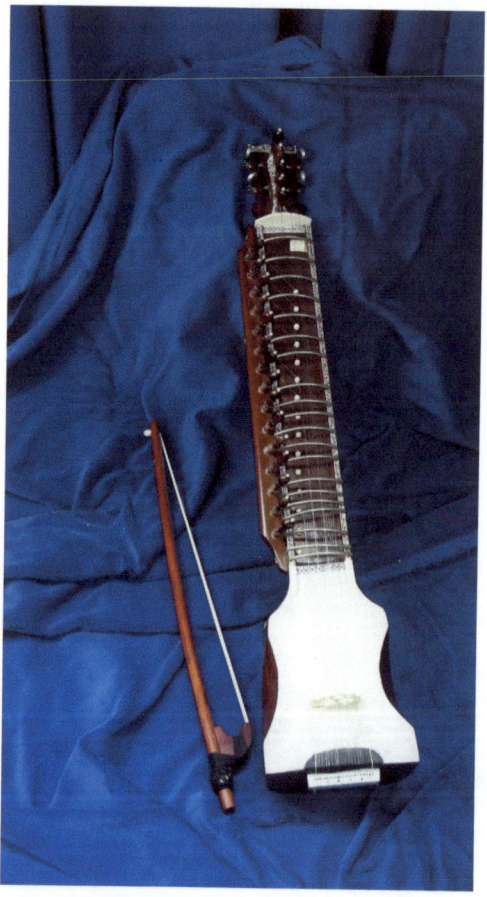

**DILRUBA** - *Dilruba* is similar to the *esraj*. It so close that most people are unable to tell them apart. The difference is to be found in the shape of the resonator and the manner in which the sympathetic strings attach. Yet they are so similar that a *dilruba* player has no trouble playing an *esraj* and *vice versa*.

Figure 4.20 - Dilruba

> Internet Resource
> "Dilruba"
> http://chandrakantha.com/articles/indian_music/dilruba.html

**SARINGDA** – *Saringda* is a folk version of the *sarangi*. It is found in Rajasthan and Northwest India.

**VIOLIN** – Although not native to the subcontinent, the violin has become so popular that it must be mentioned in this book. There appears to be no difference in construction between the Indian violin and its Western counterpart; however, the technique is different. The most refined technique is to be found in South India. Instead of holding the instrument under the chin, the musician props it between the shoulder and the foot. This gives a stability which cannot be matched by either North Indian or Occidental technique. North Indian technique, though not as refined, is still impressive.

## MEMBRANOUS PERCUSSIVE (AVANADDH)

This is a class of instruments which have struck membranes. These typically comprise the drums.

**TABLA** – This is a pair of drums. It consists of a smaller wooden drum called *dayan*, and a larger metal one called *bayan*.

The *tabla* has an interesting construction. The *dayan* (right hand drum) is almost always made of wood. The diameter at the membrane may run from just under five inches to over six inches. The *bayan* (left hand drum) may be made of iron, aluminum, copper, steel, or clay; yet brass with a nickel or chrome plate is the most common material. Undoubtedly, the most noticeable characteristic of the *tabla* is the large black spot on each of the playing surfaces. These black spots are a mixture of gum, soot, and iron filings. For the *dayan*, this creates the bell-like timbre that is characteristic of the instrument; but for the *bayan*, it is just to lower the overall pitch.

Figure 4.21 - Tabla

Internet Resource

"Tabla Site"

http://www.chandrakantha.com/tablasite/

**PAKHAWAJ** - *Pakhawaj* is an ancient barrel shaped drum with two playing heads. It was once common throughout North India, but in the last few generations, *tabla* has usurped its position of importance. It has a right head which is identical to *tabla* except somewhat larger. The left head is similar to the *tabla bayan*, except there is a temporary application of flour and water instead of the black permanent spot. It is laced with rawhide and has tuning blocks placed between the straps and shell. This instrument was very much tied to *dhrupad* style of singing, consequently as *dhrupad* has declined, the *pakhawaj* too has also fallen out of fashion. Today, this instrument is rare.

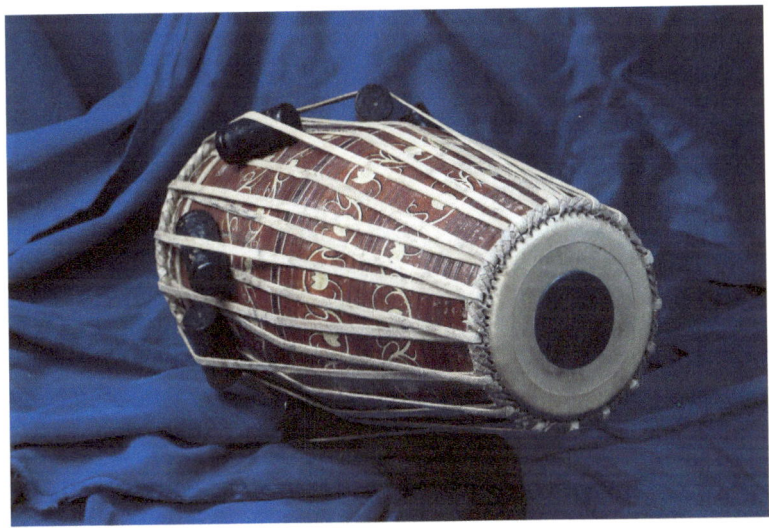

Figure 4.22 - Pakhawaj

**MRIDANGAM** - This is a South Indian version of the *pakhawaj*. It bears a strong superficial resemblance to *pakhawaj*, but there are major differences in construction and technique. The tone of the instrument is very different (Courtney 1993). This is due in part to *mridangam's* heavier annular membrane around the right side, and a number of pieces of straw which are placed radially between this annular membrane and the main membrane. The left side also uses a mixture of flour and water to provide a proper tone. The sustain of *mridangam's* left side is substantially less due to a large-double annular membrane, rather than a small single layer as found on the *pakhawaj*.

Figure 4.23 - Mridangam

**TABLA TARANG** - *Tabla tarang* consists of a number of *tabla dayan* tuned to different notes of the scale. Complete melodies are played by striking the appropriate drum.

**DHOLAK** - *Dholak* is a very popular folk drum of Northern India. It has a barrel shaped wooden body. A simple membrane is on the right side. The left hand has a single membrane with a special application on the inner surface. This application is a mixture of tar, clay, and sand (*dholak masala*) which lowers the pitch and provides a well defined tone. It is said that this instrument used to occupy a position of considerable prestige (Stewart 1974). Today, it is merely relegated to film and folk music.

**KHOL** - This instrument is also called *mridang*. It is a folk drum of northeast India. It has a body made of fired clay, a very small head on the right side (approximately 4 inches), and a larger head on the left side (approximately 10 inches).

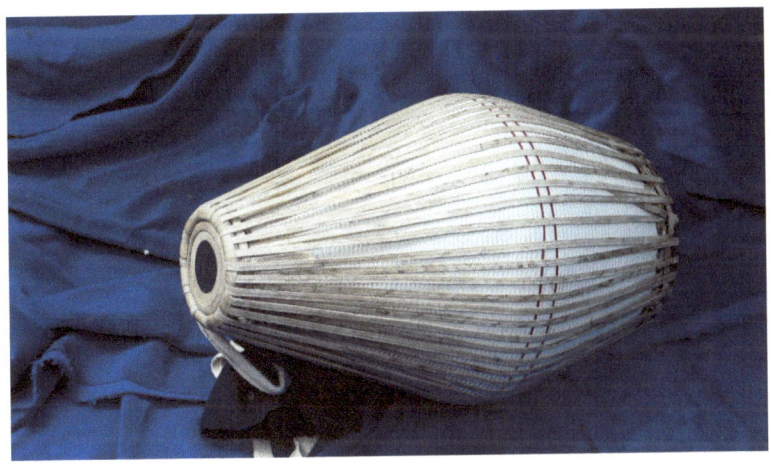

Figure 4.24 - Khol

NAGADA - These are the kettle drums of the old *naubat* (traditional ensemble of nine instruments). It is played with sticks. Today this instrument is usually used to accompany *shehnai*.

DHOLKI or NAL - *Dholki*, also called *nal* is a drum with a cylindrical shell. The left side resembles the *bayan* (large metal drum of the *tabla*), except that it uses *dholak masala* (oil based application) on the inner surface instead of a *syahi* (permanent black spot). The right side has a unique construction. Goat skin is stitched onto an iron ring. In the centre of this skin is a *syahi*, similar to that found on the *tabla*, except much thinner. The traditional *nals* were laced with rope and had sticks to function as turnbuckles. Today, metal turnbuckles have replaced the rope lacing in many models.

The *nal* is very popular in the *tamasha* (street performance) of Maharashtra. It has been absorbed into the Hindi film industry, and today the *nal* is very popular for this style.

**DAF** - *Daf* is a tambourine. It is commonly used in folk music but is rarely heard in other styles. It is also called *dapphu, dafali,* or a number of other names.

Figure 4.25 - Daf

**TAVIL** - This is an instrument found only in the deep South. It has a shell of nearly spherical proportions which is open on both sides. There are two skins wrapped around two large fibre hoops. The left side is played with a stick. The right side is played with the hands with metal thimbles placed over the fingers. These give a very sharp sound. This instrument is commonly played in South Indian temples and weddings.

**KANJIRA** – The *kanjira* is also a tambourine. It is made by stretching lizard skin over a wooden frame. The frame is about seven inches in diameter with one metal jingle mounted in it. The *kanjira* is very popular in South Indian classical performances.

Figure 4.26 - Kanjira

We have given a brief overview of the Indian instruments. It was mentioned that the instruments fall into five categories: *tat* (plucked stringed), *vitat* (bowed stringed), *sushir* (wind blown), *avanaddh* (membranous percussion), and *ghan* (non-membranous percussion). Within these five classes, there are a large number of individual instruments. Although we have talked in great detail about the instruments, we have mentioned nothing about the instrumental style of music.

# INSTRUMENTAL STYLES

There is a general tendency for the instrumental styles to follow the vocal styles quite closely. Yet, the degree to which an instrument follows is primarily linked to the dynamics of the instrument.

Dynamics is the nature of the loudness of an instrument. This is not intended to mean loudness in the usual interpretation, but rather the amplitudinal characteristics of the instrument (i.e., the envelope). The sitar and flute offer a good illustration. A flute is continuously excited; therefore, there is a steady sound as long as the breath is applied. Since it is possible to sustain a sound for a long time, it is possible to perform all kinds of delicate *meends* (*glissando*). Contrast this to a sitar with its rapid decay. The sound is essentially inaudible within about two seconds. Many types of ornamentation cannot be executed due to the quick decay.

This creates an artistic pressure for these instruments to develop their own styles. These styles enhance the strong points while avoiding the weaknesses. Over the years, they have become formalized into four major instrumental styles known as: *alap, jor, gat,* and *jhala.*

ALAP - The *alap* of instrumentalists is virtually identical to the *alap* of the vocalists. It is a slow, rhythmless exposition of the *rag*. It is usually the beginning movement. There may be a slight difference in interpretation due to the limitations of many instruments.

JOR - *Jor* is an instrumental rendition of a vocal style called *nomtom*. It is characterized by the use of a slow to medium rhythm. There is not a fully developed cycle, so it is never accompanied by *tabla*. Although the *nomtom* has fallen out of common use among vocalists, it is still a ubiquitous component of instrument concerts. The dynamics of most stringed instruments lend themselves well to this style.

**GAT** - *Gat* is a structure very much like the main theme, or *sthai* of the vocal tradition. It has a fully developed cycle and is invariably accompanied by the *tabla*. There are two basic approaches; *masitkhani* and *razakhani*. The *masitkhani gat* is the slow *gat*. The *razakhani* is the fast *gat*. In recent years, the distinction between the two styles has become blurred.

**JHALA** - *Jhala* is undoubtedly the most characteristic of the instrumental styles. Indian instruments are noted by a few special purpose drone strings called *chikari*. These strings are never fretted but are struck whenever the tonic needs to be emphasized. The *jhala* is a fast paced alternation of the main melody string and *chikari* strings. This lends itself to interesting permutations of both *rag* and *tal* simultaneously. This exciting style has become an obligatory conclusion to any sitar or *sarod* recital.

The last chapter dealt extensively with many aspects of the instrumental traditions. If we return to our definition of *sangeet*, we find that dance also occupies an important position. Let us look briefly at the Indian dance traditions.

## DANCE

There are numerous dance forms in India. The acknowledged classical dances are: *Bharatnatyam*, *Kathakali*, *Kuchipudi*, *Manipuri*, *Orissi*, and *Kathak*. Each of these styles has a strong regional connection and none can claim to be representative of the entire Indian subcontinent. Of the above styles, the *Orissi* and *Kathak* are clearly linked with the North Indian system.

# CONCLUSION

We have tried to give a good background for the instrumental styles, but have only briefly touched upon the dance traditions. This background allows us to place Indian vocal in perspective. We see that vocal music does not exist in isolation but as part of a larger musical tradition; one based upon a larger tradition comprised of vocal music, instrumental music, and dance. But each of these three disciplines has differentiated into a myriad of particular styles. Additionally, a bewildering array of musical instruments evolved.

# ENDNOTE

[1] The *Ain-i-Akbari* gives a slightly different version. According to its author Abul-Fall Allami (circa 16th century), the classes are *tata* (stringed instruments), *vitata* (instruments with skin stretched over them), *ghana* (percussive instruments based upon solid bodies), and *sushira* (wind instruments).

# WORKS CITED

Allami, Abu 1-Fazl
Circa 1590 *Ain-i Akbari*. (Translated by H. Blockmann). Delhi 1989: Reprinted by New Taj Office.

Bhatkhande, Vishnu Narayan
1934 *A Short History of the Music of Upper India*. Bombay, India: (Reprinted in 1974 by Indian Musicological Society, Baroda).
Courtney, D.R.
1980 *Introduction to Tabla*. Hyderabad, India; Anand Power Press.

1993 "Mrdangam et Tabla: un Contraste". *Percussions: Cahier Bimensiel d'Études et d'Informations sur les Arts de la Percussion.* Chailly-en-Biere, France; Vol. 28, March/April 1993; pp 11-14.

Bor, Joep
1987 "The Voice of Sarangi: An Illustrated History of Bowing in India". *Quarterly Journal for the National Centre for the Performing Arts.* Bombay: NCPA. Vol. XV and XVI Nos. 3, 4, & 1; Sept, Dec, & March 87.

Garg, Lakshminarayan
1984 *Hamare Sangeet-Ratna.* Hathras, India: Sangeet Press.

Rangacharya, Adya
1966 *Introduction to Bharata's Natya-Sastra.* Bombay, India: Popular Prakashan.

Shankar, Ravi
1968 *Ravi Shankar: My Music, My Life.* New Delhi, India; Vikas Publishing House Pvt. Ltd.

Stewart, R.M.
1974 *The Tabla in Perspective.* Ann Arbor: University Microfilms International (Ph.D. Dissertation).

# CHAPTER 5.
# VOCAL STYLES

The vocal tradition is especially strong in South Asian music. It is considered the highest of the three aspects of *sangeet* (vocal, instrumental, dance). There are many different styles and approaches.

# PARTS OF THE SONG

**ALAP** - The *alap* is an approach which is common to most of the above examples. It is a totally rhythmless style based upon a free elaboration upon the *rag*. It is usually the introductory section to any of the previously mentioned musical styles. The *alap* may vary in length from a few seconds to over an hour.

**NOMTOM** - This is an intermediate introductory movement. It contains a simple rhythm but no developed rhythmic cycle. This is found in dhrupad and related styles, but today is very rare.

**FIXED COMPOSITIONS** - The fixed composition has a special role in *Hindustani sangeet*. Such compositions may be as simple as a standard elaboration or refined as a traditional piece. In general the fixed compositions fall into two classes: pedagogic material and themes. Most fixed compositions are not complete pieces but themes used in a larger improvised performance. Such composed themes form a melodic base to which the improvisation frequently returns. Even a very heavily improvised style like *kheyal* is built around a couple of fixed themes. These themes may be several hundred years old and have been passed down for many generations.

**SWARMALIKA** - This is a style of singing where the vocalist sings the *sargam* of the song. The note-for-note relationship between the lyrics and the melody is very powerful in delineating the *swar*.

**STHAI** - The *sthai* may be thought of as the primary theme. It is fairly fixed and forms the basis for most South Asian vocal performances. This theme is typically short; generally one to three cycles in length and may be recognized by its prominence. It is usually performed in the *madhya saptak* (middle register).

**ANTARA** – This is the secondary theme of a vocal performance. It is easily recognized because it is introduced well after the *sthai*. It is also easy to recognize because it tends to be performed in the *tar saptak* (upper register). Although a classical piece has only a single *antara*, the semi-classical and light pieces may have numerous versions.

**SANCHARI** – This is the tertiary theme of a vocal performance. This is usually found in the old *dhrupad* styles and is seldom heard today.

**ABHOG** – This is the quaternary theme of a vocal performance. Like the *sanchari*, it is characteristic of the older forms like *dhrupad* and is seldom heard today.

## STYLES OF SINGING

There are many styles of singing, some old and some new. Here are some major styles:

**LAKSHAN-GEET** – This is probably the most typical fixed composition used for vocal instruction. This is a style of singing where the lyrics of the song actually describe the features of the *rag*. If the *lakshan geet* is memorized, one will never forget the *rag*. Throughout one's life, whenever the *rag* is heard the words keep coming back.

**DHRUPAD** – This is perhaps the oldest style of classical singing in North Indian music today. The heyday of this style was in the time of Tansen. It is a very heavy, masculine style performed to the accompaniment of the *pakhawaj* (an ancient *mridang*). It is known for its austere quality and strict adherence to the *tal*. The moods of *dhrupad* may vary, but themes revolving around the victories of great kings and mythological stories are common. Devotional themes are also very common.

The *dhrupad* usually adheres to a four-part structure of *sthai*, *antara*, *sanchari*, and *abhog*. It is usually set to *Chautal* of twelve beats, *Tivra tal* of seven beats, or *Sulfak tal* of ten beats. Its formal structure makes it a very difficult style to master. Unfortunately, this rigidity also made it very difficult for the average person to appreciate. Today, this style is very rare.

**DHAMMAR** - This has many similarities to *dhrupad*. Its major difference is that it is slightly more romantic. Themes of *dhammar* typically revolve around Krishna and the *Holi* festival. In fact the *dhammar* is often called "*hori*" (*holi*). It is typically performed in *Dhammar tal* of 14 beats. *Dhammar*, like its cousin the dhrupad, is rarely heard today.

**KHEYAL** - This has a special place in Indian music. The near extinction of the *dhrupad* and *dhammar* styles made the *kheyal* the *de facto* standard for classical music. It is probably the most improvised of the Indian styles.

There are two movements of *kheyal*. There is a very slow section which is called *vilambit* or *bada kheyal*, and a fast section called *drut* or *chota kheyal*. The *vilambit* section is extremely slow and usually played in *ektal* of twelve beats. The fast section is usually played in *drut Tintal* or *drut Ektal*.

**TARANA** This is a style which arose in popularity during the Mogul period. This style is based upon the use of meaningless syllables in a very fast rendition. There is an interesting legend concerning its origin:

There was once a music competition in the court of Alauddin Khilji. It had come to two finalists: a Hindu by the name of Gopal Nayak, and a Muslim named Amir Khusru. Gopal Nayak was well aware that he was up against a formidable opponent. Therefore, he sang a very fast song in Sanskrit, knowing quite well that Amir Khusru did not know the language. Amir Khusru then sang the same song, note-for-note, but substituting Persian words for the Sanskrit. The resulting performance was thrilling, even though it was unintelligible. In this way, Amir Khusru won the competition and invented *tarana*.

This legend is entertaining but highly unlikely. It is likely that the transformation from intelligible Persian lyrics to the present unintelligible syllables took a long time.

**THUMRI** - This is a common style of light classical music. The text is romantic and devotional in nature, and usually revolves around a girl's love for Krishna (Devangan 1984). The language is a dialect of Hindi called Brijbhasha. This style is characterized by a greater flexibility with the *rag*. The compositions are usually set to *Kaherava tal* of eight beats, *Adha tal* of sixteen beats, or *Dipchandi tal* of fourteen beats. It arose in popularity during the 19th century. Lighter *rags* such as *Mand* or *Khammaj* are usually used.

**DADRA** - This is a light classical style which is very similar to *thumri*. The most important difference is that the lyrics tend to be in Urdu, and the themes are purely romantic in character. The *tals* used are *Dadra tal* of six beats, *Kaherava* of eight beats, or any other light *tal*. This too is based upon lighter *rags*.

**BHAJAN** - This has been popular for many centuries. Unfortunately, it is difficult to describe musically, because the *bhajan* is defined by a sense of devotion (*bhakti*) rather than any musical characteristics.

*Bhajans* cover a broad spectrum of musical styles from the simple musical chant (*dhun*) to highly developed versions comparable to *thumri*. The poetic content of the *bhajan* also covers a broad spectrum. The more traditional ones by great saint-musicians such as Mira, Surdas, or Kabir, are considered of the highest literary quality.

Many modern ones, although more easily understood by the masses, usually have a literary value no greater than a typical film song (a popular form of music generated for the masses). The lowest poetic form is the *dhun*, which is actually nothing more than a musical version of a chant.

The structure of *bhajan* is very conventional. It contains a single *sthai* and numerous *antara*. The last *antara* has special significance because it contains the *nom de plume* of the author.

**QAWWALI** – This is an Islamic devotional song. It is a lively, light style which has a popular appeal for both Muslims and Hindus alike. The *qawwali* may or may not be based upon a *rag*, and it is usually set to *Kaherava* (eight beats), *Dadra tal* (six beats), or any of the lighter *tals*.

**TAPPA** – This is a light classical style which is declining in popularity. It is basically a classical style of music from the Punjab.

**SHABAD** – This is a style similar to *bhajan*. However, these songs are from the *Guru Granth Sahib*, the holy book of the Sikhs, while the *bhajan* is found among the Hindus.

**KIRTAN** or **DHUN** – These styles are related to *bhajan*. The major difference is that *bhajan* is usually performed by a soloist, while *kirtan* and *dhun* usually involve the audience. The musical quality is consequently much simpler to accommodate the uncertain musical abilities of the participants.

**GHAZAL** – Nowadays, this is considered a style of singing. In a strict sense this is not true; it is a style of poetic recitation (Mukri 1990). Because of its poetic origins, there is a very heavy emphasis upon the literary quality of the lyrics. Invariably, such lyrics revolve around philosophic and romantic themes. Since this is a mere musical adaptation of Urdu poetry, concepts such as *sthai* and *antara* have no significance. The flow is determined by the structure of the poem. The language is a very formal Urdu and the *tals* tend to be *Kaherava* (eight beats), *Rupak* (seven beats), or *Dadra tal* (six beats). The melodies may be based upon lighter *rags* or they may be based upon folk themes.

**GEET** – This may or may not be considered a distinct style. The word "*geet*" actually means "song". However, there is a tendency to use the term for many of the lighter styles which do not fit the rigid classification of the more classical forms. The *geet* may or may not be based upon a *rag*, and it is usually set to the lighter *tals*.

**FOLK STYLES** – Each region has its own styles of song. The text, style, and structure vary considerably.

**FILM STYLES** – This is the music from the Indian film industry. It is a commercial genre comparable to the Western "Top 40". Although it is of questionable artistic value, the industry and the extent of popular appeal make this style impossible to dismiss. Since it is a haphazard syncretism, it is impossible to define musically. Classical and traditional elements may be found, yet it is more likely to be dominated by Western jazz, rap, disco or whatever styles may be in vogue. The constant flux makes any definitive musical discussion impossible.

# WORKS CITED

Devangan, Tulsiram
1984 *Thumri–Gayaki*. Hathras; Sangeet Karyalaya.

Mukri, Naseem
1990 *Junoon*, Bombay: Intel Communications.

# CHAPTER 6.
# LANGUAGE

It is impossible to give a complete description of the South Asian languages in a music book. However, some degree of familiarity is necessary. In this chapter we will touch upon their development, dialects, and provide a small glimpse into grammar and writing.

# NORTHERN LANGUAGES

The languages of Northern India, Pakistan, and Bangladesh share a remarkable kinship to each other. The similarity between them is most striking when compared to the South Indian languages. The common South Indian languages are Tamil, Telugu, Malayalam, and Kannada, and are said to belong to the Dravidian family of languages. Conversely, the languages of the North, such as Hindi-Urdu (Hindustani), Gujarati, Punjabi, Bengali, Marathi, or Assami, belong to the Indo-European family. These two families differ drastically in terms of grammar and vocabulary.[1]

The Indo-European theory states that all the languages in this family were derived from a single language which is referred to as Proto-Indo-European. The Proto-Indo-Europeans were a group of tribes, leading a pastoral existence, whose culture began to spread in the first few centuries B.C.E. This culture traveled and differentiated until it occupied most of Europe and much of Asia (Mallory 1989). Therefore, these languages show a marked kinship with European languages such as English, French, or German.

It is convenient that the musical division within India follow the linguistic divisions. The regions of the South which speak the Dravidian languages are also the areas which follow the *Carnatic* system of music. Conversely, the northern states which speak Indo-European languages follow the *Hindustani* system of music. Since this is a book on North Indian music the South Indian languages will not be considered here.

We can begin our discussion with Sanskrit. This language was once considered to be nearly identical to Proto-Indo-European. However, contemporary linguistic thought places it at a considerably greater distance than once believed. Regardless of its position in the Indo-European family tree, there is no doubt about its importance to Indian culture.

Sanskrit is only minimally used in contemporary musical performances. The most common application is the *shloka*. *Shloka* is a prayer which is generally sung at the beginning of a performance.

Sanskrit has gone through several stages to arrive at its present position. Initially, it was a vernacular language. It later became a literary language. After it had become a literary language, it was frozen into its present form. The extreme formalization was convenient for Vedic studies, but it proclaimed the death of Sanskrit as a viable *lingua franca* (Barz 1977). A language which is frozen in this manner quickly becomes unable to deal with day-to-day affairs. From that period, numerous vernacular forms developed.

The period of Islamic expansion into the Indian subcontinent is especially important for the development of Hindustani (Hindi-Urdu). The influence of Persian, Turkish, and Arabic upon the Sanskrit derived vernaculars, created dialects which for the first time could be considered as Hindustani. Over the years, many dialects of Hindi-Urdu (Hindustani) would come and go.

Some of these dialects assumed a special significance in the period between the 15th and 17th centuries. It was in this period that the Hindu *bhakti* movement was sweeping northern India. This movement was a grassroots revolution against the pressures of Islam on one hand, and the *Brahmanic* monopoly of Hinduism on the other. The essence of the *bhakti* philosophy was that anyone, of any race, caste, or social strata, could obtain the grace of God.

This created a strong reaction away from Sanskrit and its elitist connotations towards the vernacular for religious purposes. One vernacular, called Brijbhasha, is especially important for musicians. Brijbhasha is a dialect of Hindi which was used in Mathur (Barz 1977).

Brijbhasha is one of the most widely used dialects for musical lyrics. It is used extensively in *bhajans, kheyal,* and *thumri*. It is generally used whenever there are themes revolving around Krishna. Since Krishna is a central theme in much of North Indian music, there is ample scope for the use of this dialect.

The rise of Urdu is historically linked to the formalization of Brijbhasha. Brijbhasha became so formalized that it could no longer function as an effective *lingua franca*. Urdu had not yet become a literary language, so it was not yet burdened with rigid rules and restrictions. Urdu's flexibility, coupled with its wide acceptance, made it the prime choice for administrative purposes in the 19th century.

Urdu reached its artistic zenith in the 19th century. There is an extensive amount of poetry from which much of North Indian music derives its lyrics. The poetry of Ghalib is perhaps the most famous. Urdu is extensively used in *ghazal* and *dadra* and it is sometimes found in *kheyal*.

History has a habit of repeating itself. Just as Sanskrit, Pali, and Brijbhasha began as vernaculars, evolved into literary languages, and then became frozen into a solid mass of grammatical rules and restrictions, so did Urdu. In the last century, it grew in acceptance as a literary language and quickly became formalized Today literary Urdu is flowery and poetic but impractical for day-to-day applications.

We find that a contemporary vernacular, sometimes referred to as film-Hindi, is extensively used in a number of musical genre. For many years this vernacular was confined to film music; however, in recent years it has started to be used in other forms such as *bhajan* and *ghazal*. Although such usage is not hailed as a great artistic achievement, it is certainly consistent with the natural linguistic ebb and flow.

The relationship between Hindi and Urdu deserves some discussion. Outside of academic circles, Hindi and Urdu are generally considered to be separate languages. The distinction is based upon a number of criteria. One distinction is that Hindi uses the Sanskrit alphabet while Urdu uses an Arabic script. Another difference is that the majority of Hindi speakers are Hindu while the majority of Urdu speakers are Muslim. Neither of these are academically valid criteria! It would he more correct to say that Hindi, Urdu, Brijbhasha, Pahadi, etc., are all dialects of one language which most linguists refer to as Hindustani.

## HINDI SCRIPT

The Hindi Script, also known as *Devanagari*, is a model of elegance. It is phonetic and easy. The rules are consistent and clear. It is not surprising that the majority of North Indian languages have adopted this script or one of its derivatives (e.g., Guru Mukhi, Bengali) (Greaves 1983). In the table 6.1, we see that the alphabet is clearly divided into vowels and consonants. One interesting characteristic is that the only time the vowels are written in this form is when they occur in isolation (Van Olphen 1992). Usually, the vowels are designated by a series of modifying marks placed around the consonant. Therefore, it is easier to think of the syllable as being the basic functional unit of the writing (Srinivasachari 1983). The most striking characteristic of *Devanagari* is the extremely clear phonetic nature of the script. The concept of "spelling" just doesn't even exist because words are written like they are pronounced. *Devanagari* is written from left to right, just like English. Words are clearly separated, and in modern forms one may find the full compliment of commas and other marks of punctuation.

**Vowels**

| अ | आ | इ | ई | उ | ऊ | ऋ |
|---|---|---|---|---|---|---|
| a | ā | i | ī | u | ū | ṛ |

| ए | ऐ | ओ | औ | अं | अः |
|---|---|---|---|---|---|
| e | ai | o | au | am | ah |

**Consonants**

| क | ख | ग | घ | ङ |
|---|---|---|---|---|
| k | kh | g | gh | ṅ |

| च | छ | ज | झ | ञ |
|---|---|---|---|---|
| ch | chh | j | jh | ñ |

| ट | ठ | ड | ढ | ण |
|---|---|---|---|---|
| ṭ | ṭh | ḍ | ḍh | ṇ |

| त | थ | द | ध | न |
|---|---|---|---|---|
| t | th | d | dh | n |

| प | फ | ब | भ | म |
|---|---|---|---|---|
| p | ph | b | bh | m |

| य | र | ल | व | श |
|---|---|---|---|---|
| y | r | l | v | sh |

| ष | स | ह | क्ष | त्र | ज्ञ |
|---|---|---|---|---|---|
| ṣ | s | h | ksh | tr | ñ |

Table 6.1 - Devanagri script

This finishes our brief description of the *Devanagari* script. Now it is appropriate for us to take a quick look at the Urdu script.

## URDU SCRIPT

Urdu uses a modified Arabic script. It would be more correct to say that it uses the Persian script, because there are some letters which are common in the Persian and Indian dialects but are absent in the original Arabic. The Urdu alphabet is shown in table 6.2 (Ganathe 1981). Each letter has four forms: isolate, initial, medial, and final. This reflects its position in a word section. If the letter is by itself, one uses the isolate form (table 6.2). If it comes at the beginning the initial form is used. If it comes in the middle or end, the medial and terminal forms are used.

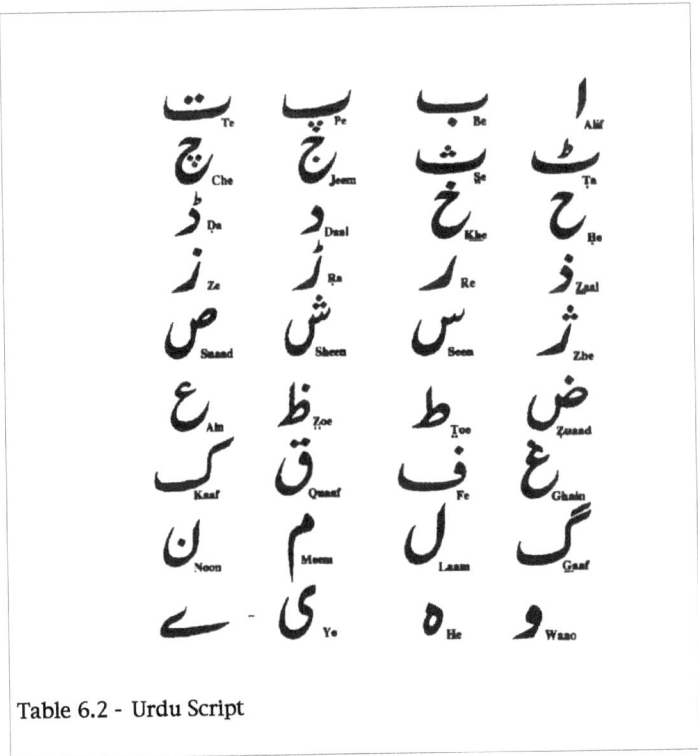

Table 6.2 - Urdu Script

There are a few things which make Urdu difficult. The most fundamental difficulty lies in the fact that the vowels are ambiguous. There is even a tendency to leave them off entirely. This creates a situation similar to English, where one must be familiar with the correct spellings.

Another problem lies in the calligraphy. Although Urdu calligraphy is exceptionally beautiful, there are such liberties taken with the placement of the various sections, that it is sometimes difficult to decipher.

## BASIC GRAMMAR

There are both similarities and differences between Hindustani and English. The grammar of Hindustani is remarkably similar to English and other Indo-European languages, yet the vocabulary is very different. It uses nouns, verbs, adjectives, etc. in a process that is remarkably similar to English. The example in table 6.3. will illustrate this very easily.

| Translation | "The book is on the table" | | | |
|---|---|---|---|---|
| Parts of speech | subject | object | preposition (postposition) | verb |
| Hindi | किताब | मेज़ | पर | है |
| Transliteration | kitab | mez | par | hai |
| Word-for-Word | book | table | on | is |

Table 6.3 - Basic sentence structure

This example illustrates quite clearly the structure of a typical sentence. There are a number of other points which should also be considered.

Gender is an area of great importance. Generally, there are three approaches to gender: masculine, feminine, and common. Animate objects may or may not be referred to according to their sex; however, even inanimate objects have a gender. For example, a hammer (*hathodi*) is considered feminine and will be grammatically treated as such. The common gender is rare and represents situations where both genders are present, for instance the word for "parents" (*mata-pita*).

The number is another area of importance. The use of the plural form verses the singular form is usually quite clear. However, there is one interesting exception. The use of the plural form is generally considered a mark of respect. This is roughly analogous to a doctor's bedside manner when he says "How are we feeling today?" Therefore, use of the term "you" is of special significance. Unlike modern English, there are three forms of the word "you". In India, you cannot even talk to another person without placing them in some social context with respect to yourself. For instance, when one is dealing with an elder, or social superior, one will use the term *aap*. If one is with friends, one will generally use the term *tum*, However, if one is dealing with children, servants, or social inferiors, one may use the term *tu*.

There are literary ramifications to this rule which are of tremendous importance to the vocalist. In India, it is customary for God to be addressed in the familiar form *Tu*. It has also been the subject of much discussion; however, this is beyond the scope of an introductory work on Indian music.

# OTHER INDO-PAKISTANI LANGUAGES

We have here-to-fore confined our discussion to the various dialects of Hindustani. We must not forget that there are other languages in the North as well.

Punjabi is a language of the area of Northwest India and Pakistan. Punjabi is used in classical, semiclassical, and folk music. In the classical and semiclassical realm, the tappa and shabad have attained a tremendous degree of sophistication. The folk music is also noteworthy for its strong popular appeal. Much of the Hindi film music has been influenced by the Punjabi folk music.

Bengali is another language which has great importance to musicians. This is a language which is used in north-east India and Bangladesh. It is especially important in the styles of music known as *Nazrul geet* and *Rabindra sangeet*.

There are other South Asian languages whose musical contributions are largely in the folk styles. Common Indian ones are Oriya from the Indian state of Orissa, Gujarati of the state of Gujarat, Assami from Assam, Kashmiri from the Indo-Pakistani states of Kashmir, and Marathi from the state of Maharashtra. In Pakistan we also have Sindhi, Multani, Balochi, and Pashto

# SUMMARY

*Hindustani* vocal music is inextricably linked to the languages of Northern India. Unfortunately, the study of these languages is such a deep matter that it is not possible to give more than the briefest glimpse. In spite of these limitations, there were a number of points that we were able to make.

Unlike the South Indian languages, most of the Northern languages are part of the Indo-European family. This implies a certain similarity to each other as well as European languages such as English, German, or French. One of the similarities is the grammatical concept of nouns, verbs, adjectives, prepositions (postpositions), etc.

There are other areas that are difficult for an English speaking person to comprehend. One area is the concept of gender. It is hard for many people to conceive of inanimate objects as having a gender; however, that is how objects are treated. Another difficult concept is having to construct sentences differently depending upon whether a person is one's social superior, equal, or inferior.

As if these differences are not enough, there is also the problem of script. There are a number of scripts used in North India, but from the standpoint of North Indian classical music, the two most important ones are Urdu (Arabic/Persian) and *Devanagari* (Sanskrit). If these points are kept in mind, then our discussion of vocal music becomes much easier.

## ENDNOTE

[1] There are a few other languages which do not fall into either of these families; however, the Indo-European and Dravidian group account for the vast majority.

# WORKS CITED

Barz, R.K.
1977 *An Introduction to Hindi and Urdu.* Canberra, Australia: Australian National University Press.

Ganathe, N.S.R.
1981 *Learn Urdu in 30 Days.* Madras: Balaji Publications.

Greaves, Edwin
1983 *Hindi Grammar.* New Delhi: Asian Educational Services.

Mallory, J. P.
1989 *In Search of the Indo-Europeans; Language Archaeology and Myth.* London: Thames and Hudson Ltd.

Srinivasachary, K.
1983 *Learn Sanskrit in 30 Days.* Madras: Balaji Publications.

Van Olphen, H.H
1992 *Hindi Pravesikaa – Beginner's Hindi: Writing and Conversation.* Austin: University of Texas.

# CHAPTER 7.
# BILAWAL THAT

*Bilawal that* is considered the most fundamental musical mode in North Indian music. This *that* consists of only natural notes; therefore, it is referred to as the *shuddha swar saptak*. This that corresponds to the Western major scale, and to the south Indian *Dhirashankarabharanam mela*. Additionally, it is believed by many to be the *Nashadi jati* of the original *shuddha jati* mentioned in the *Natya-Shastra*. Therefore, it is of great antiquity.

# THAT EXERCISES

It is obvious that one does not suddenly start singing *Bilawal*. One must begin with exercises to acquaint oneself with the basic principles. One of the most fundamental is the relationship between the *swar*. Here are a few exercises in *Bilawal that* will aid in the development of these concepts:

EXERCISE 1.

Aroh     Sa Re Ga Ma Pa Dha Ni Sa̍

Avaroh   Sa̍ Ni Dha Pa Ma Ga Re Sa


EXERCISE 2.

Aroh     Sa Re Ga Ma,   Re Ga Ma Pa,   Ga Ma Pa Dha,

            Ma Pa Dha Ni,   Pa Dha Ni Sa̍

Avaroh   Sa̍ Ni Dha Pa,   Ni Dha Pa Ma,   Dha Pa Ma Ga,

             Pa Ma Ga Re,   Ma Ga Re Sa


EXERCISE 3.

Aroh     Sa Re Ga,   Re Ga Ma,   Ga Ma Pa,

            Ma Pa Dha,   Pa Dha Ni,   Dha Ni Sa̍

Avaroh   Sa̍ Ni Dha,   Ni Dha Pa,   Dha Pa Ma,

             Pa Ma Ga,   Ma Ga Re,   Ga Re Sa


EXERCISE 4.

Aroh     Sa Re Ga Ma Ga Re,   Sa Re Ga Ma Pa Dha Ni Sa̍

Avaroh   Sa̍ Ni Dha Pa Dha Ni,   Sa̍ Ni Dha Pa Ma Ga Re Sa

EXERCISE 5.

Aroh    Sa Ga, Re Ma, Ga Pa, Ma Dha, Pa Ni, Dha Sá
Avaroh  Sá Dha, Ni Pa, Dha Ma, Pa Ga, Ma Re, Ga Sa

EXERCISE 6.

Aroh    Sa Re, Sa Re, Sa Re Ga Ma Pa Dha Ni Sá
Avaroh  Sá Ni, Sá Ni, Sá Ni Dha Pa Ma Ga Re Sa

EXERCISE 7.

Aroh    Sa,
        Sa Re Sa,
        Sa Re Ga Re Sa,
        Sa Re Ga Ma Ga Re Sa,
        Sa Re Ga Ma Pa Ma Ga Re Sa,
        Sa Re Ga Ma Pa Dha Pa Ma Ga Re Sa,
        Sa Re Ga Ma Pa Dha Ni Dha Pa Ma Ga Re Sa,
        Sa Re Ga Ma Pa Dha Ni Sá Ni Dha Pa Ma Ga Re Sa,
Avaroh  Sá,
        Sá Ni Sá,
        Sá Ni Dha Ni Sá,
        Sá Ni Dha Pa Dha Ni Sá,
        Sá Ni Dha Pa Ma Pa Dha Ni Sá,
        Sá Ni Dha Pa Ma Ga Ma Pa Dha Ni Sá,
        Sá Ni Dha Pa Ma Ga Re Ga Ma Pa Dha Ni Sá,
        Sá Ni Dha Pa Ma Ga Re Sa Re Ga Ma Pa Dha Ni Sá,

EXERCISE 8.

Aroh  Sa - Sa Re Ga Re Sa -,  Re - Re Ga Ma Ga Re -,
Ga - Ga Ma Pa Ma Ga -,  Ma - Ma Pa Dha Pa Ma - ,
Pa - Pa Dha Ni Dha Pa -,  Dha - Dha Ni Sá - Sá -,
Avaroh  Sá - Sá Ni Dha Ni Sá -,  Ni - Ni Dha Pa Dha Ni -,
Dha - Dha Pa Ma Pa Dha -,  Pa - Pa Ma Ga Ma Pa -,
Ma - Ma Ga Re Ga Ma -,  Ga - Ga Re Sa - Sa -,

# RAG BILAWAL

*Rag Bilawal* is the most basic *rag* in *Bilawal that*. Indeed the name of the *that* is derived from this *rag*. However, it has declined in popularity over the years. It is sometimes referred to as *Shuddha Bilawal* to distinguish it from the much more popular *Alhaiya Bilawal*.

Bilawal is considered by most to be *sampurna-sampurna*. However, some are of the opinion that it should be considered *shadav-sampurna* due to the weakness of *Ga* in the *arohana*. It is a morning *rag* with *Dha* as the *vadi* and *Re* as the *samavadi*. Its characteristics are:

Arohana    Sa Re Ga Ma Pa Dha Ni Sá
Avarohana  Sá Ni Dha Pa Ma Ga Re Sa
Jati       sampurna-sampurna
Vadi       Dha
Samavadi   Re
Time       morning
That       Bilawal

> Internet Resource
> "Film Songs in Rag Alhiya Bilawal"
> http://chandrakantha.com/raga_raag/film_song_raga/alhiya_bilawal.shtml

**RAG BILAWAL, SWARMALIKA – TINTAL** (Bhatkhande 1985a)

Sthai (first part)

| Ga Pa Dha Ni | Sȧ - Sȧ - | Sȧ Rė Sȧ Ni | Dha Pa Ma Ga |
|---|---|---|---|
| 3 | X | 2 | 0 |

Sthai (second Part)

| Ga Ma Pa Ga | Ma Ga Re Sa | Dha Ni Sȧ Ni | Dha Pa Ma Ga |
|---|---|---|---|
| 3 | X | 2 | 0 |

Antara (first part)

| Pa Pa Dha Ni | Sȧ - Sȧ - | Sȧ Rė Gȧ Mȧ | Gȧ Rė Sȧ - |
|---|---|---|---|
| 3 | X | 2 | 0 |

Antara (second part)

| Gȧ Rė Sȧ Rė | Sȧ Ni Dha Pa | Dha Ni Sȧ Ni | Dha Pa Ma Ga |
|---|---|---|---|
| 3 | X | 2 | 0 |

Tihai

| Ga Pa Dha Ni | Sá - Sá - | Ga Pa Dha Ni | Sá - Sá - |
|---|---|---|---|
| 3 | X | 2 | 0 |

| Ga Pa Dha Ni | Sá - - Sá - |
|---|---|
| 3 | X |

Procedure

1. Sthai (first part) 2-times
2. Sthai (second part) 2-times
3. Sthai (first part) 2-times
4. Antara (first part) 2-times
5. Antara (second part) 2-times
6. Sthai (first part) 2-times
7. Tihai

RAG BILAWAL, SWARMALIKA- TINTAL (Kulshreshtha 1983:17-18)

Arohana / Avarohana

Sa Re Ga Ma Pa Dha Ni Sȧ Sȧ Ni Dha Pa Ma Ga Re Sa

Sthai (first part)

| Sȧ - Dha Pa | Ma Ga Ma Re | Ga Ma Pa Ga | Ma Re Sa - |
| 0 | 3 | X | 2 |

Sthai (second part)

| Ga - Ma Re | Ga Pa Ni Ni | Sȧ - Rė Sȧ | Ni Dha Pa - |
| 0 | 3 | X | 2 |

Antara (first part)

| Pa - Pa Pa | Sȧ Sȧ Sȧ Sȧ | Sȧ - Sȧ - | Sȧ Rė Sȧ Sȧ |
| 0 | 3 | X | 2 |

Antara (second part)

| Sȧ - Gȧ Mȧ | Gȧ Rė Sȧ Ni | Dha Ni Sȧ Ni | Dha Pa Ma Ga |
| 0 | 3 | X | 2 |

Sthai Tans - sing sargam

1)
| Sa Re Ga Pa | Dha Ni Sȧ Rė | Sȧ Ni Dha Pa | Ma Ga Re Sa |
| 0 | 3 | X | 2 |

2)
| Sȧ Rė Gȧ Rė | Sȧ Ni Dha Ni | Sȧ Ni Dha Pa | Ma Ga Re Sa |
| 0 | 3 | X | 2 |

Antara Tans - sing sargam

| 1) Ga Pa Dha Ni | Sȧ Rė Sȧ Ni | Dha Pa Ga Pa | Dha Ni Sȧ - |
| --- | --- | --- | --- |
| 0 | 3 | X | 2 |

| 2 Sȧ Ni Dha Pa | Ma Ga Re Sa | Ga Pa Dha Ni | Sȧ - Sȧ - |
| --- | --- | --- | --- |
| 0 | 3 | X | 2 |

Tihai

| Sȧ - Dha Pa | Ma Ga Ma Re | Sȧ - Dha Pa | Ma Ga Ma Re |
| --- | --- | --- | --- |
| 0 | 3 | X | 2 |

| Sȧ - Dha Pa | Ma Ga Ma Re | Ga - Ma Pa - Ga - Ma Re Sa - - |
| --- | --- | --- |
| 0 | 3 | X |

Procedure

1. Arohana / Avarohana
2. Sthai (first part) 2-times
4. Sthai (second part) 2-times
6. Sthai (first part) 2-times
8. Antara (first part) 2-times
10. Antara (second part) 2-times
11. Sthai (first part) 2-times
12. Sthai tan #1 2-times
13. Sthai (first part)
14. Sthai Tan #2 2-times
15. Sthai (first part) 2-times
16. Antara (first part)

17. Antara Tan #1 2-times
18. Antara (first part)
19. Antara Tan #2 2-times
20. Antara (first part)
21. Antara (second part) 2-times
21. Sthai (first part) 2-times
22. Tihai

Comments

One will notice that we prefaced the last composition with the ascending and descending sequence of the *rag* (*arohana* and *avarohana*). Please pay attention to this portion. As we progress through these compositions, we will pay greater and greater attention to this section. Ultimately, we will be able to preface our composition with a full *alap*.

Another thing to consider manner in which "*Ga - Ma Pa - Ga - Ma Re Sa*" trails off at the end of the *tihai*. Notice that it is slow and easy, without any connection to the tempo of the composition. This introduces us to the concept of an extremely small *alap* which is common at the end of classical pieces.

# WORKS CITED

Bhatkhande, Vishnu Narayan
1985a  *Hindustani Sangeet Paddhati, Kramik Pustak Malika, Vol. 1.* Hathras, India: Sangeet Karyalaya
1985b  *Hindustani Sangeet Paddhati, Kramik Pustak Malika, Vol. 3.* Hathras, India: Sangeet Karyalaya

Kulshreshtha, J.S.
1983  *Sangeet Kishor.* Hathras, India: Sangeet Karyalaya.

# CHAPTER 8.
# KALYAN THAT

*Kalyan* that is characterized by the *tivra madhyam* (augmented 4th). It corresponds to the *Mechakalyani mela* of South Indian music. This that is reputed to have been *Gandharijati* (i.e., one of the seven *shuddha jatis* mentioned in the *Natya-Shastra*). Therefore, it is considered one of the oldest musical modes, predating the concept of *rag* by at least a millennium. Here are some exercises in *Kalyan that.*

# THAT EXERCISES

## EXERCISE 1.

Aroh    Sa Re Ga Má Pa Dha Ni Sá
Avaroh  Sá Ni Dha Pa Má Ga Re Sa

## EXERCISE 2.

Aroh    Sa Re Ga Má, Re Ga Má Pa, Ga Má Pa Dha,
          Má Pa Dha Ni, Pa Dha Ni Sá
Avaroh  Sá Ni Dha Pa, Ni Dha Pa Má, Dha Pa Má Ga,
          Pa Má Ga Re, Má Ga Re Sa

## EXERCISE 3.

Aroh    Sa Re Ga, Re Ga Má, Ga Má Pa,
          Má Pa Dha, Pa Dha Ni, Dha Ni Sá
Avaroh  Sá Ni Dha, Ni Dha Pa, Dha Pa Má,
          Pa Má Ga, Má Ga Re, Ga Re Sa

## EXERCISE 4.

Aroh    Sa Re Ga Má Ga Re, Sa Re Ga Má Pa Dha Ni Sá
Avaroh  Sá Ni Dha Pa Dha Ni, Sá Ni Dha Pa Má Ga Re Sa

## EXERCISE 5.

Aroh    Sa Ga, Re Má, Ga Pa, Má Dha, Pa Ni, Dha Sá
Avaroh  Sá Dha, Ni Pa, Dha Má, Pa Ga, Má Re, Ga Sa

EXERCISE 6.

Aroh    Sa Re, Sa Re, Sa Re Ga M'a Pa Dha Ni Sá
Avaroh  Sá Ni, Sá Ni, Sá Ni Dha Pa M'a Ga Re Sa

EXERCISE 7.

Aroh    Sa,
        Sa Re Sa,
        Sa Re Ga Re Sa,
        Sa Re Ga M'a Ga Re Sa,
        Sa Re Ga M'a Pa M'a Ga Re Sa,
        Sa Re Ga M'a Pa Dha Pa M'a Ga Re Sa,
        Sa Re Ga M'a Pa Dha Ni Dha Pa M'a Ga Re Sa,
        Sa Re Ga M'a Pa Dha Ni Sá Ni Dha Pa M'a Ga Re Sa,
Avaroh  Sá,
        Sá Ni Sá,
        Sá Ni Dha Ni Sá,
        Sá Ni Dha Pa Dha Ni Sá,
        Sá Ni Dha Pa M'a Pa Dha Ni Sá,
        Sá Ni Dha Pa M'a Ga M'a Pa Dha Ni Sá,
        Sá Ni Dha Pa M'a Ga Re Ga M'a Pa Dha Ni Sá,
        Sá Ni Dha Pa M'a Ga Re Sa Re Ga M'a Pa Dha Ni Sá,

EXERCISE 8.

Aroh    Sa - Sa Re Ga Re Sa -, Re - Re Ga M'a Ga Re -,
        Ga - Ga M'a Pa M'a Ga -, M'a - M'a Pa Dha Pa M'a -,
        Pa - Pa Dha Ni Dha Pa -, Dha - Dha Ni Sá - Sá -,

Avaroh  Sa̍ - Sa̍ Ni Dha Ni Sa̍ -, Ni - Ni Dha Pa Dha Ni -,
Dha - Dha Pa Ma̍ Pa Dha -, Pa - Pa Ma̍ Ga Ma̍ Pa -,
Ma̍ - Ma̍ Ga Re Ga Ma̍ -, Ga - Ga Re Sa - Sa -

# RAG KALYAN

This *rag* is known by several names; *Kalyan, Iman, Eman,* or *Yaman*. Strangely enough *Yaman Kalyan* is a different *rag*. Yaman is a *sampurna rag* which is performed at the first part of the night. The *vadi* is *Ga* and the *samavadi* is *Ni*. Typically *Sa* and *Pa* are weak in t h e *arohana*. However, such omission is not obligatory. Its structure is:

Arohana    Ni̱ Re Ga Ma̍ Pa Dha Ni Sa̍
Avarohan   Sa̍ Ni Dha Pa Ma̍ Ga Re - Ni̱ - Re - Sa
Jati       sampurna-sampurna
Vadi       Ga
Samavadi   Ni
Time       first part of night
That       Kalyan

---

Internet Resource

"Film Songs in Rag Kalyan"

http://www.chandrakantha.com/raga_raag/film_song_raga/kalyan.html

# RAG KALYAN SWARMALIKA - TINTAL (Bhatkhande 1985a;28-29)

Arohana /Avarohana / Pakad

Ṇi Re Ga Málla Dha Ni Sá - Sá Ni Dha Pa Málla Ga Re - Ṇi Re

Sa - Ṇi Re Ga - Ga Re - ‿Ga Málla Pa‿ - Re - Ṇi Re Sa

Sthai (first part)

| Ni Dha - Pa | Málla Pa Ga Málla | Pa - - - | Pa Málla Ga Re |
|---|---|---|---|
| 0 | 3 | X | 2 |

Sthai (second part)

| Sa Re Ga Re | Ga Málla Pa Dha | Pa Málla Ga Re | Ga Re Sa - |
|---|---|---|---|
| 0 | 3 | X | 2 |

Sthai (third part)

| Ṇi Re Ga Málla | Pa Dha Ni Sá | Ré Sá Ni Dha | Pa Málla Ga Málla |
|---|---|---|---|
| 0 | 3 | X | 2 |

Antara (first part)

| Ga Ga Pa Dha | Pa Sá - Sá | Ni Ré Gá Ré | Sá Ni Dha Pa |
|---|---|---|---|
| 0 | 3 | X | 2 |

Antara (second part)

| Gá Ré Sá Ni | Dha Pa Ni Dha | Pa Málla Ga Re | Ga Re Sa - |
|---|---|---|---|
| 0 | 3 | X | 2 |

Antara (third part)

| Ṇi Re Ga M'a | Pa Dha Ni Sȧ | Ṙe Sȧ Ni Dha | Pa M'a Ga M'a |
|---|---|---|---|
| 0 | 3 | X | 2 |

Tihai

| Ni Dha - Pa | M'a Pa Ga M'a | Ni Dha - Pa | M'a Pa Ga M'a |
|---|---|---|---|
| 0 | 3 | X | 2 |

| Ni Dha - Pa | M'a Pa Ga M'a | Pa - - - - Re - - - - Sa - - - |
|---|---|---|
| 0 | 3 | X |

Procedure

1. Arohana / Avarohana / Pakad
2. Sthai (first part) 2-times
3. Sthai (second part) 2-times
4. Sthai (third part) 2-times
5. Sthai (first part) 2-times
6. Antara (first part) 2-times
7. Antara (second part) 2-times
8. Antara (third part) 2-times
9. Sthai (first part) 2-times
10. Tihai

Comments

We have gone over a number of songs. In each case, the various sections of the song did not line up with the rhythmic cycle (*tal*).

That is to say that the first beat of the cycle (as denoted with the "X") did not correspond to the beginning of the song. Therefore, the first beat of the cycle, known as the *sam*, should be conceptualized as being a type of cadence or a point of emphasis.

The vocalist must conceive the starting of the song as being some number within the cycle. For example, many of the songs we covered were in 16 beats, yet began on beat number nine. But songs can actually begin on any beat, it is all determined by the composition.

As a practical matter, this means that the accompaniment patterns of the *tabla* (i.e., the theka) MUST BE COMMITTED TO MEMORY! It is probably a good idea to review the *tals* that were introduced in Chapter 3.

# RAG YAMAN, SWARMALIKA – TINTAL (Bhatkhande1985a:29-30)

Arohana / Avarohana / Pakad

Nị Re Ga Má Dha Ni Sá - Sá Ni Dha Pa Má Ga Re - Nị Re

Sa - Nị Re Ga - Ga Re - ⌣Ga Má Pa⌣ - Re - Nị Re Sa

Sthai (first part)

| Ni Dha - Pa | Má Pa Ga Má | Pa - - - | Pa Má Ga Re |
|---|---|---|---|
| 0 | 3 | X | 2 |

Sthai (second part)

| Sa Re Ga Re | Ga Má Pa Dha | Pa Má Ga Re | Ga Re Sa Sa |
|---|---|---|---|
| 0 | 3 | X | 2 |

Sthai (third part)

| Nị Re Ga Má | Pa Dha Ni Sá | Ré Sá Ni Dha | Pa Má Ga Má |
|---|---|---|---|
| 0 | 3 | X | 2 |

Antara (first part)

| Ga - Pa ⌣DhaPa⌣ | Sá - Sá - | Ni Ré Gá Ré | Sá Ni Dha Pa |
|---|---|---|---|
| 0 | 3 | X | 2 |

Antara (second part)

| Gá Ré Sá Sá | Ni Dha Má Pa | Ni Dha Pa Má | Ga Re Nị Sa |
|---|---|---|---|
| 0 | 3 | X | 2 |

Antara (third part)

| Sa Re Ga M'a | Pa Dha Ni Sá | Ṙe Sá Ni Dha | Pa M'a Ga M'a |
|---|---|---|---|
| 0 | 3 | X | 2 |

Tihai

| Ni Dha - Pa | M'a Pa Ga M'a | Pa Ni Dha Pa | M'a Pa Ga M'a |
|---|---|---|---|
| 0 | 3 | X | 2 |

| Pa Ni Dha Pa | M'a Pa Ga M'a | Pa - - - - Re - - - Sa - - - |
|---|---|---|
| 0 | 3 | X |

Procedure
1. Arohana / Avarohana / Pakad
2. Sthai (first part) 2-times
3. Sthai (second part) 2-times
4. Sthai (third part) 2-times
5. Sthai (first part) 2-times
6. Antara (first part) 2-times
7. Antara (second part) 2-times
8. Antara (third part) 2-times
9. Sthai (first part) 2-times
10. Tihai

Comment

One will notice that every song included the first beat (*sam*) as a cadence for the ending. Although the song trails off in a very small *alap*, whatever falls on the first beat is strongly emphasised.

## RAG KALYAN, KHEYAL – TINTAL (Bhatkhande 1985a:30)

guru bin kaise gun gave
guru na mane to gun nahi ave
guniyan me beguni kahave
mane to rijhave sabko
charan gahe sa dikhana ke jab
ave achpal tal sur

how can one sing the glory of the creator
without the guidance of the guru
if you fail to follow your guru
you will fail to become virtuous
and the wise will consider you to be a fool
if you follow the guru's guidance
you will become a model for those
seen as constant in following his path

Arohana / Avarohana / Pakad

Ni Re Ga M'a Dha Ni Sa - Sa Ni Dha Pa M'a Ga Re - Ni Re

Sa - Ni Re Ga - Ga Re -  Ga M'a Pa  - Re - Ni Re Sa

Sthai (first part)

| Pa Pa Ni Dha | M'a Dha Pa - | M'a Ga M'a - | Pa - - - |
|---|---|---|---|
| gu ru bi na | kai - se - | gu na ga - | ve - - - |
| 0 | 3 | X | 2 |

## Sthai (second part)

| Pa Ni Dha Pa | - M'a Ga - | Ga Re Ga Pa | Re - Sa - |
|---|---|---|---|
| gu ru na ma | - ne to - | gu na na hi | a - ve - |
| 0 | 3 | X | 2 |

## Sthai (third part)

| Ṇi Ṇi Re Re | Ga - M'a - | M'a Dha Ni Dha | M'a Dha Pa - |
|---|---|---|---|
| gu ni ya na | me - be - | gu ni - ka | ha - ve - |
| 0 | 3 | X | 2 |

## Antara (first part)

| Pa - M'a - | Ga - - Re | Ga Pa Ni Dha | Ni Rė Sȧ - |
|---|---|---|---|
| maa - ne - | to - - ri | jha - ve - | sa ba ko - |
| 0 | 3 | X | 2 |

## Antara (second part)

| Ni Rė Gȧ Rė | Ni Rė Sȧ - | Ni Dha Sȧ Sȧ | Ni Dha Pa Pa |
|---|---|---|---|
| cha ra na ga | he - sa - | de - kha na | ke - ja ba |
| 0 | 3 | X | 2 |

## Antara (third part)

| Pa Ga Pa - | Re Re Sa Sa | ⌣SaRe⌣ ⌣GaM'a⌣ | ⌣PaDha⌣ ⌣NiSȧ⌣ |
|---|---|---|---|
| a - ve - | a cha pa la | ta - - | - - |
| 0 | 3 | X | 2 |

| ⌣NiDha⌣ | ⌣PaM'a⌣ | ⌣GaRe⌣ | ⌣NiSa⌣ |
|---|---|---|---|
| - | la | su | ra |
| 2 | | | |

Tihai

| Pa Pa Ni Dha | Má Dha Pa - | Pa Pa Ni Dha | Má Dha Pa - |
| gu ru bi na | kai - se - | gu ru bi na | kai - se - |
| 0 | 3 | X | 2 |

| Pa Pa Ni Dha | Má Dha Pa - | Má - Ga Má - - Pa - - Re - - Sa - |
| gu ru bi na | kai - se - | gu - na ga - - ve - - - - - - - - |
| 0 | 3 | X |

Procedure

1. Arohana / Avarohana / Pakad
2. Sthai (first part) 2-times
3. Sthai (second part) 2-times
4. Sthai (third part) 2-times
5. Sthai (first part) 2-times
6. Antara (first part) 2-times
7. Antara (second part) 2-times
8. Antara (third part) 2-times
9. Sthai (first part) 2-times
10. Tihai

Comment

One will notice that every song ended in a *tihai*. The *tihai* is a device where a musical phrase is repeated three times. It always indicates a conclusion, therefore, every classical song will end in a *tihai*. However, the presence of the *tihai* does not necessarily mean that it is the end of the song. Many musicians will use a *tihai* to end whatever it is that they were doing.

# RAG YAMAN-SWARMALIKA - CHOUTAL (Bhatkhande 1989:60)

Arohana / Avarohana / Pakad

Ni Re Ga M'a Dha Ni Sá - Sá Ni Dha Pa M'a Ga Re - Ni Re

Sa - Ni Re Ga - Ga Re - ⌣Ga M'a Pa⌣ - Re - Ni Re Sa

Sthai (first part)

| Ga - Re - | Sa Sa Sa Ga | Re Ga | M'a Pa |
|---|---|---|---|
| X | 2 | 3 | 4 |

Sthai (second part)

| Ni Pa - M'a | - Ga Ga M'a | ⌣GaRe⌣ Ga | Re Sa |
|---|---|---|---|
| X | 2 | 3 | 4 |

Sthai (third part)

| Sa Re Ga Re | - Sa Sa Re | Ga Re | Re Sa |
|---|---|---|---|
| X | 2 | 3 | 4 |

Sthai (fourth part)

| Sa Re Ga M'a | Pa Pa Pa Re | Ga Re | ⌣SaRe⌣ Sa |
|---|---|---|---|
| X | 2 | 3 | 4 |

Antara (first part)

| * * M'a Ga | M'a Pa | Dha Pa | Ni Dha Sá Ni | Ré Sá * * |
|---|---|---|---|---|
| 2 | 3 | 4 | X | 2 |

## Antara (second part)

| * * Ni -  | Ni Ni | Dha Dha | Sȧ - Ni Ni | Pa Pa * * |
|---|---|---|---|---|
| 2 | 3 | 4 | X | 2 |

## Antara (third part)

| * * Pa Pa | Ni Dha | Má Dha |
|---|---|---|
| 2 | 3 | 4 |

| Pa Má Ga Má | Pa Pa Pa Má | Ga Re | Sa Re |
|---|---|---|---|
| X | 2 | 3 | 4 |

| Sa Sa Sa Re | Sa Sa Má Ga | Má Pa | - Pa |
|---|---|---|---|
| X | 2 | 3 | 4 |

| Ni Sȧ Ni Ni | Má Pa Pa Re | Ga Re | SaRe Sa |
|---|---|---|---|
| X | 2 | 3 | 4 |

## Tihai

| Ga - Re - | Sa Sa Ga - | Re - | Sa Sa |
|---|---|---|---|
| X | 2 | 3 | 4 |

| Ga - Re - | Sa Sa Sa Ga | Re Ga | Má Pa | - |
|---|---|---|---|---|
| X | 2 | 3 | 4 | X |

Procedure

1. Arohana / Avarohana / Pakad
2. Sthai (first part) 2-times
3. Sthai (second part) 2-times
4. Sthai (third part) 2-times
5. Sthai (fourth part) 2-times
6. Sthai (first part)
7. Sthai (first six beats of first part)
8. Antara (first part) 2-times
9. Antara (second part) 2-times
10. Antara (third part - this is a long one)
11. Sthai (first part) 2-times
11. Tihai

Comment

This piece is very different from most of the other pieces in this series. It is based upon the old *dhrupad* style. Notice how the flow of the piece was much different from anything else we have had before. Please also note that the *tihai* which resolves the piece at the end does not move like our earlier *tihais*. One other thing to note is that this piece, like many others in this work, differs from the cited Bhatkhande version.

This is a beginning series so we really should not go into further detail here.

# WORKS CITED

Bhatkhande, Vishnu Narayan
1985a *Hindustani Sangeet Paddhati, Kramik Pustak Malika, Vol. 1.* Hathras, India: Sangeet Karyalaya
1985b *Hindustani Sangeet Paddhati, Kramik Pustak Malika, Vol. 3.* Hathras, India: Sangeet Karyalaya.
1989 *Hindustani Sangeet Paddhati, Kramik Pustak Malika, Vol. 2.* Hathras, India: Sangeet Karyalaya.

Rao, B. Subba
1980 *Raganidhi: A Comparative Study Hindustani and Karnatak Ragas, Vol. 1.* Madras, India: The Music Academy.

Singh, Lal Bahadur
1977 "Rag Yaman, Tintal", *Sangeet Sagar.* Hathras, India: Sangeet Karyalaya.

# CHAPTER 9.
# KHAMMAJ THAT

*Khammaj that* is characterized by the *komal nishad* (minor seventh). This that is known as *Harikambhoji* in the *melakarta* system of the South. Two thousand years ago in the *jati* system, it was one of the seven *shuddha jatis*, where it was known as *Madhyama jati*.

# THAT EXERCISES

EXERCISE 1.

Aroh    Sa Re Ga Ma Pa Dha Ni Sa̍

Avaroh  Sa̍ Ni Dha Pa Ma Ga Re Sa

EXERCISE 2.

Aroh    Sa Re Ga Ma, Re Ga Ma Pa, Ga Ma Pa Dha,
        Ma Pa Dha Ni, Pa Dha Ni Sa̍

Avaroh  Sa̍ Ni Dha Pa, Ni Dha Pa Ma, Dha Pa Ma Ga,
        Pa Ma Ga Re, Ma Ga Re Sa

EXERCISE 3.

Aroh    Sa Re Ga, Re Ga Ma, Ga Ma Pa, Ma Pa Dha,
        Pa Dha Ni, Dha Ni Sa̍

Avaroh  Sa̍ Ni Dha, Ni Dha Pa, Dha Pa Ma, Pa Ma Ga,
        Ma Ga Re, Ga Re Sa

EXERCISE 4.

Aroh    Sa Re Ga Ma Ga Re, Sa Re Ga Ma Pa Dha Ni Sa̍

Avaroh  Sa̍ Ni Dha Pa Dha Ni, Sa̍ Ni Dha Pa Ma Ga Re Sa

EXERCISE 5.

Aroh    Sa Ga, Re Ma, Ga Pa, Ma Dha, Pa Ni, Dha Sa̍

Avaroh  Sa̍ Dha, Ni Pa, Dha Ma, Pa Ga, Ma Re, Ga Sa

EXERCISE 6.

Aroh   Sa Re, Sa Re, Sa Re Ga Ma Pa Dha <u>Ni</u> Sả

Avaroh  Sả <u>Ni</u>, Sả <u>Ni</u>, Sả <u>Ni</u> Dha Pa Ma Ga Re Sa

EXERCISE 7.

Aroh   Sa,
       Sa Re Sa,
       Sa Re Ga Re Sa,
       Sa Re Ga Ma Ga Re Sa,
       Sa Re Ga Ma Pa Ma Ga Re Sa,
       Sa Re Ga Ma Pa Dha Pa Ma Ga Re Sa,
       Sa Re Ga Ma Pa Dha <u>Ni</u> Dha Pa Ma Ga Re Sa,
       Sa Re Ga Ma Pa Dha <u>Ni</u> Sả <u>Ni</u> Dha Pa Ma Ga Re Sa

Avaroh  Sả,
        Sả <u>Ni</u> Sả,
        Sả <u>Ni</u> Dha <u>Ni</u> Sả,
        Sả <u>Ni</u> Dha Pa Dha <u>Ni</u> Sả,
        Sả <u>Ni</u> Dha Pa Ma Pa Dha <u>Ni</u> Sả,
        Sả <u>Ni</u> Dha Pa Ma Ga Ma Pa Dha <u>Ni</u> Sả,
        Sả <u>Ni</u> Dha Pa Ma Ga Re Ga Ma Pa Dha <u>Ni</u> Sả,
        Sả <u>Ni</u> Dha Pa Ma Ga Re Sa Re Ga Ma Pa Dha <u>Ni</u> Sả

EXERCISE 8.

Aroh   Sa - Sa Re Ga Re Sa -, Re - Re Ga Ma Ga Re -,
       Ga - Ga Ma Pa Ma Ga -, Ma - Ma Pa Dha Pa Ma -,
       Pa - Pa Dha <u>Ni</u> Dha Pa -, Dha - Dha <u>Ni</u> Sả - Sả -

Avaroh Sả - Sả N̲i̲ Dha N̲i̲ Sả -, N̲i̲ - N̲i̲ Dha Pa Dha N̲i̲ -,
Dha - Dha Pa Ma Pa Dha -, Pa - Pa Ma Ga Ma Pa -,
Ma - Ma Ga Re Ga Ma -, Ga - Ga Re Sa - Sa -

# RAG KHAMMAJ

This *rag* is one of the most common in Indian music. Although it is used in the classical styles, its romantic character makes it much more common in the classical and lighter styles. It is traditionally ascribed to the second part of the night.

It has a clear musical structure. It is a *shadav-sampurna rag* due to the omission of *rishabh* in the *arohana*. Even in the *avarohana*, the *rishabh* is *durbul* (i.e., weak). The *vadi* is *gandhar* and the *samavadi* is *nishad*. Undoubtedly, the use of *nishad* is its most defining characteristic. It is *shuddha nishad* in the *arohana* but *komal* in the *avarohana*. Therefore, structures like Sả Ni Sả N̲i̲ Dha Ni Sả are very common.

Its characteristics are:

| | |
|---|---|
| Arohana | Sa - Ga Ma - Pa - Dha Ni Sả |
| Avarohana | Sả N̲i̲ Dha Pa - Ma Ga Re Sa |
| Jati | shadav-sampurna |
| Vadi | Ga |
| Samavadi | Ni |
| Time | second part of night |
| That | Khammaj |
| Pakad | Ga Ma Pa Dha N̲i̲ - Dha - Pa - Dha Ga Ma - Ga |

Internet Resource
"Film Songs in Rag Khammaj"
http://www.chandrakantha.com/raga_raag/film_song_raga/khammaj.shtml

**RAG KHAMMAJ, SWARMALIKA – TINTAL** (Bhatkhande 1985a;35-36)

Arohana / Avarohana / Pakad

Sa Ga Ma Pa Dha Ni Sa᷄ – Sa᷄ Ni Dha Pa Ma Ga Re Sa

Ga Ma Pa Dha Ni – Dha – Pa – – Dha Ga Ma – Ga –

Sthai

| Ga Ga Sa Ga | Ma Pa Ga Ma | Ni Dha – Ma | Pa Dha – Ma |
| X | 2 | 0 | 3 |

| Ga – – – | Dha Ni Sa᷄ – | Sa᷄ Ni Dha Pa | Ma Ga Re Sa |
| X | 2 | 0 | 3 |

Antara (first part)

| Ga Ma Dha Ni | Sa᷄ – Ni Sa᷄ | Sa᷄ Ga᷄ Ma᷄ Ga᷄ | Ni Ni Sa᷄ – |
| X | 2 | 0 | 3 |

Antara (second part)

| Sa᷄ Re᷄ Sa᷄ Ni | Dha Ni Dha Pa | Dha Ma Pa Ga | Ma Ga Re Sa |
| X | 2 | 0 | 3 |

Sthai (alternate)

| Ni Sa Ga Ma | Pa Ga - Ma | Ni Dha - Ma | Pa Dha - Ma |
| X | 2 | 0 | 3 |
| Ga - - - | Dha Ni Sȧ - | Sȧ Ni Dha Pa | Ma Ga Re Sa |
| X | 2 | 0 | 3 |

Sthai / Tihai

| Ga Ga Sa Ga | Ma Pa Ga Ma | Ni Dha - Ma | Pa Dha - Ma |
| X | 2 | 0 | 3 |
| Ga - - - | Dha Ni Sȧ - | Sȧ Ni Dha Pa | Ma Ga Re Sa |
| X | 2 | 0 | 3 |
| Sȧ Ni Dha Pa | Ma Ga Re Sa | Sȧ Ni Dha Pa | Ma Ga Re Sa | Sa - - |
| X | 2 | 0 | 3 | X |

Procedure

1. Arohana / Avarohana / Pakad
2. Sthai 2-times
3. Antara (first part) 2-times
4. Antara (second part) 2-times
5. Sthai (alternate) 2-times
6. Sthai / Tihai

# RAG KHAMMAJ, SWARMALIKA - TINTAL (Bhatkhande 1985a:36-37)

Arohana / Avarohana / Pakad

Sa Ga Ma Pa Dha Ni Sá - Sá Ni Dha Pa Ma Ga Re Sa

Ga Ma Pa Dha Ni - Dha - Pa - - Dha Ga Ma - Ga -

Sthai (first part)

| * * * Sá | | | |
|---|---|---|---|
| 2 | | | |

| Ni Ni DhaPa Ma | Pa Ma Ga Ga | Ma - Pa Ma | Pa - - * |
|---|---|---|---|
| 0 | 3 | X | 2 |

Sthai (second part)

| Sá Ni Sá Ré | Sá Ni Dha Pa | Ma Ga Ma GaRe | Sa Re Ni Sa |
|---|---|---|---|
| 0 | 3 | X | 2 |

Sthai (third part)

| Ni Sa Ga Ma | Pa Pa Ni Ni | Sá Ni Sá Ré | Sá Ni Dha Sá |
|---|---|---|---|
| 0 | 3 | X | 2 |

Antara (first part)

| Ga Ma Dha Ni | Sá - Sá Sá | Ni - Sá Ré | Ni Sá Ni Dha |
|---|---|---|---|
| 0 | 3 | X | 2 |

## Sargam

| Sa̍ Ni Sa̍ Re̍ | Sa̍ <u>Ni</u> Dha Pa | Sa̍ <u>Ni</u> Dha Pa | Ma Ga Re Sa |
|---|---|---|---|
| 0 | 3 | X | 2 |

## Antara (second part)

| Ni̠ Sa Ga Ma | Pa Pa Ni Ni | Sa̍ Ni Sa̍ Re̍ | Sa̍ <u>Ni</u> Dha Sa̍ |
|---|---|---|---|
| 0 | 3 | X | 2 |

## Tihai

| * * * Sa̍ |
|---|
| 2 |

| <u>Ni Ni</u> DhaPa Ma | Pa Ma - Sa̍ | <u>Ni Ni</u> DhaPa Ma | Pa Ma - Sa |
|---|---|---|---|
| 0 | 3 | X | 2 |

| <u>Ni Ni</u> DhaPa Ma | Pa Ma Ga Ga | Ma - Pa - Ma - Pa - - |
|---|---|---|
| 0 | 3 | X |

## Procedure

1. Arohana / Avarohana / Pakad
2. Sthai (first part) 2-times – The last iteration should have an extra pause to carry the melody to the *khali* which is where the second part of the *sthai* begins.
3. Sthai (second part) 2-times
4. Sthai (third part) 2-times

5. Sthai (first part) 2-times – Notice that the first beat of the first part is actually the last beat of the third part.
6. Antara (first part) 2-times
7. Sargam 2-times
8. Antara (second part) 2-times
9. Sthai 2-times – Again this starts from the last beat of the second part of the *antara*.
10. Tihai

# WORKS CITED

Bhatkhande, Vishnu Narayan
1985a  *Hindustani Sangeet Paddhati, Kramik Pustak Malika, Vol. 1.* Hathras, India: Sangeet Karyalaya
1985b  *Hindustani Sangeet Paddhati, Kramik Pustak Malika, Vol. 3.* Hathras, India: Sangeet Karyalaya
1989  *Hindustani Sangeet Paddhati, Kramik Pustak Malika, Vol. 2.* Hathras, India: Sangeet Karyalaya

# CHAPTER 10.
# KAFI THAT

*Kafi* that is a very ancient musical mode. In Bharata's time it was known as *Shadaj-jati*. In the *melakarta* system of the South it is known as *Kharaharapriya*. It is characterized by a *komal gandhar* and a *komal nishad*.

# THAT EXERCISES

EXERCISE 1.

Aroh    Sa Re G̲a̲ Ma Pa Dha N̲i̲ Sȧ
Avaroh  Sȧ N̲i̲ Dha Pa Ma G̲a̲ Re Sa

EXERCISE 2.

Aroh    Sa Re G̲a̲ Ma, Re G̲a̲ Ma Pa, G̲a̲ Ma Pa Dha,
        Ma Pa Dha N̲i̲, Pa Dha N̲i̲ Sȧ
Avaroh  Sȧ N̲i̲ Dha Pa, N̲i̲ Dha Pa Ma, Dha Pa Ma G̲a̲,
        Pa Ma G̲a̲ Re, Ma G̲a̲ Re Sa

EXERCISE 3.

Aroh    Sa Re G̲a̲, Re G̲a̲ Ma, G̲a̲ Ma Pa, Ma Pa Dha,
        Pa Dha N̲i̲, Dha N̲i̲ Sȧ
Avaroh  Sȧ N̲i̲ Dha, N̲i̲ Dha Pa, Dha Pa Ma, Pa Ma G̲a̲,
        Ma G̲a̲ Re, G̲a̲ Re Sa

EXERCISE 4.

Aroh    Sa Re G̲a̲ Ma G̲a̲ Re, Sa Re G̲a̲ Ma Pa Dha N̲i̲ Sȧ
Avaroh  Sȧ N̲i̲ Dha Pa Dha N̲i̲, Sȧ N̲i̲ Dha Pa Ma G̲a̲ Re Sa

EXERCISE 5.

Aroh    Sa G̲a̲, Re Ma, G̲a̲ Pa, Ma Dha, Pa N̲i̲, Dha Sȧ
Avaroh  Sȧ Dha, N̲i̲ Pa, Dha Ma, Pa G̲a̲, Ma Re, G̲a̲ Sa

EXERCISE 6.

Aroh    Sa Re, Sa Re, Sa Re Ga Ma Pa Dha Ni Sȧ
Avaroh  Sȧ Ni, Sȧ Ni, Sȧ Ni Dha Pa Ma Ga Re Sa

EXERCISE 7.

Aroh    Sa,
        Sa Re Sa,
        Sa Re Ga Re Sa,
        Sa Re Ga Ma Ga Re Sa,
        Sa Re Ga Ma Pa Ma Ga Re Sa,
        Sa Re Ga Ma Pa Dha Pa Ma Ga Re Sa,
        Sa Re Ga Ma Pa Dha Ni Dha Pa Ma Ga Re Sa,
        Sa Re Ga Ma Pa Dha Ni Sȧ Ni Dha Pa Ma Ga Re Sa
Avaroh  Sȧ,
        Sȧ Ni Sȧ,
        Sȧ Ni Dha Ni Sȧ,
        Sȧ Ni Dha Pa Dha Ni Sȧ,
        Sȧ Ni Dha Pa Ma Pa Dha Ni Sȧ,
        Sȧ Ni Dha Pa Ma Ga Ma Pa Dha Ni Sȧ,
        Sȧ Ni Dha Pa Ma Ga Re Ga Ma Pa Dha Ni Sa,
        Sȧ Ni Dha Pa Ma Ga Re Sa Re Ga Ma Pa Dha Ni Sȧ

EXERCISE 8.

Aroh    Sa - Sa Re Ga Re Sa -, Re - Re Ga Ma Ga Re -,
        Ga - Ga Ma Pa Ma Ga -, Ma - Ma Pa Dha Pa Ma -,
        Pa - Pa Dha Ni Dha Pa -, Dha - Dha Ni Sȧ - Sȧ -

Avaroh  Sȧ - Sȧ N̠i Dha N̠i Sȧ -, N̠i - N̠i Dha Pa Dha N̠i -,
  Dha - Dha Pa Ma Pa Dha -, Pa - Pa Ma G̠a Ma Pa -,
  Ma - Ma G̠a Re G̠a Ma -, G̠a - G̠a Re Sa - Sa -

# RAG KAFI

*Rag Kafi* is the primary *rag* in *Kafi that*. One common song in this *rag* is *Biraj Me, Holi Khelat Nand Lal*. It is a *sampurna-sampurna rag* that is very straight-forward in its execution. There is some disagreement concerning the *vadi* and the *samavadi*. Some suggest that the *vadi* and *samavadi* are *pancham* and *shadaj*, respectively. However, many are of the opinion that it should be *gandhar* for the *vadi* and *nishad* for the *samavadi*. Its characteristics are:

| | |
|---|---|
| Arohana | Sa Re G̠a Ma Pa Dha N̠i Sȧ |
| Avarohana | Sȧ N̠i Dha Pa Ma G̠a Re Sa |
| Jati | sampurna-sampurna |
| Vadi | Pa (disputed) |
| Samavadi | Sa (disputed) |
| Time | evening |
| That | Kafi |
| Pakad | Sa Ma - G̠a Re - Re G̠a Ma Pa - Dha Pa Ma Pa G̠a Re Sa |

---

Internet Resource

"Film Songs in Rag Kafi"

http://www.chandrakantha.com/raga_raag/film_song_raga/kafi.shtml

# RAG KAFI, SWARMALIKA - JHAPTAL (Bhatkhande1989:318)

Arohana / Avarohana / Pakad

Sa Re G̲a̲ Ma Pa Dha N̲i̲ Sá - Sá N̲i̲ Dha Pa Ma G̲a̲ Re Sa

Sa Ma - G̲a̲ Re - Re G̲a̲ Ma Pa - Dha Pa Ma Pa G̲a̲ Re Sa

Sthai (first part)

| G̲a̲ G̲a̲ | Re Sa Re | Pa -  | Ma Pa Dha |
|----|----------|-------|-----------|
| X  | 2        | 0     | 3         |

Sthai (second part)

| G̲a̲ G̲a̲ | Re Sa Re | Pa -  | Ma Pa Pa |
|----|----------|-------|----------|
| X  | 2        | 0     | 3        |

Sthai (third part)

| Ma Dha | N̲i̲ Sá N̲i̲ | Dha Ma | Pa G̲a̲ Re |
|--------|-----------|--------|-----------|
| X      | 2         | 0      | 3         |

Sthai (fourth part)

| Re G̲a̲ | Re Ma G̲a̲ | Re Sa | Re N̲i̲ Sa |
|-------|-----------|-------|-----------|
| X     | 2         | 0     | 3         |

Sthai (fifth part)

| N̲i̲ Dha | Sá N̲i̲ Dha | Ma Pa | Dha G̲a̲ Re |
|--------|------------|-------|-------------|
| X      | 2          | 0     | 3           |

## Antara (first part)

| Ma Ma | Pa Dha <u>Ni</u> | Sá - | Dha <u>Ni</u> Sá |
|---|---|---|---|
| X | 2 | 0 | 3 |

## Antara (second part)

| Ré <u>Gá</u> | Ré Sá Ré | <u>Ni</u> Sá | <u>Ni</u> Dha Dha |
|---|---|---|---|
| X | 2 | 0 | 3 |

## Antara (third part)

| Pa Ré | Sá Sá Ré | <u>Ni</u> Sá | <u>Ni</u> Dha Dha |
|---|---|---|---|
| X | 2 | 0 | 3 |

## Antara (fourth part)

| Sá - | <u>Ni</u> Dha Ma | Pa Dha | <u>Ga</u> <u>Ga</u> Re |
|---|---|---|---|
| X | 2 | 0 | 3 |

## Antara (fifth part)

| Re <u>Ga</u> | Re Ma <u>Ga</u> | Re Sa | Re <u>Ni</u> Sa |
|---|---|---|---|
| X | 2 | 0 | 3 |

## Antara (sixth part)

| <u>Ni</u> Dha | Sá <u>Ni</u> Dha | Ma Pa | Dha <u>Ga</u> Re |
|---|---|---|---|
| X | 2 | 0 | 3 |

## Tihai

| Pa - | Ma Pa Pa | Pa - | Ma Pa Pa |
|---|---|---|---|
| 0 | 3 | X | 2 |

| Pa  - | Ma Pa Pa | Pa - - - - - |
| 0     | 3        | X            |

## Procedure

1. Arohana / Avarohana / Pakad
2. Sthai (first part) 2-times
3. Sthai (second part) 2- times
4. Sthai (third part) 2-times
5. Sthai (fourth part) 2-times
6. Sthai (fifth part) 2-times
7. Sthai (first part)
8. Sthai (second part)
9. Antara (first part) 2-times
10. Antara (second part) 2-times
11. Antara (third part) 2-times
12. Antara (fourth part) 2-times
13. Antara (fifth part) 2-times
14. Antara (sixth part) 2-times
15. Sthai (first part) 2-times
16. Sthai (half of second part)
17. Tihai

# RAG KAFI, LAKSHAN-GEET – EKTAL (Bhatkhande 1989:320)

guni gavat kafi rag
karaharapriya mel jaanit
komal ga ni ujval par
sur pancham vadi sadha
saral svarup vipashchit
maanat sab sudhaavikal
ashray guni chatur kahat


to sing rag kafi well you must know
that it is from the kharaharapriya mode
komal ga ni display the brilliance of the rag
pancham is the vadi note,
kafi is simple in form
it is sweet to sing and is easy
the learned classify it as a host rag


Arohana / Avarohana / Pakad
Sa Re Ga Ma Pa Dha Ni Sá  - Sá Ni Dha Pa Ma Ga Re Sa


Sa Ma - Ga Re - Re Ga Ma Pa - Dha Pa Ma Pa Ga Re Sa


Sthai (first part)

| PaDha | MaPa | Ga - | ReSa  Re | Ga - | Ma Pa | - Pa |
|-------|------|------|----------|------|-------|------|
| gu    | ni   | ga - | va    ta | ka - | fi ra | - g  |
| 0     |      | 3    | 4        | X    | 0     | 2    |

## Sthai (second part)

| Sȧ Rė  | Sȧ Ni  | Dha Pa | Ga -  | Re Sa | Re Sa |
| kha ra | ha ra  | pri ya | me -  | la ja | ni ta |
| 0      | 3      | 4      | X     | 0     | 2     |

## Sthai (third part)

| Sa -  | Re Re  | Ga Ga | Ma -  | Pa Pa  | Dha Dha |
| ko -  | ma la  | ga ni | u -   | jva l  | pa   r  |
| 0     | 3      | 4     | X     | 0      | 2       |

## Sthai (fourth part)

| Ni Sȧ | NiSȧ, Rė | Sȧ Ni  | Dha - | Ma Pa  | - MaPa |
| su ra | pan   -  | cha m  | va  - | di sa  | - dha  |
| 0     | 3        | 4      | X     | 0      | 2      |

## Antara (first part)

| Ma Ma | Pa Pa  | Dha -  | Ni Ni | Sȧ -   | Sȧ Sȧ   |
| sa ra | la sva | ru  -  | p  vi | pa -   | sh chit |
| 0     | 3      | 4      | X     | 0      | 2       |

## Antara (second part)

| Ni Sȧ | Rė Gȧ | Rė Sa | Rė Sȧ  | Rė Ni | Sȧ Sȧ |
| ma -  | na t  | sa b  | su dha | a vi  | ka la |
| 0     | 3     | 4     | X      | 0     | 2     |

## Antara (third part)

| Sȧ -  | Ni Dha   | Ma Pa | Ga Ga  | Re Sa  | Re Ni |
| a -   | shra ya  | gu ni | cha tu | ra ka  | ha ta |
| 0     | 3        | 4     | X      | 0      | 2     |

## Antara (fourth part)

| Sa -  | Re Re | Ga Ga | Ma - | Pa Pa | Dha Dha |
|-------|-------|-------|------|-------|---------|
| ko -  | ma l  | ga ni | u -  | jva l | pa  r   |
| 0     | 3     | 4     | X    | 0     | 2       |

## Antara (fifth part)

| Ni Sa | NiSȧ Ṙe | Sȧ Ni  | Dha - | Ma Pa | - MaPa |
|-------|---------|--------|-------|-------|--------|
| su ra | pan  -  | cha m  | va -  | di sa | - dha  |
| 0     | 3       | 4      | X     | 0     | 2      |

## Tihai

| PaDha | MaPa | Ga - | ReSa Re |
|-------|------|------|---------|
| gu    | ni   | ga - | va   ta |
| 0     |      | 3    | 4       |

| PaDha | MaPa | Ga - | ReSa Re |
|-------|------|------|---------|
| gu    | ni   | ga - | va   ta |
| X     |      | 0    | 2       |

| PaDha | MaPa | Ga - | ReSa Re | Ga - | - Ma Pa - Pa - |
|-------|------|------|---------|------|----------------|
| gu    | ni   | ga - | va   ta | ka - | - fi ra - g -  |
| 0     |      | 3    | 4       | X    |                |

Procedure

1. Arohana / Avarohana / Pakad
2. Sthai (first part) 2-times
3. Sthai (second part) 2-times

4. Sthai (third part) 2-times
5. Sthai (fourth part) 2-times
6. Sthai (first part) 2-times
7. Antara (first part) 2-times
8. Antara (second part) 2-times
9. Antara (third part) 2-times
10. Antara (fourth part) 2-times
11. Antara (fifth part) 2-times
12. Sthai (first part) 2-times
13. Tihai


**RAG KAFI, SWARMALIKA – TINTAL** (Kulshreshtha 1983:26)

Arohana / Avarohana / Pakad

Sa Re Ga Ma Pa Dha Ni Sa  -  Sa Ni Dha Pa Ma Ga Re Sa


Sa Ma - Ga Re - Re Ga Ma Pa - Dha Pa Ma Pa - Ga Re Sa


Pickup

```
*  *  Sa  Ni |
2
```

Sthai

```
Sa Sa Re Re | Ga - Ma - | Pa - Pa Ma | Ga Re Sa Ni |
0           | 3         | X          | 2           |
```

### Sthai (alternative)

| Sa Sa Re Re | Ga - Ma - | Pa Pa Pa Ma | Pa Dha Ni Sá |
|---|---|---|---|
| 0 | 3 | X | 2 |

| Ni Dha Pa Ma | Ga Ga Re - | Re Ni Dha Ni | Pa Dha Ma Pa |
|---|---|---|---|
| 0 | 3 | X | 2 |

| Ga Ma Ga Pa | Ma Ma Sa Ni | Sa Ga Re Ma | Ga Re Sa Ni |
|---|---|---|---|
| 0 | 3 | X | 2 |

### Sthai (transition)

| Sa Sa Re Re | Ga - Ma - |
|---|---|
| 0 | 3 |

### Antara (first part)

| Pa - Pa Dha | Ma Pa Ni Sá | Ré Gá Ré Sá | Ré Ni Sá Sá |
|---|---|---|---|
| X | 2 | 0 | 3 |

### Antara (second part)

| Ni - Ni Ni | Dha Ni Pa Dha | Ni Ré Sá Ré | Ni Dha Pa Pa |
|---|---|---|---|
| X | 2 | 0 | 3 |

### Antara (third part)

| Pa Ni Dha Ni | Pa Dha Ma Pa | Ga Ma Ga Pa | Ma - PaDha Ni |
|---|---|---|---|
| X | 2 | 0 | 3 |

Antara (alternative third part)

| Pa Ni Dha Ni | Pa Dha Ma Pa | Ga Ma Ga Pa | Ma - Sa Ni |
|---|---|---|---|
| X | 2 | 0 | 3 |

| Sa Ga Re Ma | Ga - ReSa Ni |
|---|---|
| X | 2 |

Sthai Tans – sing sargam

1)
| Sa Re Ga Ma | Pa Dha Ni Sà | Ni Dha Pa Ma | Ga Re Sa - |
|---|---|---|---|
| 0 | 3 | X | 2 |

2)
| Sa Re Ga Ma | Pa Ma Ga Re | Sa Re Ga Ma | Pa Dha Ma Pa |
|---|---|---|---|
| 0 | 3 | X | 2 |

Antara Tans

1)
| Sà Ni Dha Pa | Ma Ga Re Sa | Sa Re Ga Ma | Pa Dha Ni Sà |
|---|---|---|---|
| X | 2 | 0 | 3 |

2)
| Sa Re Ga Ma | Pa Ma Ga Re | Sa Re Ga Ma | Pa Dha Ni Sà |
|---|---|---|---|
| X | 2 | 0 | 3 |

Tihai

| Sa Sa Re Re | Ga - Ma - | Sa Sa Re Re | Ga - Ma - |
|---|---|---|---|
| 0 | 3 | X | 2 |

| Sa Sa Re Re | Ga - Ma - | Dha - Ma - Pa - |
|---|---|---|
| 0 | 3 | X |

Procedure

1. Arohana / Avarohana / Pakad
2. Pickup
3. Sthai – 2-times
4. Sthai (alternative)
5. Sthai (first part) – 2-times
6. Sthai (transition)
7. Antara (first part) – 2-times
8. Antara (second part) 2-times
9. Antara (third part)
10. Antara (alternative third part)
11. Sthai – 2-times
12. Sthai Tan #1 – 2-times
13. Sthai
14. Sthai Tan #2 – 2-times
15. Sthai
16. Sthai (transition)
17. Antara (first part) – 2-times
18. Antara Tan #1 – 2-times
19. Antara (first part)
20. Antara Tan #2 – 2-times
21. Antara (first part)
22. Antara (second part) – 2-times
23. Antara (third part)
24. Antara (alternative third part)
25. Sthai – 2-times
26. Tihai

# WORKS CITED

Bhatkhande, V.N.
1989  *Hindustani Sangeet Paddhati, Kramik Pustak Malika, Vol. 2.* Hathras, India: Sangeet Karyalaya

Garg, Lakshminarayan
1973  *Bal Sangeet Shiksha, Vol. 2.* Hathras, India: Sangeet Karyalaya.

Kulshreshtha, J.S.
1983  *Sangeet Kishor.* Hathras, India: Sangeet Karyalaya.

# CHAPTER 11.
# ASAWARI THAT

*Asawari that* is a very common musical mode. It was one of the ancient *jatis* mentioned by Bharata in the *Natya-shastra*. In this work it was known as *Panchami jati*. It is characterized by *komal gandhar*, *komal dhaivat*, and *komal nishad*. In the *melakarta* system of the South it is known as *Natabhairavi*.

# THAT EXERCISES

EXERCISE 1.

Aroh    Sa Re <u>Ga</u> Ma Pa <u>Dha</u> Ni Sȧ
Avaroh  Sȧ <u>Ni</u> <u>Dha</u> Pa Ma <u>Ga</u> Re Sa

EXERCISE 2.

Aroh    Sa Re <u>Ga</u> Ma, Re <u>Ga</u> Ma Pa, <u>Ga</u> Ma Pa <u>Dha</u>,
         Ma Pa <u>Dha</u> <u>Ni</u>, Pa <u>Dha</u> <u>Ni</u> Sȧ
Avaroh  Sȧ <u>Ni</u> Dha Pa, <u>Ni</u> <u>Dha</u> Pa Ma, <u>Dha</u> Pa Ma <u>Ga</u>,
         Pa Ma <u>Ga</u> Re, Ma <u>Ga</u> Re Sa

EXERCISE 3.

Aroh    Sa Re <u>Ga</u>, Re <u>Ga</u> Ma, <u>Ga</u> Ma Pa, Ma Pa <u>Dha</u>,
         Pa <u>Dha</u> <u>Ni</u>, <u>Dha</u> <u>Ni</u> Sȧ
Avaroh  Sȧ <u>Ni</u> <u>Dha</u>, <u>Ni</u> <u>Dha</u> Pa, <u>Dha</u> Pa Ma, Pa Ma <u>Ga</u>,
         Ma <u>Ga</u> Re, Ga Re Sa

EXERCISE 4.

Aroh    Sa Re <u>Ga</u> Ma <u>Ga</u> Re, Sa Re <u>Ga</u> Ma Pa <u>Dha</u> <u>Ni</u> Sȧ
Avaroh  Sȧ <u>Ni</u> <u>Dha</u> Pa <u>Dha</u> <u>Ni</u>, Sȧ <u>Ni</u> <u>Dha</u> Pa Ma <u>Ga</u> Re Sa

EXERCISE 5.

Aroh    Sa <u>Ga</u>, Re Ma, <u>Ga</u> Pa, Ma <u>Dha</u>, Pa <u>Ni</u>, <u>Dha</u> Sȧ
Avaroh  Sȧ <u>Dha</u>, <u>Ni</u> Pa, <u>Dha</u> Ma, Pa <u>Ga</u>, Ma Re, <u>Ga</u> Sa

EXERCISE 6.

Aroh    Sa Re, Sa Re, Sa Re Ga Ma Pa Dha Ni Sa̍
Avaroh  Sa̍ Ni, Sa̍ Ni, Sa̍ Ni Dha Pa Ma Ga Re Sa

EXERCISE 7.

Aroh    Sa,
        Sa Re Sa,
        Sa Re Ga Re Sa,
        Sa Re Ga Ma Ga Re Sa,
        Sa Re Ga Ma Pa Ma Ga Re Sa,
        Sa Re Ga Ma Pa Dha Pa Ma Ga Re Sa,
        Sa Re Ga Ma Pa Dha Ni Dha Pa Ma Ga Re Sa,
        Sa Re Ga Ma Pa Dha Ni Sa̍ Ni Dha Pa Ma Ga Re Sa
Avaroh  Sa̍,
        Sa̍ Ni Sa̍,
        Sa̍ Ni Dha Ni Sa̍,
        Sa̍ Ni Dha Pa Dha Ni Sa̍,
        Sa̍ Ni Dha Pa Ma Pa Dha Ni Sa̍,
        Sa̍ Ni Dha Pa Ma Ga Ma Pa Dha Ni Sa̍,
        Sa̍ Ni Dha Pa Ma Ga Re Ga Ma Pa Dha Ni Sa̍,
        Sa̍ Ni Dha Pa Ma Ga Re Sa Re Ga Ma Pa Dha Ni Sa̍

EXERCISE 8.

Aroh    Sa - Sa Re Ga Re Sa -, Re - Re Ga Ma Ga Re -,
        Ga - Ga Ma Pa Ma Ga -, Ma - Ma Pa Dha Pa Ma,
        Pa - Pa Dha Ni Dha Pa -, Dha - Dha Ni Sa̍ - Sa̍ -

133

Avaroh  Sá - Sá Ni Dha Ni Sá -, Ni - Ni Dha Pa Dha Ni -,
Dha - Dha Pa Ma Pa Dha -, Pa - Pa Ma Ga Ma Pa -,
Ma - Ma Ga Re Ga Ma -, Ga - Ga Re Sa - Sa -

# RAG ASAWARI

*Rag Asawari* is considered to be the fundamental *rag* in *Asawari that*. *Asawari* is a morning *rag*. It is *audav-sampurna* due to the omission of the *gandhar* and *nishad* in the ascending structure. The *vadi* is *dhaivat* and the *samavadi* is *gandhar*.

There are several *rags* which share the same that. *Jaunpuri* and *Darbari Kanada* are two of the most common examples. Therefore, it is important to pay attention to the *pakad* to keep from impinging upon them. *Asawari's* characteristics are:

| | |
|---|---|
| Arohana | Sa - Re Ma Pa - Dha Sá |
| Avarohan | Sá Ni Dha - Pa - Ma Ga - Re - Sa |
| Jati | audav-sampurna |
| Vadi | Dha |
| Samavadi | Ga |
| Time | morning |
| That | Asawari |
| Pakad | Re Ma Pa - Ni Dha Pa - Ma Pa Dha Ma Pa - - Ga - Re Sa |

---

Internet Resource

"Film Songs in Rag Asawari"

http://www.chandrakantha.com/raga_raag/film_song_raga/asavari.shtml

# RAG ASAWARI SWARMALIKA - TINTAL (J.V.S. Rao - personal interview)

Arohana / Avarohana / Pakad

Sa Re Ma Pa Dha Sá - Sá Ni Dha Pa Ma Ga Re Sa -

Re Ma Pa Ni - Dha Pa - Ma Pa Dha Ma Pa Ga - Re - Sa -

Sthai (first part)

| Re Ma Pa Sá | Dha Dha Pa Pa | Ma Pa Dha Pa | Ga Ga Re Sa |
|---|---|---|---|
| 3 | X | 2 | 0 |

Sthai (second part)

| Re Sa Dha Pạ | Mạ Pạ Dha Sa | Re Ma Pa Dha | Ga Ga Re Sa |
|---|---|---|---|
| 3 | X | 2 | 0 |

Antara (first part)

| Ma Pa Dha Dha | Sá - Ré Sá | Dha Sá Ré Gá | Ré Sá Dha Pa |
|---|---|---|---|
| 3 | X | 2 | 0 |

Antara (second part)

| Dha Gá Ré Sá | Ré Ni Dha Pa | Ma Pa Dha Pa | Ga Ga Re Sa |
|---|---|---|---|
| 3 | X | 2 | 0 |

Tihai

| Re Ma Pa Sȧ | Dha Dha Pa Pa | Ma Pa Dha Pa | Ga Ga Re Sa |
| 3 | X | 2 | 0 |

| Re Ma Pa Sȧ | Dha - Dha - Pa - Pa - |
| 3 | X |

Procedure

1. Arohana / Avarohana / Pakad
2. Sthai (first part) 2-times
3. Sthai (second part) 2-times
4. Sthai (first part) 2-times
5. Antara (first part) 2-times
6. Antara (second part) 2-times
7. Sthai (first part) 2-times
8. Tihai

# RAG ASAWARI, LAKSHAN-GEET – TINTAL (Bhatkhande 1989:358)

kaan mohe asaavari rag sunaae
ga ni ko adhirohan me chupaae
dhaivat vaadi ga samvaadi
madhyam sur grah nyaas supancham
avarohana sampurna dikhaaye

sing rag asawari to me
ga and ni are absent while ascending
dhaivat is vadi and ga is samavadi
madhyam is the grah and pancham is nyas
all the notes are used while descending

Arohana / Avarohana / Pakad

Sa Re Ma Pa Dha Sȧ - Sȧ Ni Dha Pa Ma Ga Re Sa -

Re Ma Pa Ni - Dha Pa - Ma Pa Dha Ma Pa Ga - Re - Sa -

Sthai (first part)

| Ma PaSȧ | Dha Pa | Dha Ma | PaDha | MaPa |
|---------|--------|--------|-------|------|
| ka  na  | mo he  | a   sa | va    | ri   |
| 0       |        | 3      |       |      |

| Ga - Re Sa | Re Ma Pa - |
| ra - ga su | na - ye - |
| X | 2 |

## Sthai (second part)

| Dha Dha Dha - | Ni Dha Pa DhaMa |
| ga ni ko - | a dhi ro - |
| 0 | 3 |

| Ma Pa PaDha MaPa | Ga - Re Sa |
| ha na me chu | pa - - ye |
| X | 2 |

## Sthai Tan - sing sargam

| Sa Re Ma Re | Ma Pa Dha Pa | Dha Gȧ Rė Sȧ | Rė Ni Dha Pa |
| 0 | 3 | X | 2 |

## Antara (first part)

| Ma - Pa Pa | Dha - Dha - | Sȧ - Sȧ Sȧ | Sȧ - Sȧ - |
| dhai - va ta | va - di - | ga - sa ma | va - di - |
| 0 | 3 | X | 2 |

## Antara (second part)

| Dha - Dha Dha | Sȧ Sȧ Sȧ Sȧ |
| ma - dhya me | su ra gra ha |
| 0 | 3 |

⌒SȧRė⌒  Gȧ Rė Sȧ  | Sȧ ⌒RėNi⌒  Dha Pa
nya       - sa su  | pan -       cha ma
X                  | 2

Antara (third part)
Ma Pa Sȧ -  | Dha Pa ⌒PaDha⌒  ⌒MaPa⌒  | Ga Ga Re Sa  | Re - Sa Sa
a va ro -   | ha na sum        -       | pu ra na di  | kha - ye -
0           | 3                         | X            | 2

Antara Tan
Sa Re Ma Re  | Ma Pa Dha Pa  | Dha Gȧ Rė Sȧ  | Rė Ni Dha Pa
0            | 3             | X             | 2

Tihai
Ma ⌒PaSȧ⌒  Dha Pa  | Dha Ma ⌒PaDha⌒  ⌒MaPa⌒
ka   na    mo he   | a   sa   va      ri
0                  | 3

Ma ⌒PaSȧ⌒  Dha Pa  | Dha Ma ⌒PaDha⌒  ⌒MaPa⌒
ka   na    mo he   | a   sa   va      ri
X                  | 2

Ma ⌒PaSȧ⌒  Dha Pa  | Dha Ma ⌒PaDha⌒  ⌒MaPa⌒
ka   na    mo he   | a   sa   va      ri
0                  | 3

Ga - - Re - Sa Re Ma Pa -
ra - - ga - su na - ye -
X

Procedure
1. Arohana, Avarohana, Pakad
2. Sthai (first part) (2x)
3. Sthai (second part) (2x)
4. Sthai Tan (2x)
5. Sthai (first part) (2x)
6. Antara (first part) (2x)
7. Antara (second part) (2x)
8. Antara (third part) (2x)
9. Antara Tan (2x)
10. Sthai (first part) (2x)
11. Tihai

# RAG ASAWARI, SWARMALIKA - TINTAL (Kulshreshtha 1983:42)

Arohana / Avarohana / Pakad

Sa Re Ma Pa Dha Sá - Sá Ni Dha Pa Ma Ga Re Sa -

Re Ma Pa Ni - Dha Pa - Ma Pa Dha Ma Pa Ga - Re - Sa -

Sthai (first part)

| Ma Ma Pa Sá | Dha Pa PaDha MaPa |
| 0 | 3 |

| Ga Ga Re Sa | Re Ma Pa - |
| X | 2 |

Sthai (second part)

| Ga Ga Re Sa | Re - Sa - | Gá - Ré Sá | Dha Dha Pa - |
| 0 | 3 | X | 2 |

Antara (first part)

| Ma Ma Pa Pa | Dha Dha Dha - | Sá - Sá - | Sá Sá Sá Sá |
| 0 | 3 | X | 2 |

Antara (second part)

| Dha - Dha Dha | Sá Sá Sá - | Gá - Ré Sá | Ni Sa Dha Pa |
| 0 | 3 | X | 2 |

Antara (third part)

| Pa Pa Gá Gá | Ré Ré Sá Sá | Ré - Sá Sá | Ré Sá Dha Pa |
| 0 | 3 | X | 2 |

Sthai Tans - sing sargam

1) | Sa Re Ma Pa | Dha Dha Sá Sá | Ni Dha Pa Ma | Ga Re Sa - |
   | 0           | 3             | X            | 2          |

2) | Ma Pa Dha Sá | Gá Gá Ré Sá | Ni Dha Pa Ma | Ga Re Sa - |
   | 0            | 3           | X            | 2          |

Antara Tans

1) | Sá Ni Dha Pa | Ma Ga Re Sa | Sa Re Ma Pa | Dha Dha Sá - |
   | 0            | 3           | X           | 2            |

2) | Sa Re Ma Ma | Re Ma Pa Pa | Ma Pa Dha Dha | Pa Dha Sá - |
   | 0           | 3           | X             | 2           |

Tihai

| Ma Ma Pa Sá | Dha Pa ⌣PaDha⌣ ⌣MaPa⌣ |
| 0           | 3                       |

| Ma Ma Pa Sá | Dha Pa ⌣PaDha⌣ ⌣MaPa⌣ |
| X           | 2                       |

| Ma Ma Pa Sá | Dha Pa ⌣PaDha⌣ ⌣MaPa⌣ |
| 0           | 3                       |

Ga - Ga - Re Sa - Re Ma Pa -
X

Procedure
1. Araohana / Avarohana / Pakad
2. Sthai (first part) 2x
3. Sthai (second part) 2x
4. Sthai (first part) 2x
5. Antara (first part) 2x
6. Antara (second part) 2x
7. Antara (third part) 2x
8. Sthai (first part) 2x
9. Sthai Tan #1 2x
10. Sthai (first part) 2x
11. Sthai Tan #2 2x
12. Sthai (first part) 2x
13. Antara (first part) 2x
14. Antara tan #1 2x
15. Antara (first part) 2x
16. Antara tan#2 2x
17. Antara (first part) 2x
18. Antara (second part) 2x
19. Antara (third part) 2x
20. Sthai (first part) 2x
21. Tihai

## WORKS CITED

Bhatkhande, V.N,
1985   *Hindustani Sangeet Paddhati, Kramik Pustak Malika, Vol. 4.* Hathras, India: Sangeet Karyalaya
1989   *Hindustani Sangeet Paddhati, Kramik Pustak Malika, Vol. 2.* Hathras, India: Sangeet Karyalaya.

Kulshreshtha, J.S,
1983   *Sangeet Kishor.* Hathras, India: Sangeet Karyalaya.

# CHAPTER 12.
# BHAIRAV THAT

*Bhairav* is an interesting *that*. It is known as *Mayamalawagoula* in the *melakarta* system. South Indians consider it to be their *shuddha-swar-saptak* (natural scale). Although Western music is modally impoverished, Hollywood seized upon this scale to be used anytime the background music requires an oriental feel. Therefore in the West, it is known as "Arabic minor". It is characterized by a *komal rishabh* and a *komal dhaivat*.

# THAT EXERCISES

EXERCISE 1.

Aroh    Sa <u>Re</u> Ga Ma Pa <u>Dha</u> Ni Sȧ
Avaroh  Sȧ Ni <u>Dha</u> Pa Ma Ga <u>Re</u> Sa


EXERCISE 2.

Aroh    Sa <u>Re</u> Ga Ma, <u>Re</u> Ga Ma Pa, Ga Ma Pa <u>Dha</u>,
Ma Pa <u>Dha</u> Ni, Pa <u>Dha</u> Ni Sȧ
Avaroh  Sȧ Ni <u>Dha</u> Pa, Ni <u>Dha</u> Pa Ma, <u>Dha</u> Pa Ma Ga,
Pa Ma Ga <u>Re</u>, Ma Ga <u>Re</u> Sa


EXERCISE 3.

Aroh    Sa <u>Re</u> Ga, <u>Re</u> Ga Ma, Ga Ma Pa, Ma Pa <u>Dha</u>,
Pa <u>Dha</u> Ni, <u>Dha</u> Ni Sȧ
Avaroh  Sȧ Ni <u>Dha</u>, Ni <u>Dha</u> Pa, <u>Dha</u> Pa Ma, Pa Ma Ga,
Ma Ga <u>Re</u>, Ga <u>Re</u> Sa


EXERCISE 4.

Aroh    Sa <u>Re</u> Ga Ma Ga <u>Re</u>, Sa Re Ga Ma Pa <u>Dha</u> Ni Sȧ
Avaroh  Sȧ Ni <u>Dha</u> Pa <u>Dha</u> Ni, Sȧ Ni <u>Dha</u> Pa Ma Ga <u>Re</u> Sa


EXERCISE 5.

Aroh    Sa Ga, <u>Re</u> Ma, Ga Pa, Ma <u>Dha</u>, Pa Ni, <u>Dha</u> Sȧ
Avaroh  Sȧ <u>Dha</u>, Ni Pa, <u>Dha</u> Ma, Pa Ga, Ma <u>Re</u>, Ga Sa

EXERCISE 6.

Aroh   Sa Re, Sa Re, Sa Re Ga Ma Pa Dha Ni Sá
Avaroh  Sá Ni, Sá Ni, Sá Ni Dha Pa Ma Ga Re Sa


EXERCISE 7.

Aroh   Sa,
       Sa Re Sa,
       Sa Re Ga Re Sa,
       Sa Re Ga Ma Ga Re Sa,
       Sa Re Ga Ma Pa Ma Ga Re Sa,
       Sa Re Ga Ma Pa Dha Pa Ma Ga Re Sa,
       Sa Re Ga Ma Pa Dha Ni Dha Pa Ma Ga Re Sa,
       Sa Re Ga Ma Pa Dha Ni Sá Ni Dha Pa Ma Ga Re Sa
Avaroh Sá,
       Sá Ni Sá,
       Sá Ni Dha Ni Sá,
       Sá Ni Dha Pa Dha Ni Sá,
       Sá Ni Dha Pa Ma Pa Dha Ni Sá,
       Sá Ni Dha Pa Ma Ga Ma Pa Dha Ni Sá,
       Sá Ni Dha Pa Ma Ga Re Ga Ma Pa Dha Ni Sá,
       Sá Ni Dha Pa Ma Ga Re Sa Re Ga Ma Pa Dha Ni Sá


EXERCISE 8.

Aroh   Sa - Sa Re Ga Re Sa -, Re - Re Ga Ma Ga Re -,
       Ga - Ga Ma Pa Ma Ga -, Ma - Ma Pa Dha Pa Ma -,
       Pa - Pa Dha Ni Dha Pa -, Dha - Dha Ni Sá - Sá -

Avaroh  Sȧ - Sȧ Ni Dha Ni Sȧ -, Ni - Ni Dha Pa Dha Ni -,
Dha - Dha Pa Ma Pa Dha -, Pa - Pa Ma Ga Ma Pa -,
Ma - Ma Ga Re Ga Ma -, Ga - Ga Re Sa - Sa -

## RAG BHAIRAV

*Rag Bhairav* is very common. According to mythology it was the first *rag*. It is a very well known *rag*, yet seldom heard in performances. This is due to the fact that it is a morning *rag*, and most performances are in the evening.

It has a very simple structure. It is *sampurna-sampurna* with *dhaivat* as the *vadi* and *rishabh* as the *samavadi*. Rishabh and *dhaivat* should have a heavy *andolan* (slow shake) to define its character. *Bhairav's* characteristics are:

| | |
|---|---|
| Arohana | Sa Re Ga - Ma - Pa Dha - Ni Sȧ |
| Avarohana | Sȧ Ni Dha - Pa Ma Ga - Re - Sa |
| Jati | sampurna-sampurna |
| Vadi | Dha |
| Samavadi | Re |
| Time | morning |
| That | Bhairav |
| Pakad | Ga Ma Dha Dha Pa - ⸝Ga Ma Pa Ga Re⸍ Re - Sa - |

---

Internet Resource

"Film Songs in Rag Bhairav"

http://www.chandrakantha.com/raga_raag/film_song_raga/bhairav.shtml

# RAG BHAIRAV, SWARMALIKA – JHAPTAL (Bhatkhande1985:40)

Arohana / Avarohana / Pakad

Sa Re Ga Ma Pa Dha Ni Sȧ - Sȧ Ni Dha Pa Ma Ga Re Sa -

Ga Ma Dha - Dha - Pa - ⌢Ga Ma Pa Ga Ma Re⌣ Re - Sa -

Sthai (first part)

| Sa Dha | Pa Pa Dha | Ma Pa | Ma Ga Re |
|---|---|---|---|
| X | 2 | 0 | 3 |

Sthai (second part)

| Ga Re | Ga Ma Pa | Ma Ga | Re Re Sa |
|---|---|---|---|
| X | 2 | 0 | 3 |

Sthai (third part)

| Ṇi Sa | Re Re Sa | Dha Dha | Ṇi Sa - |
|---|---|---|---|
| X | 2 | 0 | 3 |

Sthai (fourth part)

| Ga Re | Ga Ma Pa | Ma Ga | Re Re Sa |
|---|---|---|---|
| X | 2 | 0 | 3 |

Antara (first part)

| Pa Pa | Dha Dha Ni | Sȧ - | Dha Ni Sȧ |
|---|---|---|---|
| X | 2 | 0 | 3 |

| Dha Dha | Ni Sȧ Rė | Sȧ Ni | Dha Dha Pa |
|---|---|---|---|
| X | 2 | 0 | 3 |

Antara (second part)

| Ma Ga | Ma Pa Dha | Rė Sȧ | Dha Dha Pa |
|---|---|---|---|
| X | 2 | 0 | 3 |

Antara (third part)

| Sȧ Ni | Dha Dha Pa | Ma Ga | Re Re Sa |
|---|---|---|---|
| X | 2 | 0 | 3 |

Tihai

| Ma Pa | Ma Ga Re | Ma Pa | Ma Ga Re |
|---|---|---|---|
| 0 | 3 | X | 2 |

| Ma Pa | Ma Ga Re | Sa - |
|---|---|---|
| 0 | 3 | X |

Procedure

1. Arohana / Avarohana / Pakad
2. Sthai (first part) 2-times
3. Sthai (second part) 2-times
4. Sthai (third part) 2-times
5. Sthai (fourth part) 2-times
6. Sthai (first part) 2-times
7. Antara (first part) 2-times
8. Antara (second part) 2-times
9. Antara (third part) 2-times
11. Sthai (first part) 2-times
12. Sthai (half of first part)
12. Tihai

# RAG BHAIRAV, SWARMALIKA – TINTAL (Bhatkhande 1985:41)

Arohana / Avarohana / Pakad

Sa Re Ga Ma Pa Dha Ni Sá  - Sá Ni Dha Pa Ma Ga Re Sa -

Ga Ma Dha - Dha - Pa - ⌒Ga Ma Pa Ga Ma Re⌒ - Ré - Sá -

Sthai (first part)

| * * Pa Ma | Re - - Sa | - Re Ṇi Sa | Ma - - - | Re Re * * |
|2|0|3|X|2|

Sthai (second part)

| * * Ma Ma | Pa - Pa Dha | Sá - Sá ⌒SáNi⌒ |
|2|0|3|

| Dha Ni Dha Pa | Ma Re * * |
|X|2|

Two Beat Pause

| * * - - |
|2|

Antara (first part)

| Ma - Pa - | Dha - Ni Ni | Sá Sá Sá Sá | Ni Sá Sá Sá |
|0|3|X|2|

## Antara (2nd part)

| Dha - Dha Dha | Ni - Sȧ Sȧ | Rė Rė Sȧ Sȧ | Ni Sȧ Dha Pa |
|---|---|---|---|
| 0 | 3 | X | 2 |

## Antara (3nd part)

| Ga Ma Pa Dha | Sȧ - Sȧ ⌣SȧNi⌣ | Dha Ni Dha Pa | Ma Re Pa ⌣MaGa⌣ |
|---|---|---|---|
| 0 | 3 | X | 2 |

## Tihai (pickup)

| * * Pa Ma | Re - - Sa | - - Pa Ma | Re - - Sa |
|---|---|---|---|
| 2 | 0 | 3 | X |

## Tihai

| - - Pa Ma | Re - - Sa | - Re Ṇi Sa | Ma - Re - Sa Sa |
|---|---|---|---|
| 2 | 0 | 3 | X |

Procedure

1. Arohana / Avarohana / Pakad
2. Sthai (first part) 2-times
3. Sthai (second part) 2-times
4. Sthai (first part) 2-times
5. Two Beat Pause
6. Antara (first part) 2-times
7. Antara (second part) 2-times
8. Antara (third part)
9. Antara (third part) (subtract two beats from the end)
10. Sthai (first part) 2-times
11. Tihai (pickup)
12. Tihai

Comments

Up to now, the *sthais* and *antaras* always started on the same beat. This is not always the case. This shows how we can handle this situation. In this example, the *sthai* starts on beat number seven, while the *antara* starts on beat number nine. This means that we must add two beats before starting the *antara* and subtract two beats before returning to the *sthai*. At first this may seem to be complicated, but it is really easy when we remember to always listen to the *tabla*. Its *theka* will always tell us where we are.

# RAG BHAIRAV, SWARMALIKA – TINTAL (Bhatkhande1985:42)

Arohana / Avarohana / Pakad

Sa Re Ga Ma Pa Dha Ni Sá – Sá Ni Dha Pa Ma Ga Re Sa –

Ga Ma Dha – Dha – Pa – Ga Ma Pa Ga Ma Re , – Rė – Sá –

**Sthai (first part)**

| Ga Ma Dha Dha | Pa – Dha Ma | Dha – PaMa, Pa | Ma – Ga – |
| 0 | 3 | X | 2 |

**Sthai (second part)**

| Ga Ga Ma Ga | Re – Ga Pa | Ma Ga Ma Ga | Re – Sa – |
| 0 | 3 | X | 2 |

**Sthai (third part)**

| Ni Sa Ga Ma | Pa Dha Ni Sá | Rė – Sá Ni | Dha Pa Ma Ga |
| 0 | 3 | X | 2 |

**Antara (first part)**

| Pa Pa Pa Pa | Dha Dha Ni Ni | Sá Sá Sá Sá | Rė – Sá – |
| 0 | 3 | X | 2 |

**Antara (second part)**

| Dha – Dha Dha | Ni Ni Sá Sá | Rė – Sá Sá | Ni Sá Dha Pa |
| 0 | 3 | X | 2 |

## Antara (third part)

| Ga Ma Pa Dha | Sȧ Ni Dha Pa | Ma Ga Ma Ga | Re - Sa Sa |
|---|---|---|---|
| 0 | 3 | X | 2 |

## Antara (fourth part)

| Ṇi Sa Ga Ma | Pa Dha Ni Sȧ | Ṙe - Sȧ Ni | Dha Pa Ma Ga |
|---|---|---|---|
| 0 | 3 | X | 2 |

## Sthai Tans - sing sargam

1) 
| Ṇi Sa Ga Ma | Pa Dha Sȧ - | Ni Dha Pa Ma | Ga Re Sa - |
|---|---|---|---|
| 0 | 3 | X | 2 |

2) 
| Ga Ma Pa Dha | Ni Sȧ Ṙe Sȧ | Ni Dha Pa Ma | Ga Re Sa - |
|---|---|---|---|
| 0 | 3 | X | 2 |

## Antara Tans - sing sargam

1) 
| Sȧ Ni Dha Pa | Ma Ga Re Sa | Sa Re Ga Ma | Pa Dha Ni Sȧ |
|---|---|---|---|
| 0 | 3 | X | 2 |

2) 
| Dha Ni Sȧ Ṙe | Sȧ Ni Dha Pa | Ma Ga Ma Pa | Dha Ni Sȧ - |
|---|---|---|---|
| 0 | 3 | X | 2 |

## Tihai

| Ga Ma Dha Dha | Pa - Dha Ma | Ga Ma Dha Dha | Pa - Dha Ma |
|---|---|---|---|
| ja - go - | mo - ha n | ja - go - | mo - ha n |
| 0 | 3 | X | 2 |

| Ga Ma Dha Dha | Pa - Dha Ma | Dha - Pa Ma Pa Ma - Ga - Re - Sa |
|---|---|---|
| 0 | 3 | X |

Procedure

1. Arohana / Avarohana / Pakad
2. Sthai (first part) 2-times
3. Sthai (second part) 2-times
4. Sthai (third part) 2-times
5. Sthai (first part) 2-times
6. Antara (first part) 2-times
7. Antara (second part) 2-times
8. Antara (third part) 2-times
9. Antara (fourth part) 2-times
10. Sthai (first part) 2-times
11. Sthai Tan #1 (single time)
12. Sthai Tan #1 (double time) 2-times
13. Sthai (first part) 2-times
14. Sthai Tan #2 (single time)
15. Sthai Tan #2 (double time) 2-times
16. Sthai (first part) 2-times
17. Antara (first part) 2-times
18. Antara Tan #1 (single time)
19. Antara Tan #1 (double time) 2-times
20. Antara (first part) 2-times
21. Antara Tan #2 (single time)
22. Antara Tan #2 (double time) 2-times
23. Antara (first part) 2-times
24. Antara (second part) 2-times
25. Antara (third part) 2-times
26. Antara (fourth part) 2-times
27. Sthai (first part) 2-times
28. Tihai

# WORKS CITED

Bhatkhande, V.N.
1985 *Hindustani Sangeet Paddhati, Kramik Pustak Malika, Vol. 1.* Hathras, India: Sangeet Karyalaya.

# CHAPTER 13
# BHAIRAVI THAT

This is a very ancient musical mode. In Bharata's time it was referred to as *Arshabi jati*. In the South, it is known as *Hanumantodi*. It is characterized by a *komal rishabh, komal gandhar, komal dhaivat,* and *komal nishad*.

# THAT EXERCISES

EXERCISE 1.

Aroh    Sa Re Ga Ma Pa Dha Ni Sả
Avaroh  Sả Ni Dha Pa Ma Ga Re Sa


EXERCISE 2.

Aroh    Sa Re Ga Ma, Re Ga Ma Pa, Ga Ma Pa Dha,
        Ma Pa Dha Ni, Pa Dha Ni Sả
Avaroh  Sả Ni Dha Pa, Ni Dha Pa Ma, Dha Pa Ma Ga,
        Pa Ma Ga Re, Ma Ga Re Sa


EXERCISE 3.

Aroh    Sa Re Ga, Re Ga Ma, Ga Ma Pa,
        Ma Pa Dha, Pa Dha Ni, Dha Ni Sả,
Avaroh  Sả Ni Dha, Ni Dha Pa, Dha Pa Ma,
        Pa Ma Ga, Ma Ga Re, Ga Re Sa,


EXERCISE 4.

Aroh    Sa Re Ga Ma Ga Re, Sa Re Ga Ma Pa Dha Ni Sả
Avaroh  Sả Ni Dha Pa Dha Ni, Sả Ni Dha Pa Ma Ga Re Sa


EXERCISE 5.

Aroh    Sa Ga, Re Ma, Ga Pa, Ma Dha, Pa Ni, Dha Sả
Avaroh  Sả Dha, Ni Pa, Dha Ma, Pa Ga, Ma Re, Ga Sa

EXERCISE 6.

Aroh    Sa Re, Sa Re, Sa Re Ga Ma Pa Dha Ni Sà
Avaroh  Sà Ni, Sà Ni, Sà Ni Dha Pa Ma Ga Re Sa


EXERCISE 7.

Aroh    Sa,
        Sa Re Sa,
        Sa Re Ga Re Sa,
        Sa Re Ga Ma Ga Re Sa,
        Sa Re Ga Ma Pa Ma Ga Re Sa,
        Sa Re Ga Ma Pa Dha Pa Ma Ga Re Sa,
        Sa Re Ga Ma Pa Dha Ni Dha Pa Ma Ga Re Sa,
        Sa Re Ga Ma Pa Dha Ni Sà Ni Dha Pa Ma Ga Re Sa

Avaroh  Sà,
        Sà Ni Sà,
        Sà Ni Dha Ni Sà,
        Sà Ni Dha Pa Dha Ni Sà,
        Sà Ni Dha Pa Ma Pa Dha Ni Sà,
        Sà Ni Dha Pa Ma Ga Ma Pa Dha Ni Sà,
        Sà Ni Dha Pa Ma Ga Re Ga Ma Pa Dha Ni Sà,
        Sà Ni Dha Pa Ma Ga Re Sa Re Ga Ma Pa Dha Ni Sà


Exercise 8.

Aroh    Sa - Sa Re Ga Re Sa -, Re - Re Ga Ma Ga Re -,
        Ga - Ga Ma Pa Ma Ga -, Ma - Ma Pa Dha Pa Ma -,
        Pa - Pa Dha Ni Dha Pa -, Dha - Dha Ni Sà - Sà -

Avaroh   Sá - Sá N̲i D̲h̲a̲ N̲i Sá -, N̲i - N̲i D̲h̲a̲ Pa D̲h̲a̲ N̲i -,
   D̲h̲a̲ - D̲h̲a̲ Pa Ma Pa D̲h̲a̲ -, Pa - Pa Ma G̲a̲ Ma Pa -,
   Ma - Ma G̲a̲ R̲e̲ G̲a̲ Ma -, G̲a̲ - G̲a̲ R̲e̲ Sa - Sa -

## RAG BHAIRAVI

This *rag* is the main representative of *Bhairavi that*. It has traditionally been sung in the early morning hours. However, due to the fact that performances went all night, it became common to consider *Bhairavi* the finale. Today, it is played at any time, provided it is the end of a concert.

There are two approaches to the performance of *Bhairavi; Shuddha Bhairavi* and *Sindhi (Sindhu) Bhairavi*. In *Shuddha Bhairavi*, only the notes of *Bhairavi that* are used. In *Sindhi Bhairavi*, all of the notes may be used. These are opposite extremes of philosophy. Contemporary practice tends to be somewhere in between, although the degree is strictly a question of individual artistic interpretation.

The structure is very simple and flexible. The *vadi* is usually considered to be *madhyam* and the *samavadi* is *shadaj*. However, *gandhar, dhaivat,* and *pancham,* have also been suggested for the *vadi* and *samavadi.*

The characteristics are:

| | |
|---|---|
| Arohana | Sa Re Ga Ma Pa Dha Ni Sá |
| Avarohana | Sá Ni Dha Pa Ma Ga Re Sa |
| Jati | sampurna-sampurna |
| Vadi | Ma (disputed) |
| Samavadi | Sa (disputed) |
| Time | early morning or end of concert (anytime) |
| That | Bhairavi |
| Pakad | Ga Ma Pa Dha - Pa - Ma Ga Re Ga - Re - Sa |

---

Internet Resource

"Film Songs in Rag Bhairavi"

http://www.chandrakantha.com/raga_raag/film_song_raga/bhairavi.html

# RAG BHAIRAVI, SWARMALIKA – TINTAL (Bhatkhande1989:392)

Arohana / Avarohana / Pakad

Sa Re Ga Ma Pa Dha Ni Sá – Sá Ni Dha Pa Ma Ga Re Sa –

Ga Ma Pa Dha – Pa – Ma Ga Re – Ga – Re – Sa

Sthai (first part)

| Ma Ga Re Sa | Ni Sa Dha – | Ni Dha – Ga | Ma Dha Ma Pa |
|---|---|---|---|
| 0 | 3 | X | 2 |

Sthai (second part)

| Ga Ma Ga Re | Sa Ni Dha – | Dha Ni Sa Ga | – Ma Dha – |
|---|---|---|---|
| 0 | 3 | X | 2 |

Sthai (third part)

| Ni Sá – Ré | Sá Ni Dha Ma | Pa Ni Dha Pa | Ma Ga Re Sa |
|---|---|---|---|
| 0 | 3 | X | 2 |

Antara (first part)

| Ni Ni Dha Ni | Dha Pa Ma Ga | Ma Dha Ni Sá | Dha Ni Sá – |
|---|---|---|---|
| 0 | 3 | X | 2 |

Antara (second part)

| Gá Má Gá Ré | Sá Ni Dha Ni | Gá – Sá – | Ré Ni Sá – |
|---|---|---|---|
| 0 | 3 | X | 2 |

Antara (third part)

| Dha - Ni Ma | - Dha Ga - | Ma Ni Dha Pa | Ma Ga Re Sa |
|---|---|---|---|
| 0 | 3 | X | 2 |

Tihai

| Ma Ga Re Sa | Ni Sa Dha - | Ma Ga Re Sa | Ni Sa Dha - |
|---|---|---|---|
| 0 | 3 | X | 2 |

| Ma Ga Re Sa | Ni Sa Dha - | Pa |
|---|---|---|
| 0 | 3 | X |

Procedure

1. Arohana / Avarohana / Pakad
2. Sthai (first part) 2-times
3. Sthai (second part) 2-times
4. Sthai (third part) 2-times
5. Sthai (first part) 2-times
6. Antara (first part) 2-times
7. Antara (second part) 2-times
8. Antara (third part) 2-times
9. Sthai (first part) 2-times
10. Tihai

# RAG BHAIRAVI, LAKSHAN-GEET - JHAPTAL (J.V.S. Rao-personal interview)

jayati jay ragini, bhairavi naamini
bhakti ras purini, pratah gaavat guni
-
sapt sur rupini, sakal mrudu svairini
shadaj samvaadini, pancham suvaadini


hail rag bhairavi, which is full of devotion
this rag is best performed in the early morning hours
this rag uses all seven notes in a flattened form
shadaj is the samavadi and pancham is the vadi


Arohana / Avarohana / Pakad

Sa Re Ga Ma Pa Dha Ni Sá - Sá Ni Dha Pa Ma Ga Re Sa -

Ga Ma Pa Dha - Pa - Ma Ga Re - Ga - Re - Sa -


Sthai (first part)

| Pa Dha | Pa Ga Ma | Pa Ni | ⌒DhaPa⌒ | Ga Ma |
|--------|----------|-------|---------|-------|
| ja ya  | ti ja ya | ra -  | gi      | ni -  |
| X      | 2        | 0     | 3       |       |

Sthai (second part)

| Pa Dha | ⌒SáNi⌒ | Dha Pa | Ga Ma | ⌒PaMa⌒ | Re Sa |
|--------|--------|--------|-------|--------|-------|
| bhai - | ra     | vi -   | na -  | mi     | ni -  |
| X      | 2      |        | 0     | 3      |       |

**Sthai (third part)**

| Ga -  | Ga Ma Ma  | SaGa MaPa | Ma Re Sa |
|---|---|---|---|
| bha - | kti ra sa | pu    -   | ri ni -  |
| X     | 2         | 0         | 3        |

**Sthai (fourth part)**

| GaMa PaNi | Dha Pa Ga | Pa Ma   | Re Sa -  |
|---|---|---|---|
| pra   -   | ta  ga -  | va ta   | gu ni -  |
| X         | 2         | 0       | 3        |

**Antara (first part)**

| Ga Ga | Ma Dha Ni  | Sȧ Ni | SȧGȧ Rė Sȧ |
|---|---|---|---|
| sa -  | pta su ra  | ru -  | pi    ni - |
| X     | 2          | 0     | 3          |

**Antara (second part)**

| Ni Ni | Ni Sȧ Sȧ   | DhaNi SȧRė | Sȧ Dha Pa |
|---|---|---|---|
| sa ka | la mru du  | svai -     | ri ni -   |
| X     | 2          | 0          | 3         |

**Antara (third part)**

| Dha Dha | Ni Sȧ -   | SȧRė Gȧ | Rė Sȧ -  |
|---|---|---|---|
| sha da  | ja sam -  | va -    | di ni -  |
| X       | 2         | 0       | 3        |

**Antara (fourth part)**

| Sȧ -   | Ni Dha Pa  | Ga Ma | PaMa Rė Sa |
|---|---|---|---|
| pan -  | cha ma su  | va -  | di ni -    |
| X      | 2          | 0     | 3          |

Filler

| Pa Dha | Pa Ga Ma |
|---|---|
| ja ya | ti ja ya |
| X | 2 |

Tihai

| Pa Ni | DhaPa  Ga Ma | Pa Ni | DhaPa  Ga Ma |
|---|---|---|---|
| ra - | gi    ni - | ra - | gi    ni - |
| 0 | 3 | X | 2 |

| Pa Ni | DhaPa  Ga Ma | Pa  -  |
|---|---|---|
| ra - | gi    ni - | -   - |
| 0 | 3 | X |

Procedure

1. Arohana / Avarohana / Pakad
2. Sthai (first part) 2-times
3. Sthai (second part) 2-times
4. Sthai (third part) 2-times
5. Sthai (fourth part) 2-times
6. Sthai (first part) 2-times
7. Antara (first part) 2-times
8. Antara (second part) 2-times
9. Antara (third part) 2-times
10. Antara (fourth part) 2-times
11. Sthai (first part) 2-times
12. Filler
13. Tihai

RAG BHAIRAVI, SWARMALIKA – TINTAL (Kulshreshth 1983:36-37)

Arohana / Avarohana / Pakad

Sa Re Ga Ma Pa Dha Ni Sá - Sá Ni Dha Pa Ma Ga Re Sa -

Ga Ma Pa Dha - Pa - Ma Ga Re - Ga - Re - Sa -

Sthai (first part)

| Pa Pa Pa Dha | PaMa Pa Ga Ma | Pa Ni Dha Pa | Ma Ga Re Sa |
|---|---|---|---|
| 0 | 3 | X | 2 |

Sthai (second part)

| Re  - Ga Ma | Ga Ga Re Sa | Pa Dha Ni Sá | Pa Dha Pa - |
|---|---|---|---|
| 0 | 3 | X | 2 |

Antara (first part)

| Ga Ma Dha Ni | Sá Sá Ré Sá | Ni - Sá Sá | RéNi Sá Dha Pa |
|---|---|---|---|
| 0 | 3 | X | 2 |

Antara (second part)

| Pa - Pa Pa | Pa Dha Ni Sá | Pa Dha Pa Ma | Ga Re - Sa |
|---|---|---|---|
| 0 | 3 | X | 2 |

Sthai Tans – sing sargam

| 1) Ni Sa Ga Ma | Pa Dha Ni Sá | Ni Dha Pa Ma | Ga Re Sa - |
|---|---|---|---|
| 0 | 3 | X | 2 |

2) Pa <u>Dha Ni</u> Sȧ | <u>Ni Dha</u> Pa Ma | <u>Ga</u> Ma Pa Ma | <u>Ga Re</u> Sa  - |
   0              | 3               | X               | 2              |

3) Sȧ <u>Ni Dha</u> Pa | Ma Pa <u>Ga</u> Ma | Pa <u>Dha</u> Pa Ma | <u>Ga Re</u> Sa  - |
   0                | 3                | X                 | 2              |

4) Sa <u>Re Ga</u> Ma | <u>Re Ga</u> Ma Pa | <u>Ga</u> Ma Pa <u>Dha</u> | Ma Pa <u>Dha Ni</u> |
   0               | 3                | X                      | 2                |

Pa <u>Dha Ni</u> Sȧ | Sȧ <u>Ni Dha</u> Pa | <u>Ni Dha</u> Pa Ma | <u>Ga Re</u> Sa  - |
0                | 3                | X                | 2              |

Antara Tans - sing sargam

1) Sȧ <u>Ni Dha</u> Pa | Ma <u>Ga Re</u> Sa | <u>Ni</u> Sa <u>Ga</u> Ma | Pa <u>Dha Ni</u> Sȧ |
   0                | 3               | X                      | 2                 |

2) Sȧ <u>Ṙe</u> Sȧ <u>Ni</u> | <u>Dha</u> Pa Ma <u>Ga</u> | <u>Re Ga</u> Ma Pa | <u>Dha Ni</u> Sȧ  - |
   0                   | 3                    | X                | 2               |

Tihai

Pa Pa Pa <u>Dha</u> | <u>PaMa</u> Pa <u>Ga</u> Ma | Pa Pa Pa <u>Dha</u> | <u>PaMa</u> Pa <u>Ga</u> Ma |
0                | 3                      | X                 | 2                      |

Pa Pa Pa <u>Dha</u> | <u>PaMa</u> Pa <u>Ga</u> Ma |
0                | 3                      |

Pa - <u>Ni</u> - <u>Dha</u> - Pa - Ma - <u>Ga</u> - <u>Re</u> - Sa
X

Procedure

1. Arohana / Avarohana / Pakad
2. Sthai (first part) 2-times
3. Sthai (second part) 2-times
4. Sthai (first part) 2-times
5. Antara (first part) 2-times
6. Antara (second part) 2-times
7. Sthai (first part) 2-times
8. Sthai Tan #1 (single time)
9. Sthai Tan #1 (double time)
10. Sthai Tan #1 (double time - "aahkar")
11. Sthai (first part) 2-times
12. Sthai Tan #2 (single time)
13. Sthai Tan #2 (double time)
14. Sthai Tan #2 (double time - "aahkar")
15. Sthai (first part) 2-times
16. Sthai Tan #3 (single time)
17. Sthai Tan #3 (double time)
18. Sthai Tan #3 (double time - "aahkar")
19. Sthai (first part) 2-times
20. Sthai Tan #4 (single time)
21. Sthai Tan #4 (double time)
22. Sthai (first part) 2-times
23. Antara (first part) 2-times
24. Antara Tan #1 (single time)
25. Antara Tan #1 (double time)
26. Antara Tan #1 (double time - "aahkar")
27. Antara (first part) 2-times
28. Antara Tan #2 (single time)
29. Antara Tan #2 (double time)
30. Antara Tan #2 (double time - "aahkar")

31. Antara (first part) 2-times
32. Antara (second part) 2-times
33. Sthai (first part) 2-times
34. Tihai

## WORKS CITED

Bhatkhande, V. N.
1989 *Hindustani Sangeet Paddhati, Kramik Pustak Malika, Vol. 2.* Hathras, India: Sangeet Karyalaya.

Kulshreshth, Jagdish Sahay
1983 *Sangeet Kishor*, Hathras, India: Sangeet Karyalaya.

# CHAPTER 14.
# PURVI THAT

*Purvi that* is one of the ten *thats* mentioned by Bhatkhande. It is known in the South as *Kamavardhini mela*. It is characterized by a *komal rishabh, tivra madhyam*, and a *komal dhaivat*.

## THAT EXERCISES

EXERCISE 1.

Aroh    Sa Re Ga M'a Pa Dha Ni Sȧ
Avaroh  Sȧ Ni Dha Pa M'a Ga Re Sa

EXERCISE 2.

Aroh    Sa Re Ga M'a, Re Ga M'a Pa, Ga M'a Pa Dha,
        M'a Pa Dha Ni, Pa Dha Ni Sȧ
Avaroh  Sȧ Ni Dha Pa, Ni Dha Pa M'a, Dha Pa M'a Ga,
        Pa M'a Ga Re, M'a Ga Re Sa

EXERCISE 3.

Aroh    Sa Re Ga, Re Ga M'a, Ga M'a Pa, M'a Pa Dha,
        Pa Dha Ni, Dha Ni Sȧ
Avaroh  Sȧ Ni Dha, Ni Dha Pa, Dha Pa M'a, Pa M'a Ga,
        M'a Ga Re, Ga Re Sa

EXERCISE 4.

Aroh    Sa Re Ga M'a Ga Re, Sa Re Ga M'a Pa Dha Ni Sȧ
Avaroh  Sȧ Ni Dha Pa Dha Ni, Sȧ Ni Dha Pa M'a Ga Re Sa

EXERCISE 5.

Aroh    Sa Ga, Re M'a, Ga Pa, M'a Dha, Pa Ni, Dha Sȧ
Avaroh  Sȧ Dha, Ni Pa, Dha M'a, Pa Ga, M'a Re, Ga Sa

EXERCISE 6.

Aroh    Sa Re, Sa Re, Sa Re Ga M'a Pa Dha Ni Sȧ
Avaroh  Sȧ Ni, Sȧ Ni, Sȧ Ni Dha Pa M'a Ga Re Sa


EXERCISE 7.

Aroh    Sa,
        Sa Re Sa,
        Sa Re Ga Re Sa,
        Sa Re Ga M'a Ga Re Sa,
        Sa Re Ga M'a Pa M'a Ga Re Sa,
        Sa Re Ga M'a Pa Dha Pa M'a Ga Re Sa,
        Sa Re Ga M'a Pa Dha Ni Dha Pa M'a Ga Re Sa,
        Sa Re Ga M'a Pa Dha Ni Sȧ Ni Dha Pa M'a Ga Re Sa
Avaroh  Sȧ,
        Sȧ Ni Sȧ,
        Sȧ Ni Dha Ni Sȧ,
        Sȧ Ni Dha Pa Dha Ni Sȧ,
        Sȧ Ni Dha Pa M'a Pa Dha Ni Sȧ,
        Sȧ Ni Dha Pa M'a Ga M'a Pa Dha Ni Sȧ,
        Sȧ Ni Dha Pa M'a Ga Re Ga M'a Pa Dha Ni Sȧ,
        Sȧ Ni Dha Pa M'a Ga Re Sa Re Ga M'a Pa Dha Ni Sȧ,


EXERCISE 8.

Aroh    Sa - Sa Re Ga Re Sa -, Re - Re Ga M'a Ga Re -,
        Ga - Ga M'a Pa M'a Ga -, M'a - M'a Pa Dha Pa M'a -,
        Pa - Pa Dha Ni Dha Pa -, Dha - Dha Ni Sȧ - Sȧ -,

Avaroh  Sá - Sá Ni <u>Dha</u> Ni Sá -, Ni - Ni <u>Dha</u> Pa <u>Dha</u> Ni -,
<u>Dha</u> - <u>Dha</u> Pa M'a Pa <u>Dha</u> -, Pa - Pa M'a Ga M'a Pa -,
M'a - M'a Ga <u>Re</u> Ga M'a -, Ga - Ga <u>Re</u> Sa - Sa -

# RAG PURVI

*Purvi* is considered the fundamental *rag* for *Purvi that*. It is sung around sunset (*sandhi-prakash*). There are two philosophies to this *rag*. The first is to use only the notes of *Purvi that*. Unfortunately, this impinges upon *Puriyadhanashri*. The second and more common philosophy is to use a touch of *shuddha madhyam*. We will only discuss the second approach.

The structure of *Purvi* is a bit complex. The inclusion of *shuddha madhyam* forces a somewhat convoluted approach. This *rag* is *sampurna- sampurna* with *gandhar* as the *vadi* and *nishad* as the *samavadi*. Its characteristics are:

| | |
|---|---|
| Arohana | Sa - <u>Re</u> Ga - M'a Pa <u>Dha</u> - Ni Sá |
| Avarohana | Sá Ni <u>Dha</u> Pa - M'a Ga - <u>Re</u> Ma Ga - <u>Re</u> Ga <u>Re</u> Sa |
| Jati | sampurna-sampurna |
| Vadi | Ga |
| Samavadi | Ni |
| Time | sunset |
| That | Purvi |
| Pakad | Ṇi - Sa <u>Re</u> Ga - Ma Ga - M'a Ga - <u>Re</u> Ma Ga - <u>Re</u> Ga <u>Re</u> Sa |

---

Internet Resource

"Film Songs in Rag Purvi (Poorvi)"

http://www.chandrakantha.com/raga_raag/film_song_raga/purvi.shtml

**RAG PURVI, SWARMALIKA – TINTAL** (Bhatkhande 1985:14)

Arohana / Avarohana / Pakad

Sa Re Ga M'a Pa Dha Ni Sȧ - Sȧ Ni Dha Pa M'a Ga Re - Ma - Ga - Re

Ga - Re - Sa - Ṇi - Sa Re Ga - Ma - Ga - M'a Ga - Re Ga Re - Sa

Sthai (first part)

| Sa Dha M'a Pa | Ga Ma Ga Re | Ma Ga - Re | Ga M'a Pa - |
|---|---|---|---|
| 0 | 3 | X | 2 |

Sthai (second part)

| Pa Dha M'a Pa | Ga Ma Ga - | Re Ga - M'a | Ga Re Sa - |
|---|---|---|---|
| 0 | 3 | X | 2 |

Sthai (third part)

| Ṇi Ṇi Sa Re | Ga - Ma Ga | M'a Dha Rė Ni | Dha Ni Dha Pa |
|---|---|---|---|
| 0 | 3 | X | 2 |

Sthai (fourth part)

| Pa Dha M'a Pa | Ga Ma Ga Re | Ma Ga - Re | Ga M'a Pa - |
|---|---|---|---|
| 0 | 3 | X | 2 |

Antara (first part)

| M'a Ga M'a Dha | M'a Sȧ - Sȧ | Ni Rė Gȧ Re | Sȧ Ni Dha Pa |
|---|---|---|---|
| 0 | 3 | X | 2 |

## Antara (second part)

| Ṙe Ni Dha Ni | Dha Pa Dha Pa | M'a Ga - M'a | Ga Re Sa - |
|---|---|---|---|
| 0 | 3 | X | 2 |

## Antara (third part)

| Ṇi Ṇi Sa Re | Ga - Ma Ga | M'a Dha Ṙe Ni | Dha Ni Dha Pa |
|---|---|---|---|
| 0 | 3 | X | 2 |

## Antara (fourth part)

| Pa Dha M'a Pa | Ga Ma Ga Re | Ma Ga - Re | Ga M'a Pa - |
|---|---|---|---|
| 0 | 3 | X | 2 |

## Tihai

| Sa Dha M'a Pa | Ga Ma Ga Re | Sa Dha M'a Pa | Ga Ma Ga Re |
|---|---|---|---|
| 0 | 3 | X | 2 |

| Sa Dha M'a Pa | Ga Ma Ga Re | Ma - Ga - Re - Ga M'a Pa - |
|---|---|---|
| 0 | 3 | X |

Procedure

1. Arohana / Avarohana / Pakad
2. Sthai (first part) 2-times
3. Sthai (second part) 2-times
4. Sthai (third part) 2-times
5. Sthai (fourth part) 2-times
6. Sthai (first part) 2-times
7. Antara (first part) 2-times
8. Antara (second part) 2-times
9. Antara (third part) 2-times
10. Antara (first part) 2-times
11. Sthai (first part) 2-times
12. Tihai

Comment

There are two things to take note of on this piece: the *arohana / avarohana / pakad* section and the structure of the antara.

One will notice that the *pakad* shown in the *arohana / avarohana / pakad* section deviates from the *pakad* shown just a few pages earlier. This is not an oversight. First, it gives us an idea of the latitude that is extended to us in describing the *pakad*. But more importantly, it starts to prepare us for the performance of the *alap*. We will deal with *alap* in greater detail in the next volume, but we should still make a small mental note about it.

There is also a peculiarity in the *antara*. Notice that the notes of the fourth part are exactly the same as the notes for the fourth part of the *sthai*. Presumably, at some time in the past there were lyrics which differentiated the *antara* from the *sthai*, but somewhere along the pedagogic chain, the lyrics were stripped away.

## RAG PURVI, SWARMALIKA – TINTAL (Bhatkhande 1985:46)

Arohana / Avarohana / Pakad

Sa Re Ga M'a Pa Dha Ni Sȧ - Sȧ Ni Dha Pa M'a Ga Re - Ma Ga Re

Ga - Re - Sa - Ni - Sa Re Ga - Ma - Ga - M'a Ga - Re Ga Re - Sa -

Sthai (first part)

| Pa - Dha M'a | - PaM'a, Ga Ma | Ga - - M'a | Ga Re Sa - |
|---|---|---|---|
| 0 | 3 | X | 2 |

Sthai (second part)

| M'a Dha Ni M'a | Dha M'a Ga Ma | Ga - - M'a | Ga Re Sa - |
|---|---|---|---|
| 0 | 3 | X | 2 |

Sthai (third part)

| Ni - Dha Ni | Rė Ni M'a M'a | Ga - - M'a | Ga Re Sa - |
|---|---|---|---|
| 0 | 3 | X | 2 |

Sthai (fourth part)

| Sa Dha Dha M'a | - PaM'a, Ga Ma | Ga - - M'a | Ga Re Sa - |
|---|---|---|---|
| 0 | 3 | X | 2 |

Antara (first part)

| M'a - Ga Ga | M'a M'a Dha M'aDha, | Sȧ - Sȧ Sȧ | Sȧ Rė Sȧ - |
|---|---|---|---|
| 0 | 3 | X | 2 |

Antara (second part)

| Ni Rė Gȧ Ni | Rė Ni M'a M'a | Ga - - M'a | Ga Re Sa - |
|---|---|---|---|
| 0 | 3 | X | 2 |

Antara (third part)

| Ma - Dha Ni | Rė Ni Ma Ma | Ga - - Ma | Ga Re Sa - |
| 0 | 3 | X | 2 |

Sthai Tans – sing sargam

1) | Ni Re Ga Ga | Ma Ga Re Ga | Re Sa Ni Re | Sa - Sa - |
   | 0 | 3 | X | 2 |

2) | Ma Dha Ni Dha | Ma Dha Ma Ga | Re Ga Ma Ga | Ma Ga Re Sa |
   | 0 | 3 | X | 2 |

Antara Tans

1) | Ni Dha Ni Rė | Sa̅ - Sa̅ - | Ni Dha Ma Dha | Ni Dha Pa - |
   | 0 | 3 | X | 2 |

2) | Ni Rė Ga̅ Ni | Rė Ni Ma Ga | Ma Dha Ni Sa̅ | Ni Rė Sa̅ - |
   | 0 | 3 | X | 2 |

Tihai

| Pa - Dha Ma | - PaMa Ga Ma |
| 0 | 3 |

| Pa - Dha Ma | - PaMa Ga Ma |
| X | 2 |

| Pa - Dha Ma | - PaMa Ga Ma | Ga - - Ma - Ga - Re - Sa - |
| 0 | 3 | X |

Procedure
1. Arohana / Avarohana / Pakad
2. Sthai (first part) 2-times
3. Sthai (second part) 2-times
4. Sthai (third part) 2-times
5. Sthai (fourth part) 2-times
6. Antara (first part) 2-times
7. Antara (second part) 2-times
8. Antara (third part) 2-times
9. Sthai (first part) 2-times
10. Sthai Tan #1 (single time)
11. Sthai Tan #1 (double time)
12. Sthai Tan #1 (double time, "aahkar")
13. Sthai (first part) 2-times
14. Sthai Tan #2 (single time)
15. Sthai Tan #2 (double time)
16. Sthai Tan #2 (double time, "aahkar")
17. Sthai (first part) 2-times
18. Antara (first part) 2-times
19. Antara Tan #1 (single time)
20. Antara Tan #1 (double time)
21. Antara Tan #1 (double time, "aahkar")
22. Antara (first part) 2-times
23. Antara Tan #2 (single time)
24. Antara Tan #2 (double time)
25. Antara Tan #2 (double time, "aahkar")
26. Antara (first part) 2-times
27. Antara (second part) 2-times
28. Antara (third part) 2-times
29. Sthai (first part) 2-times
30. Tihai

# WORKS CITED

Bhatkhande, V.N.
1985 *Hindustani Sangeet Paddhati, Kramik Pustak Malika, Vol. 1.* Hathras, India: Sangeet Karyalaya.

# CHAPTER 15.
# MARWA THAT

*Marwa* is one of the lesser used *thats* in the *Hindustani* system. It is characterized by a *komal rishabh* and a *tivra madhyam*. It is known as *Gamanashrama mela* in the South.

# THAT EXERCISES

EXERCISE 1.

Aroh    Sa Re Ga M'a Pa Dha Ni Sȧ
Avaroh  Sȧ Ni Dha Pa M'a Ga Re Sa

EXERCISE 2.

Aroh    Sa Re Ga M'a,  Re Ga M'a Pa,  Ga M'a Pa Dha,
        M'a Pa Dha Ni, Pa Dha Ni Sȧ
Avaroh  Sȧ Ni Dha Pa,  Ni Dha Pa M'a,  Dha Pa M'a Ga,
        Pa M'a Ga Re,  M'a Ga Re Sa

EXERCISE 3.

Aroh    Sa Re Ga,  Re Ga M'a,  Ga M'a Pa,
        M'a Pa Dha,  Pa Dha Ni,  Dha Ni Sȧ
Avaroh  Sȧ Ni Dha,  Ni Dha Pa,  Dha Pa M'a,
        Pa M'a Ga,  M'a Ga Re,  Ga Re Sa

EXERCISE 4.

Aroh    Sa Re Ga M'a Ga Re,  Sa Re Ga M'a Pa Dha Ni Sȧ
Avaroh  Sȧ Ni Dha Pa Dha Ni,  Sȧ Ni Dha Pa M'a Ga Re Sa

EXERCISE 5.

Aroh    Sa Ga,  Re M'a,  Ga Pa,  M'a Dha,  Pa Ni,  Dha Sȧ
Avaroh  Sȧ Dha,  Ni Pa,  Dha M'a,  Pa Ga,  M'a Re,  Ga Sa

EXERCISE 6.

Aroh    Sa Re, Sa Re, Sa Re Ga M'a Pa Dha Ni Sá
Avaroh  Sá Ni, Sá Ni, Sá Ni Dha Pa M'a Ga Re Sa

EXERCISE 7.

Aroh    Sa,
         Sa Re Sa,
         Sa Re Ga Re Sa,
         Sa Re Ga M'a Ga Re Sa,
         Sa Re Ga M'a Pa M'a Ga Re Sa,
         Sa Re Ga M'a Pa Dha Pa M'a Ga Re Sa,
         Sa Re Ga M'a Pa Dha Ni Dha Pa M'a Ga Re Sa,
         Sa Re Ga M'a Pa Dha Ni Sá Ni Dha Pa M'a Ga Re Sa
Avaroh  Sá,
         Sá Ni Sá,
         Sá Ni Dha Ni Sá,
         Sá Ni Dha Pa Dha Ni Sá,
         Sá Ni Dha Pa M'a Pa Dha Ni Sá,
         Sá Ni Dha Pa M'a Ga M'a Pa Dha Ni Sá,
         Sá Ni Dha Pa M'a Ga Re Ga M'a Pa Dha Ni Sá,
         Sá Ni Dha Pa M'a Ga Re Sa Re Ga M'a Pa Dha Ni Sá

EXERCISE 8.

Aroh    Sa - Sa Re Ga Re Sa -, Re - Re Ga M'a Ga Re -,
         Ga - Ga M'a Pa M'a Ga -, M'a - M'a Pa Dha Pa M'a -,
         Pa - Pa Dha Ni Dha Pa -, Dha - Dha Ni Sá - Sá -
Avaroh  Sá - Sá Ni Dha Ni Sá -, Ni - Ni Dha Pa Dha Ni -,
         Dha - Dha Pa M'a Pa Dha -, Pa - Pa M'a Ga M'a Pa -,
         M'a - M'a Ga Re Ga M'a -, Ga - Ga Re Sa - Sa -

# RAG MARWA

*Marwa* is considered the most fundamental *rag* in *Marwa that*. It is an evening *rag* that is quite popular. It is unusual in that there is a compromise in its tonic foundation. The *pancham* is totally absent and the *madhyam* is *tivra*. Therefore, the harmonic base of the 4th /5th is missing. This imbalance creates a very distinctive character. Considering this imbalance, the structure is surprisingly simple. *Rishabh* is the *vadi* and *dhaivat* is the *samavadi*. It is *shadav-shadav* due to the exclusion of pancham. One well know song in this rag is *Payalia Banwari Baje*. *Marwa's* characteristics are:

| | |
|---|---|
| Arohana | Sa Re - Ga Ma̋ Dha - Ni Dha Sȧ |
| Avarohana | Sȧ - Rė - Ni Dha - Ma̋ Ga Re - Sa |
| Jati | shadav-shadav |
| Vadi | Re |
| Samavadi | Dha |
| Time | evening |
| That | Marwa |
| Pakad | Dha Ma̋ Ga Re - Ga Ma̋ Ga - Re - Sa |

> Internet Resource
>
> "Film Songs in Rag Marwa"
>
> http://www.chandrakantha.com/raga_raag/film_song_raga/marwa.shtml

The drone for *Marwa* is a bit complicated. One would think that in the absence of *Pa*, simply tuning to *Ma* would be acceptable. But it isn't (remember the *Ma* in *Marwa* is tivra). This is problematic because the musical interval between low *Sa* and *tivra Ma* is the same interval as *tivra Ma* to high *Sa*. Therefore, even if you were able to avoid making an accidental inversion in the performance, the listener might invert it in their own mind. A *Sa-Ma̋-Sȧ* will not properly ground the *rag*. In the companion disks which accompany this book, we use one *tanpura* set to *Sa-Dha-Sȧ* and another tuned to *Sa-Ni-Sȧ*. Either of which is commonly used with *Marwa*.

# SWARMALIKA, RAG MARWA – EKTAL (JVS Rao – personal interview)

Arohana / Avarohana / Pakad

Sa Re Ga M'a Dha Ni Dha Sȧ - Sȧ Ṙė Ni Dha - M'a Ga Re - Sa

Dha M'a Ga Re - Ga M'a Ga Re - Sa

Sthai (first part)

| Dha M'a | Dha M'a | Ga Re | Ga M'a | Ga Re | Sa - |
|---------|---------|-------|--------|-------|------|
| X       | 0       | 2     | 0      | 3     | 4    |

Sthai (second part)

| Ni Re | Ni Dha | M'a Dha | Sa - | Re Re | Sa - |
|-------|--------|---------|------|-------|------|
| X     | 0      | 2       | 0    | 3     | 4    |

Sthai (third part)

| Ni Re | Ga Ga | M'a Dha | M'a Dha | Sȧ - | Ṙė Sȧ |
|-------|-------|---------|---------|------|-------|
| X     | 0     | 2       | 0       | 3    | 4     |

Sthai (fourth part)

| Ni Ṙė | Ni Dha | M'a Dha | Ni Dha | M'a Ga | Re Sa |
|-------|--------|---------|--------|--------|-------|
| X     | 0      | 2       | 0      | 3      | 4     |

Antara (first part)

| Ga Ga | M'a Dha | M'a Dha | Sȧ - | Ni Ṙė | Sȧ - |
|-------|---------|---------|------|-------|------|
| X     | 0       | 2       | 0    | 3     | 4    |

Antara (second part)

| Ni Ni | Ṙė Ṙė | Ni Ṙė | Ni Dha | M'a Dha | M'a Ga |
|-------|-------|-------|--------|---------|--------|
| X     | 0     | 2     | 0      | 3       | 4      |

Antara (third part)

| Re Re | Ga Ga | Ma̱ Ma̱ | Ni Dha | Ma̱ Ga | Re Sa |
|---|---|---|---|---|---|
| X | 0 | 2 | 0 | 3 | 4 |

Antara (fourth part)

| Ni Re̍ | Ni Dha | Ma̱ Dha | Ma̱ Ga | Ma̱ Ga | Re Sa |
|---|---|---|---|---|---|
| X | 0 | 2 | 0 | 3 | 4 |

Tihai

| Dha Ma̱ | Dha Ma̱ | Ga Re | Dha Ma̱ | Dha Ma̱ | Ga Re |
|---|---|---|---|---|---|
| X | 0 | 2 | 0 | 3 | 4 |

| Dha Ma̱ | Dha Ma̱ | Ga Re | Ga Ma̱ | Ga Re | Sa - - | - |
|---|---|---|---|---|---|---|
| X | 0 | 2 | 0 | 3 | 4 | X |

Procedure
1. Arohana / Avarohana / Pakad
2. Sthai (first part) 2-times
3. Sthai (second part) 2-times
4. Sthai (third part) 2-times
5. Sthai (fourth part) 2-times
6. Sthai (first part) 2-times
7. Antara (first part) 2-times
8. Antara (second part) 2-times
9. Antara (third part) 2-times
10. Antara (fourth part) 2-times
11. Sthai (first part) 2-times
12. Tihai

# RAG MARWA, SWARMALIKA - TINTAL (Bhatkhande 1989:287)

Arohana / Avarohana / Pakad

Sa Re Ga M'a Dha Ni Dha Sȧ - Sȧ Rė Ni Dha - M'a Ga Re - Sa -

Dha M'a Ga Re - Ga M'a Ga Re - Sa -

Sthai (first part)

| Nị Nị Re Ga | Ga Ga M'a Dha | Sȧ - Ni Ni | M'a Dha M'a Ga |
|---|---|---|---|
| 0 | 3 | X | 2 |

Sthai (second part)

| M'a Ga - Re | Re Sa Sa Sa | Dha Dha Dha M'a | Dha Sa Sa Sa |
|---|---|---|---|
| 0 | 3 | X | 2 |

Sthai (third part)

| Nị Nị Re Ga | Ga Ga M'a Dha | Ni Ni Dha M'a | Ga Re Sa Sa |
|---|---|---|---|
| 0 | 3 | X | 2 |

Antara (first part)

| M'a - Dha Sȧ | - Sȧ Sȧ - | Sȧ Sȧ Sȧ Sȧ | Sȧ Rė Sȧ - |
|---|---|---|---|
| 0 | 3 | X | 2 |

Antara (second part)

| Ni Ni Rė Rė | Ni Ni Rė Ni | - Rė Ni Dha | M'a Dha M'a Ga |
|---|---|---|---|
| 0 | 3 | X | 2 |

Antara (third part)

| M'a Re - Ga | - Ga M'a Dha | M'a Ga - M'a | Ga Re Sa - |
| 0 | 3 | X | 2 |

## Antara (fourth part)

| Nị Nị Re Ga | Ga Ga M'a Dha | Ni Ni Dha M'a | Ga Re Sa Sa |
| 0 | 3 | X | 2 |

## Sthai Tans - sing sargam

1)
| Nị Re Ga M'a | Dha Ni Dha M'a | Ga Re Ga M'a | Ga Re Nị Sa |
| 0 | 3 | X | 2 |

2)
| Ga M'a Dha Ni | Rė Ni Dha M'a | Ga M'a Dha M'a | Ga Re Sa - |
| 0 | 3 | X | 2 |

3)
| Nị Re Ga M'a | Re Ga M'a Dha | Ga M'a Dha Ni | M'a Dha Ni Rė |
| 0 | 3 | X | 2 |

| Dha Ni Rė Gȧ | Rė Ni Dha M'a | Ga Re Ga M'a | Ga Re Nị Sa |
| 0 | 3 | X | 2 |

## Antara Tans

1)
| M'a Dha Ni Sȧ | Ni Dha M'a Ga | M'a Dha Ni Sȧ | Ni Rė Sȧ - |
| 0 | 3 | X | 2 |

2)
| Ga M'a Dha Ni | Sȧ Ni Rė Sȧ | Ni Dha M'a Ga | M'a Dha Ni Sȧ |
| 0 | 3 | X | 2 |

Tihai

| Ṇi Ṇi Re Ga | Ga Ga M'a M'a | Ṇi Ṇi Re Ga | Ga Ga M'a M'a |
|---|---|---|---|
| 0 | 3 | X | 2 |

| Ṇi Ṇi Re Ga | Ga Ga M'a Dha | Sȧ Ni Rė - Rė - Gȧ - Rė - M'a Gȧ Rė - Sȧ - |
|---|---|---|
| 0 | 3 | X |

Procedure
1. Arohana / Avarohana / Pakad
2. Sthai (first part) 2-times
3. Sthai (second part) 2-times
4. Sthai (third part) 2-times
5. Sthai (first part) 2-times
6. Antara (first part) 2-times
7. Antara (second part) 2-times
8. Antara (third part) 2-times
9. Antara (fourth part) 2-times
10. Sthai (first part) 2-times
11. Sthai Tan#1
12. Sthai Tan#1 (double tempo)
13. Sthai Tan#1 (double tempo)(akar)
14. Sthai (first part) 2-times
15. Sthai Tan#2
16. Sthai Tan#2 (double tempo)
17. Sthai Tan#2 (double tempo)(akar)
18. Sthai (first part) 2-times
19. Sthai Tan#3
20. Sthai Tan#3 (double tempo)
21. Sthai Tan#3 (double tempo)(akar)
22. Sthai (first part) 2-times
23. Atara (first part) 2-times
24. Antara Tan#1

25. Antara Tan#1 (double tempo)
26. Antara Tan#1 (double tempo)(akar)
27. Atara (first part) 2-times
28. Antara Tan#2
29. Antara Tan#2 (double tempo)
30. Antara Tan#2 (double tempo)(akar)
31. Atara (first part) 2-times
32. Atara (second part) 2-times
33. Atara (third part) 2-times
34. Sthai (first part) 2-times
35. Tihai

# WORKS CITED

Bhatkhande V. N.
1989 *Hindustani Sangeet Paddhati, Kramik Pustak Malika, Vol. 2.* Hathras, India: Sangeet Karyalaya.

Jairazbhoy, NA.
1971 *The Rags of North Indian Music.* Middletown CT: Wesleyan University Press.

# CHAPTER 16.
# TODI THAT

Todi that is characterized by *komal rishabh, komal gandhar, tivra madhyam,* and *komal dhaivat.* It is called *Shubhapantuvarali mela* in the South.

# THAT EXERCISES

### EXERCISE 1.

Aroh    Sa <u>Re</u> <u>Ga</u> M'a Pa <u>Dha</u> Ni Sȧ
Avaroh  Sȧ Ni <u>Dha</u> Pa M'a <u>Ga</u> <u>Re</u> Sa

### EXERCISE 2.

Aroh    Sa <u>Re</u> <u>Ga</u> M'a, <u>Re</u> <u>Ga</u> M'a Pa, <u>Ga</u> M'a Pa <u>Dha</u>,
          M'a Pa <u>Dha</u> Ni, Pa <u>Dha</u> Ni Sȧ
Avaroh  Sȧ Ni <u>Dha</u> Pa, Ni <u>Dha</u> Pa M'a, <u>Dha</u> Pa M'a <u>Ga</u>,
          Pa M'a <u>Ga</u> <u>Re</u>, M'a <u>Ga</u> <u>Re</u> Sa

### EXERCISE 3.

Aroh    Sa <u>Re</u> <u>Ga</u>, <u>Re</u> <u>Ga</u> M'a, <u>Ga</u> M'a Pa,·
          M'a Pa <u>Dha</u>, Pa <u>Dha</u> Ni, <u>Dha</u> Ni Sȧ
Avaroh  Sȧ Ni <u>Dha</u>, Ni <u>Dha</u> Pa, <u>Dha</u> Pa M'a,
          Pa M'a <u>Ga</u>, M'a <u>Ga</u> <u>Re</u>, <u>Ga</u> <u>Re</u> Sa

### EXERCISE 4.

Aroh    Sa <u>Re</u> <u>Ga</u> M'a <u>Ga</u> <u>Re</u>, Sa <u>Re</u> <u>Ga</u> M'a Pa <u>Dha</u> Ni Sȧ
Avaroh  Sȧ Ni <u>Dha</u> Pa <u>Dha</u> Ni, Sȧ Ni <u>Dha</u> Pa M'a <u>Ga</u> <u>Re</u> Sa

### EXERCISE 5.

Aroh    Sa <u>Ga</u>, <u>Re</u> M'a, <u>Ga</u> Pa, M'a <u>Dha</u>, Pa Ni, <u>Dha</u> Sȧ
Avaroh  Sȧ <u>Dha</u>, Ni Pa, <u>Dha</u> M'a, Pa <u>Ga</u>, M'a <u>Re</u>, <u>Ga</u> Sa

EXERCISE 6.

Aroh     Sa Re, Sa Re, Sa Re Ga M'a Pa Dha Ni Sȧ
Avaroh  Sȧ Ni, Sȧ Ni, Sȧ Ni Dha Pa M'a Ga Re Sa

EXERCISE 7.

Aroh    Sa,
         Sa Re Sa,
         Sa Re Ga Re Sa,
         Sa Re Ga M'a Ga Re Sa,
         Sa Re Ga M'a Pa M'a Ga Re Sa,
         Sa Re Ga M'a Pa Dha Pa M'a Ga Re Sa,
         Sa Re Ga M'a Pa Dha Ni Dha Pa M'a Ga Re Sa,
         Sa Re Ga M'a Pa Dha Ni Sȧ Ni Dha Pa M'a Ga Re Sa,
Avaroh Sȧ,
         Sȧ Ni Sȧ,
         Sȧ Ni Dha Ni Sȧ,
         Sȧ Ni Dha Pa Dha Ni Sȧ,
         Sȧ Ni Dha Pa M'a Pa Dha Ni Sȧ,
         Sȧ Ni Dha Pa M'a Ga M'a Pa Dha Ni Sȧ,
         Sȧ Ni Dha Pa M'a Ga Re Ga M'a Pa Dha Ni Sȧ,
         Sȧ Ni Dha Pa M'a Ga Re Sa Re Ga M'a Pa Dha Ni Sȧ

EXERCISE 8.

Aroh     Sa - Sa Re Ga Re Sa -, Re - Re Ga M'a Ga Re -,
         Ga - Ga M'a Pa M'a Ga -, M'a - M'a Pa Dha Pa M'a -,
         Pa - Pa Dha Ni Dha Pa -, Dha - Dha Ni Sȧ - Sȧ -

Avaroh Sa̍ - Sa̍ Ni D̲h̲a̲ Ni Sa̍ -, Ni - Ni D̲h̲a̲ Pa D̲h̲a̲ Ni -,
D̲h̲a̲ - D̲h̲a̲ Pa M'a Pa D̲h̲a̲ -, Pa - Pa M'a G̲a̲ M'a Pa -,
M'a - M'a G̲a̲ R̲e̲ G̲a̲ M'a -,  G̲a̲ - G̲a̲ R̲e̲ Sa - Sa -

## RAG MIAN-KI-TODI

*Todi*, also known as *Mian-ki-Todi*, is a very common morning *rag* in this *that*. There is disagreement as to its structure. According to some, all seven notes are used, so it is *sampurna-sampurna* in its character. However, according to others, *pancham* is absent in the *aroh*, so it is *shadav-sampurna*. We will show the *sampurna-sampurna* version because it is easier for a beginner. There is also disagreement as to the *vadi* and *samavadi*. Some consider the *vadi* to be *dhaivat* while others consider it to be *madhyam*. The *samavadi* is *gandhar*. Its structure is:

| | |
|---|---|
| Arohana | Sa R̲e̲ G̲a̲ M'a Pa D̲h̲a̲ Ni Sa̍ (disputed) |
| Avarohana | Sa̍ Ni D̲h̲a̲ Pa M'a G̲a̲ R̲e̲ Sa |
| Jati | sampurna-sampurna (disputed) |
| Vadi | Dha (disputed) |
| Samavadi | Ga |
| Time | morning |
| That | Todi |
| Pakad | D̲h̲a̲ - N̩i Sa R̲e̲ - G̲a̲ - R̲e̲ - Sa - M'a - G̲a̲ - R̲e̲ G̲a̲ - R̲e̲ Sa |

---

Internet Resource

"Film Songs in Rag Mian-ki-Todi"

http://www.chandrakantha.com/raga_raag/film_song_raga/mian_ki_todi.shtml

# RAG MIAN-KI-TODI, SWARMALIKA - TINTAL (Bhatkhande 1985:63)

Arohana / Avarohana / Pakad

Sa <u>Re</u> <u>Ga</u> M'a Pa <u>Dha</u> Ni Sȧ - Sȧ Ni <u>Dha</u> Pa M'a <u>Ga</u> <u>Re</u> Sa -

<u>Dha</u> Ṇi Sa <u>Re</u> - <u>Ga</u> <u>Re</u> Sa - M'a <u>Ga</u> - <u>Re</u> <u>Ga</u> - <u>Re</u> - Sa -

Sthai (first part)

| <u>Dha</u> <u>Dha</u> Pa Pa | M'a M'a Pa <u>Dha</u> | M'a <u>Ga</u> - <u>Re</u> | <u>Ga</u> M'a Pa - |
| 0 | 3 | X | 2 |

Sthai (second part)

| <u>Ga</u> M'a Pa <u>Dha</u> | Ni <u>Dha</u> Pa M'a | <u>Ga</u> M'a Pa M'a | <u>Ga</u> <u>Ga</u> <u>Re</u> Sa |
| 0 | 3 | X | 2 |

Sthai (third part)

| Ṇi Sa <u>Ga</u> <u>Ga</u> | M'a <u>Ga</u> M'a <u>Dha</u> | Ni <u>Dha</u> <u>Rė</u> Ni | <u>Dha</u> Ni <u>Dha</u> Pa |
| 0 | 3 | X | 2 |

Antara (first part)

| M'a <u>Ga</u> M'a <u>Dha</u> | Ni Ni Sȧ - | <u>Dha</u> Ni Sȧ <u>Gȧ</u> | <u>Rė</u> Sȧ Ni <u>Dha</u> |
| 0 | 3 | X | 2 |

Antara (second part)

| <u>Gȧ</u> <u>Gȧ</u> <u>Rė</u> Sȧ | <u>Rė</u> Ni <u>Dha</u> <u>Dha</u> | M'a <u>Dha</u> Ni <u>Dha</u> | M'a <u>Ga</u> <u>Re</u> Sa |
| 0 | 3 | X | 2 |

Antara (third part)

| Ṇi Sa G̲a̲ G̲a̲ | Ma̋ G̲a̲ Ma̋ D̲h̲a̲ | Ni D̲h̲a̲ R̲ė̲ Ni | D̲h̲a̲ Ni D̲h̲a̲ Pa |
|---|---|---|---|
| 0 | 3 | X | 2 |

Tihai

| D̲h̲a̲ D̲h̲a̲ Pa Pa | Ma̋ Ma̋ Pa D̲h̲a̲ | D̲h̲a̲ D̲h̲a̲ Pa Pa | Ma̋ Ma̋ Pa D̲h̲a̲ |
|---|---|---|---|
| 0 | 3 | X | 2 |

| D̲h̲a̲ D̲h̲a̲ Pa Pa | Ma̋ Ma̋ Pa D̲h̲a̲ |
|---|---|
| 0 | 3 |

Ma̋ - G̲a̲ - - R̲e̲    - G̲a̲ - Ma̋ - Pa -
X

Procedure

1. Arohana / Avarohana / Pakad
2. Sthai (first part) 2-times
3. Sthai (second part) 2-times
4. Sthai (third part) 2-times
5. Sthai (first part) 2-times
6. Antara (first part) 2-times
7. Antara (second part) 2-times
8. Antara (third part) 2-times
9. Sthai (first part) 2-times
10. Tihai

# Rag Mian-ki-Todi, Kheyal - Tintal (Bhatkhande 1989:438)

langar kaankariya jin maaro  
langar kaankariya jin maaro  
more angva lag jaaye langar  
-  
sunpave mori sas nanadiya  
dauri dauri ghar ave  
langar kaankariya jin maaro  

someone struck me with a pebble  
someone struck me with a pebble  
i wished that he would embrace me  
i hope that my mother-in-law and sister-in-laws will hear  
and that the one who struck me will go scurrying home  

Arohana / Avarohana / Pakad  
Sa Re Ga M'a Pa Dha Ni Sȧ - Sȧ Ni Dha Pa M'a Ga Re Sa -

Dha Ni Sa - Re - Ga Re Sa - M'a Ga - Re - Ga - Re - Sa -

Sthai (pickup)

| - Re Sa Sa |
| - lan ga r  |
| 3           |

Sthai (first part)

| Pa - Pa Pa | M'a - Pa Dha | M'a Ga - Re | Ga Re Sa Sa |
| kan - ka ri | ya - ji na  | ma - - ro   | - lan ga r  |
| X           | 2           | 0           | 3           |

## Sthai (second part)

| Dha - Pa Pa | ↘M̀aPa↙ Dha Dha Ni | Ma̋ Ga - Re | Ga Re Sa Sa |
|---|---|---|---|
| kan - ka ri | ya - ji na | ma - - ro | - lan ga r |
| X | 2 | 0 | 3 |

## Transition #1

Ga Re - Sa
- mo - re
3

## Sthai (third part)

| Ni Re Ga - | M̀a - Pa Dha | M̀a - Ga Re | Ga Re Sa Sa |
|---|---|---|---|
| an ga va - | - - la g | ja - - ye | - mo - re |
| X | 2 | 0 | 3 |

## Transition #2

Ga Re Sa Sa
e lan ga r
3

## Antara (first part)

| Pa Pa Ga - | M̀a - Dha Dha | Ni - Sȧ Ni | Sȧ Sȧ Sȧ - |
|---|---|---|---|
| su na pa - | ve - mo ri | sa - sa n | na di ya - |
| X | 2 | 0 | 3 |

Antara (second part)

| SaRe Ga Re Ni<br>dau - ri dau<br>X | - Ni Sa Re<br>- ri gha r<br>2 | Ni Dha Ni Dha<br>a - - ve<br>0 | - Pa Ga M'a<br>- lan ga r<br>3 |

Antara (third part)

| Dha - Dha Ni<br>kan - ka ri<br>X | M'a - Pa Dha<br>ya - ji na<br>2 | M'a Ga - Re<br>ma - - ro<br>0 | Ga Re Sa Sa<br>- lan ga r<br>3 |

Sthai Tans - sing sargam

1) | Ni Re Ga M'a<br>X | Dha Ni Sa Ni<br>2 | Dha Pa M'a Ga<br>0 | Re Ga Re Sa<br>3 |

2) | Dha Ni Sa Ni<br>X | Dha Pa M'a Ga<br>2 | Re Ga M'a Ga<br>0 | Re Sa Ni Sa<br>3 |

Antara Tans - sing sargam

1) | Sa Ni Dha Pa<br>X | M'a Ga Re Sa<br>2 | Re Ga M'a Dha<br>0 | Ni Sa Re Sa<br>3 |

2) | Ni Re Ga Ga<br>X | Re Sa Ni Dha<br>2 | M'a Dha Ni Sa<br>0 | Dha Ni Sa -<br>3 |

Tihai (filler)

| Pa - Pa Pa<br>kan - ka ri<br>X | M'a - Pa *<br>ya - ji *<br>2 |

Tihai

| * * * <u>Dha</u> | Mȧ <u>Ga Ga</u> <u>Dha</u> | Mȧ <u>Ga Ga</u> <u>Dha</u> |
|---|---|---|
| * * *  na | ma - ro  na | ma ro -  na |
| 2 | 0 | 3 |

Mȧ - <u>Ga</u> - <u>Dha</u>   - <u>Re</u> - Sa - Sa
ma - ro -  na      - lan - ga - r
X

Procedure
1. Arohana / Avarohana / Pakad
2. Pickup
3. Sthai (first part) 2-times
4. Sthai (second part)
5. Sthai (second part) - only the first three measures
6. Transition #1
7. Sthai (third part)
8. Sthai (third part) - only the first three measures
9. Transition #2
10. Sthai (first part) 2-times
11. Antara (first part) 2-times
12. Antara (second part) 2-times
13. Antara (third part) 2-times
14. Sthai (first part) 2-times
15. Sthai Tan#1 2-times
16. Sthai (first part) 2-times
17. Sthai Tan#2 2-times
18. Sthai (first part) 2-times
19. Antara (first part) 2-times

20. Antara Tan#1 2-times
21. Antara (first part) 2-times
22. Antara Tan#2 2-times
23. Antara (first part) 2-times
24. Antara (second part) 2-times
25. Antara (third part) 2-times
26. Sthai (first part) 2-times
27. Tihai (filler)
28. Tihai

## WORKS CITED

Bhatkhande, Vishnu Narayan
1985 *Hindustani Sangeet Paddhati, Kramik Pustak Malika, Vol. 1.* Hathras, India: Sangeet Karyalaya.
1989 *Hindustani Sangeet Paddhati, Kramik Pustak Malika, Vol. 2.* Hathras, India: Sangeet Karyalaya.

# CHAPTER 17.
# CONCLUSION

We have covered a lot of material, probably much more material than would ever be necessary for a typical institutional setting. But the music is very vast and hopefully this modest work creates a thirst for more knowledge, both in yourself and your students.

# APPENDICES

# APPENDIX 1
# COMMON THATS IN THE KEY OF C

**Bilawal**

**Kalyan**

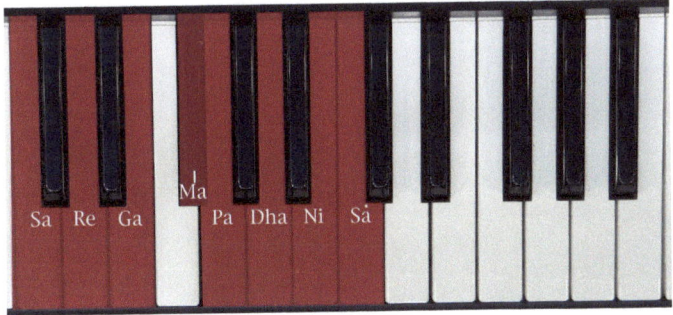

## Khammaj

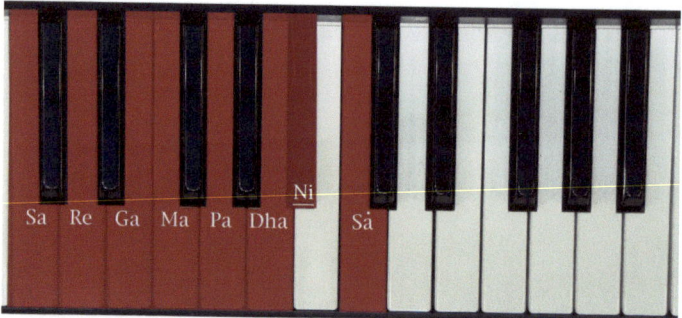

## Kafi

## Asawari

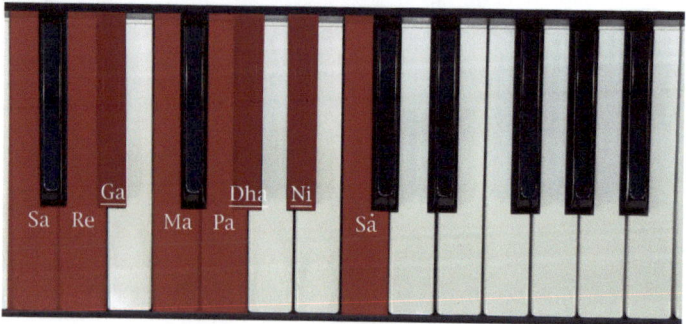

## Bhairav

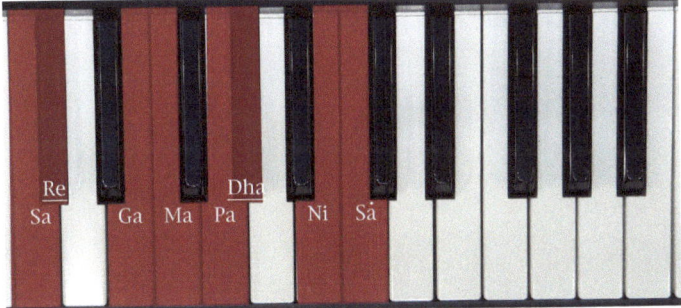

## Bhairavi

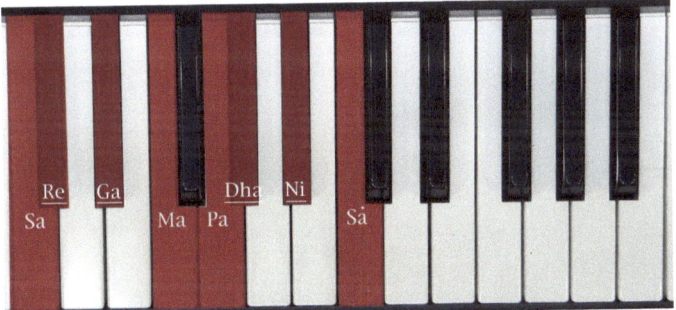

## Purvi

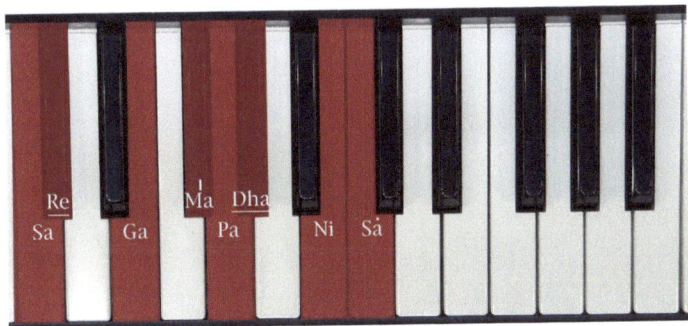

**Marwa**

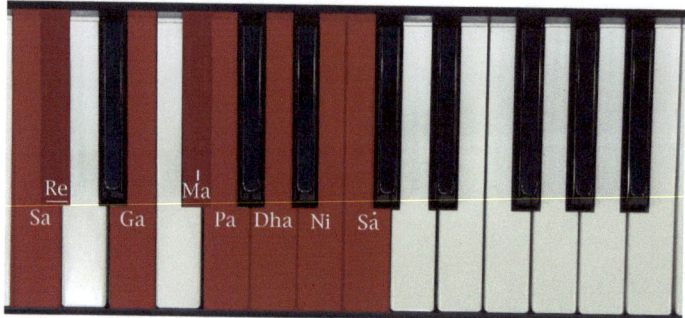

**Todi**

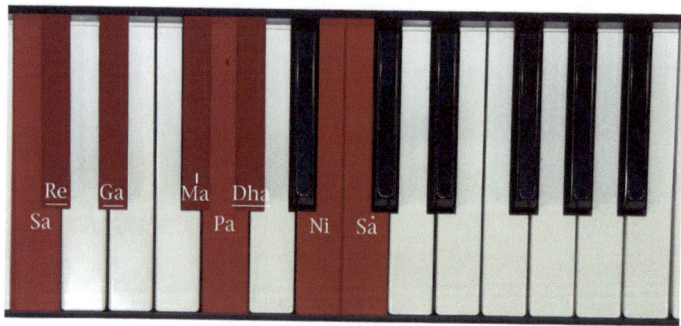

# APPENDIX 2
# COMMON THATS IN THE KEY OF C#

**Bilawal**

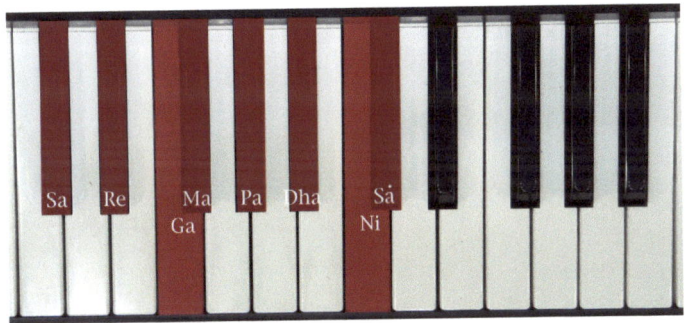

**Kalyan**

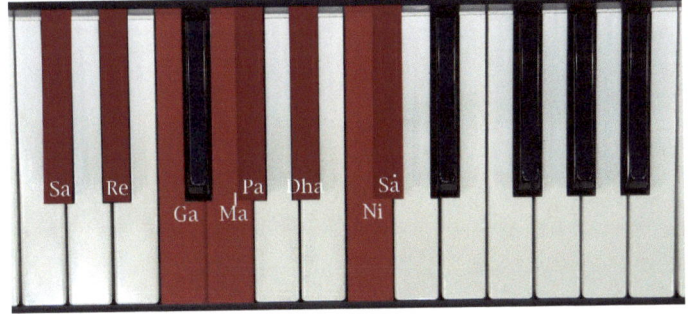

## Khammaj

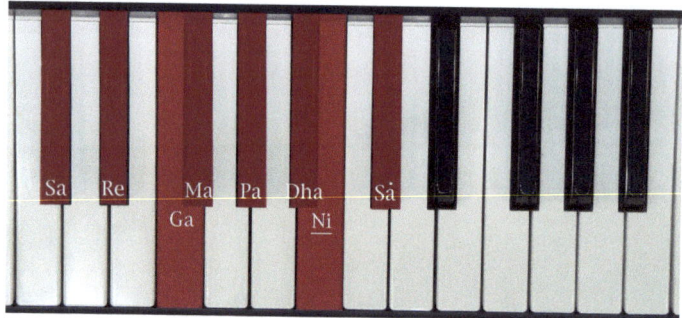

## Kafi

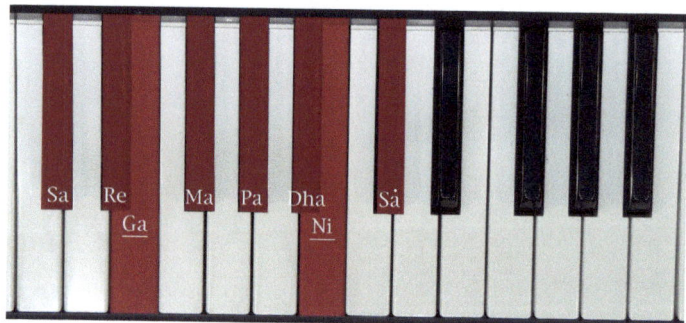

## Asawari

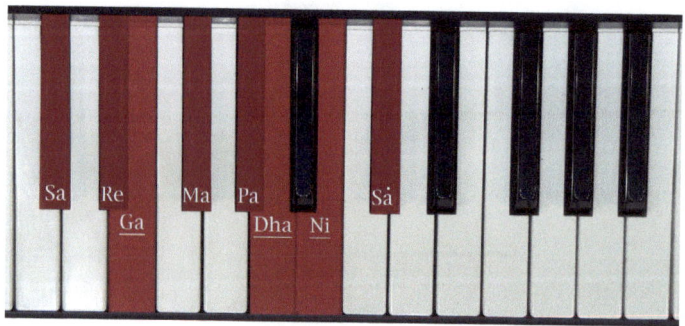

## Bhairav

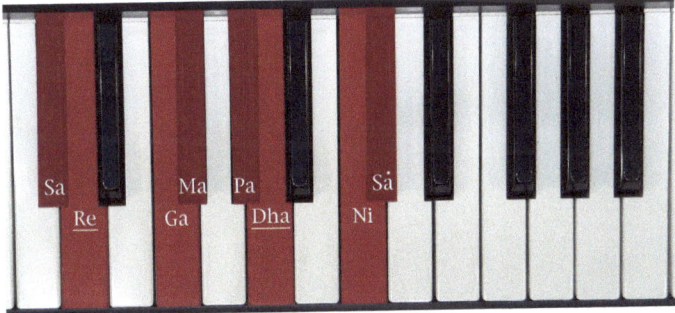

## Bhairavi

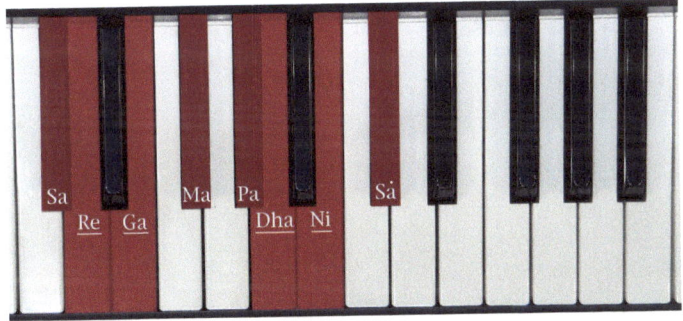

## Purvi

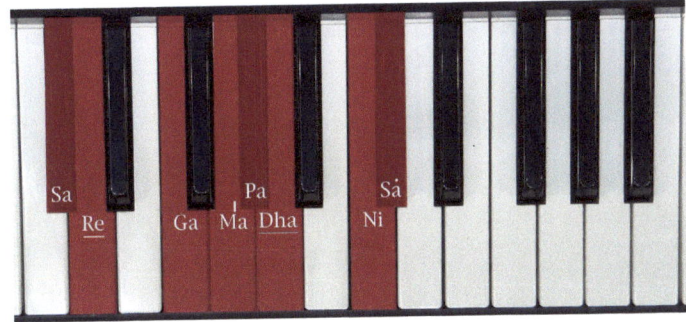

## Marwa

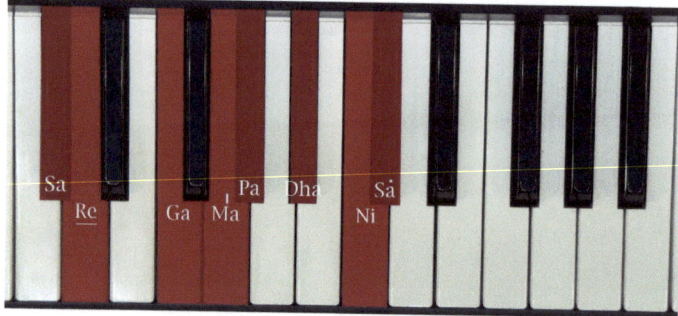

## Todi

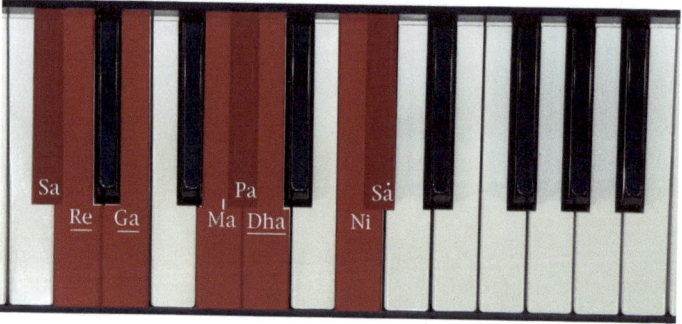

# APPENDIX 3
# COMMON THATS IN THE KEY OF D

Bilawal

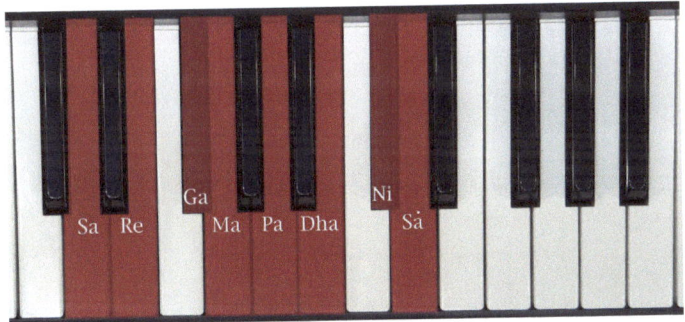

Kalyan

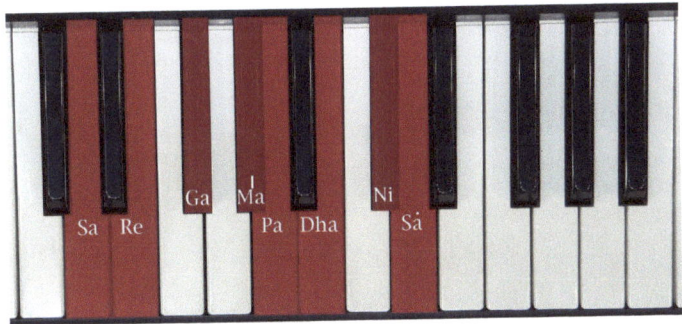

## Khammaj

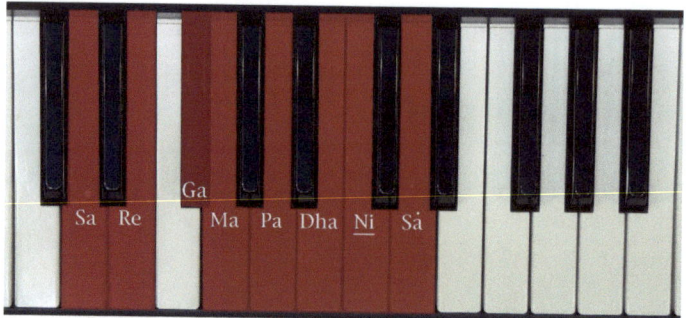

## Kafi

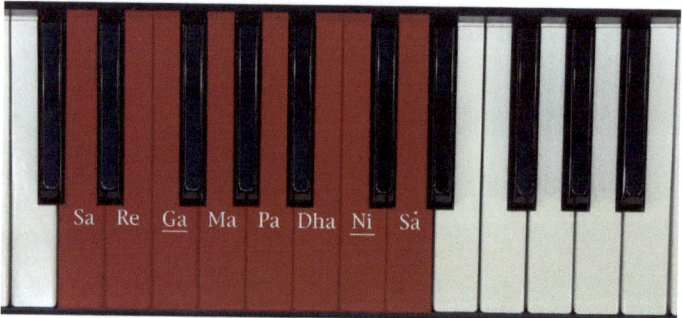

## Asawari

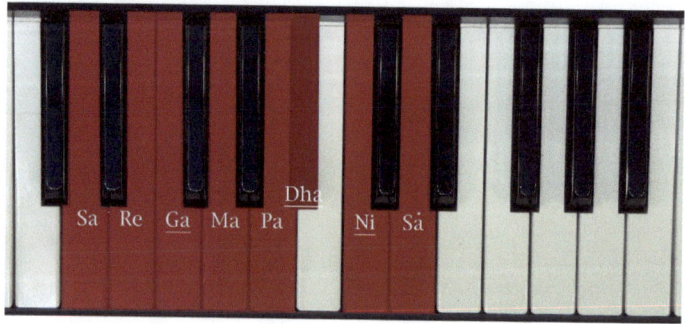

## Bhairav

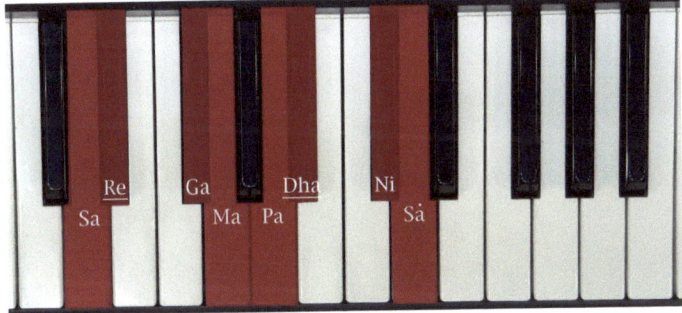

## Bhairavi

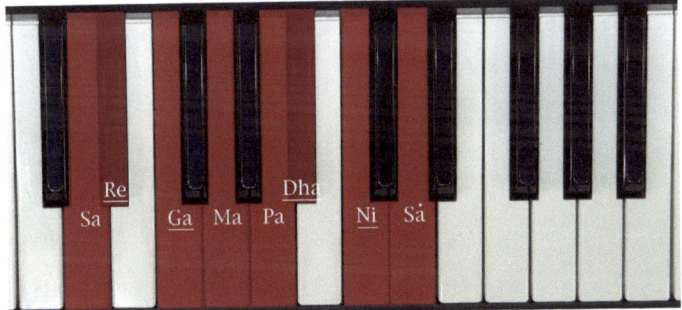

## Purvi

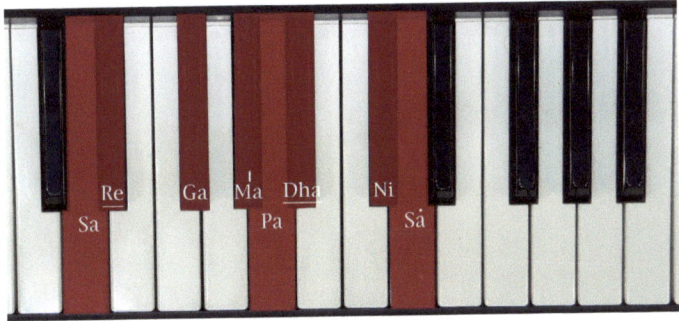

## Marwa

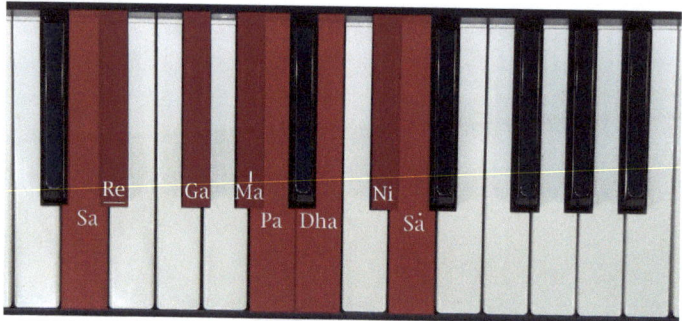

## Todi

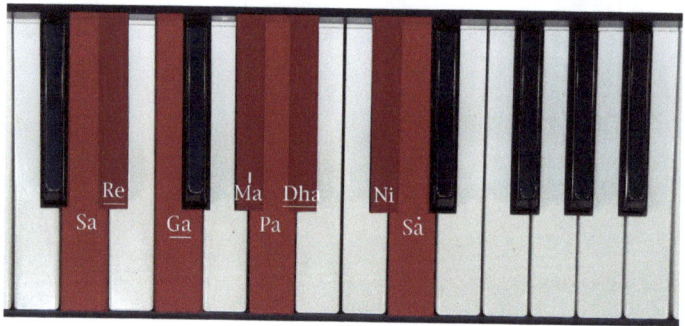

# APPENDIX 4
# COMMON THATS IN THE KEY OF D#

Bilawal

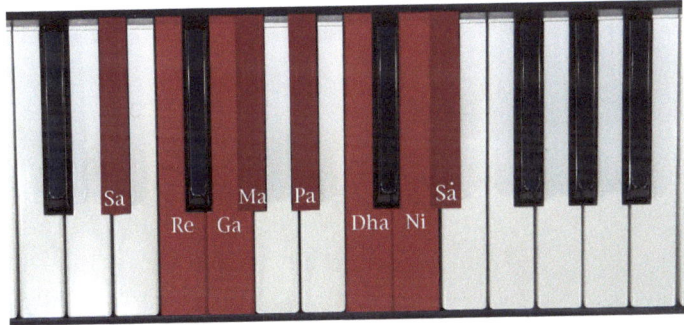

Kalyan

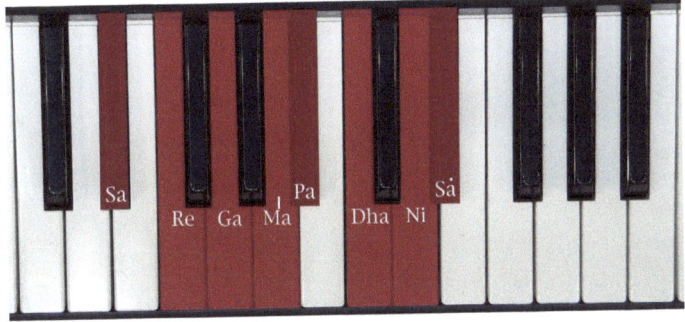

## Khammaj

## Kafi

## Asawari

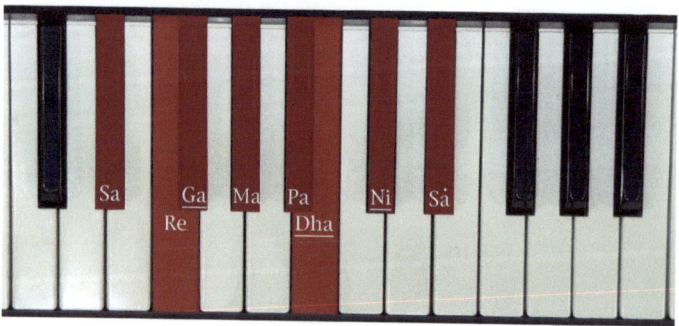

## Bhairav

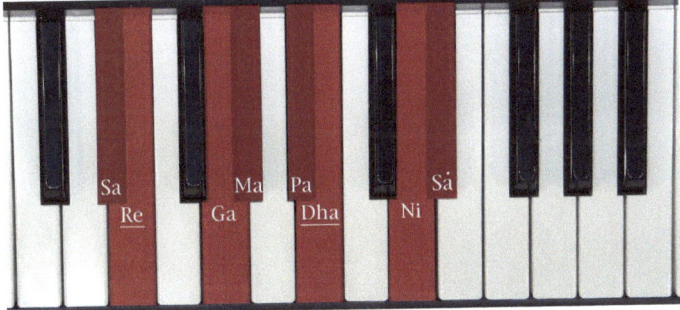

## Bhairavi

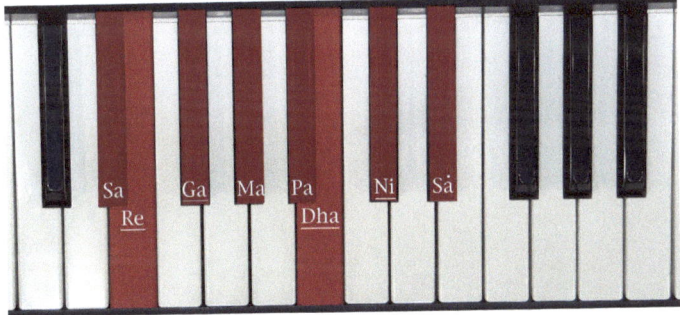

## Purvi

## Marwa

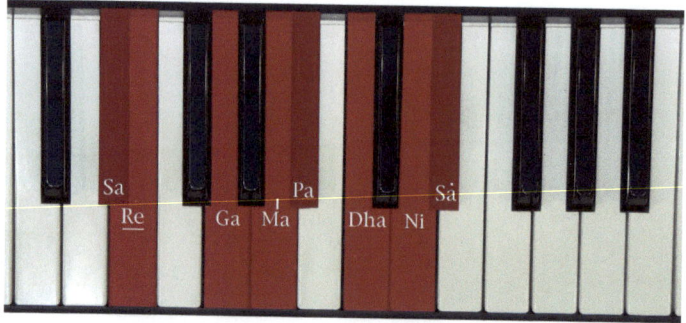

## Todi

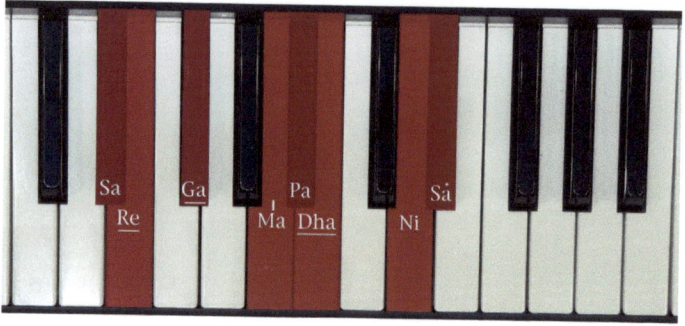

# APPENDIX 5
# COMMON THATS IN THE KEY OF E

Bilawal

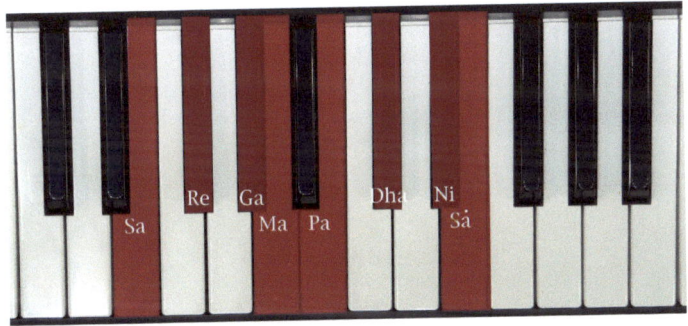

Kalyan

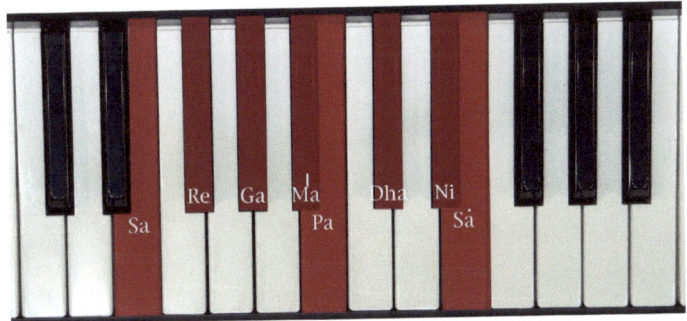

## Khammaj

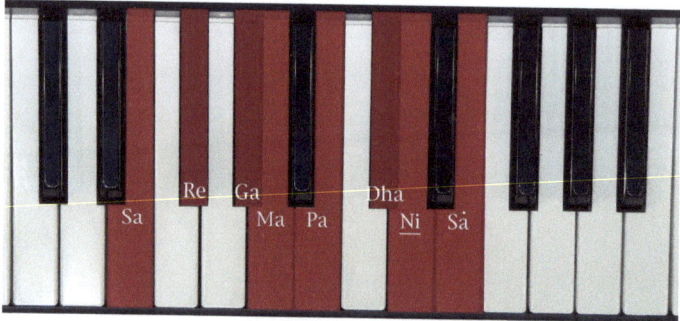

## Kafi

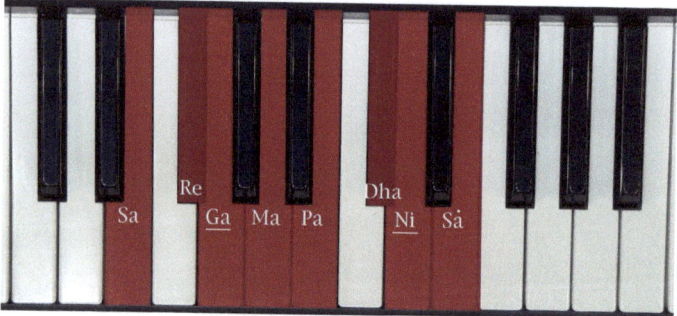

## Asawari

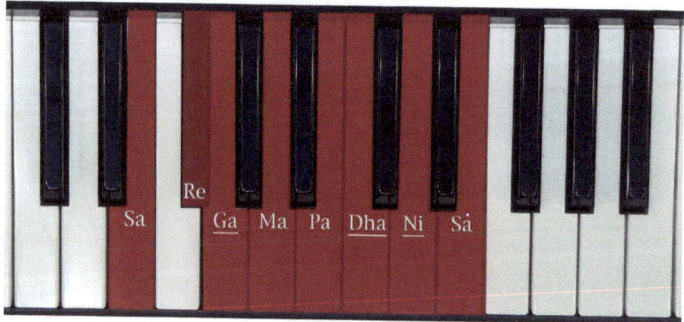

## Bhairav

## Bhairavi

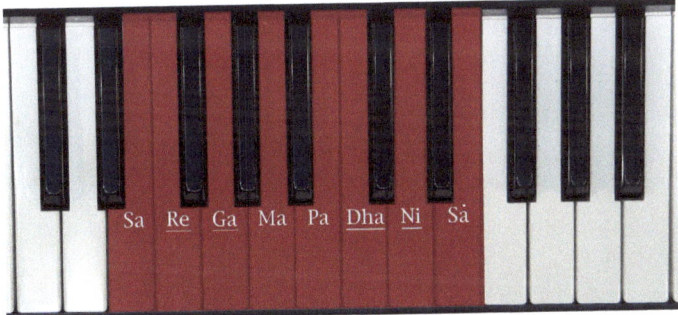

## Purvi

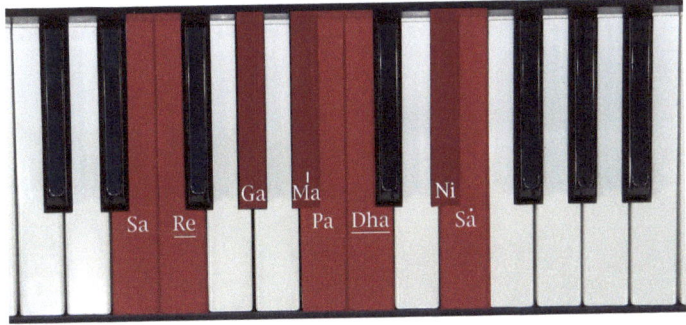

## Marwa

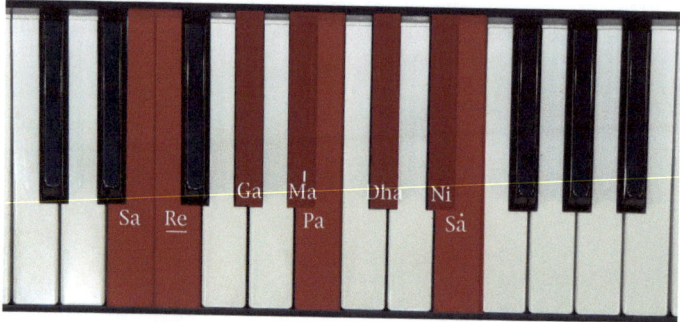

## Todi

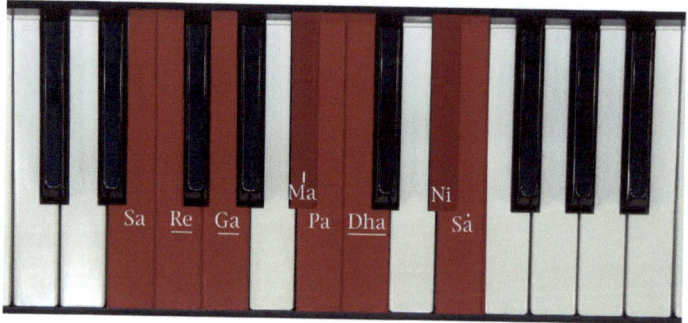

# APPENDIX 6
# COMMON THATS IN THE KEY OF F

Bilawal

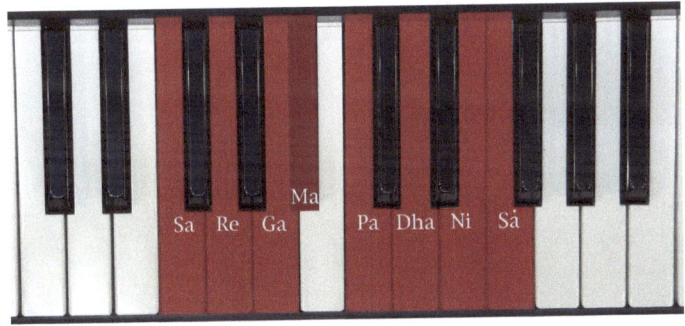

Kalyan

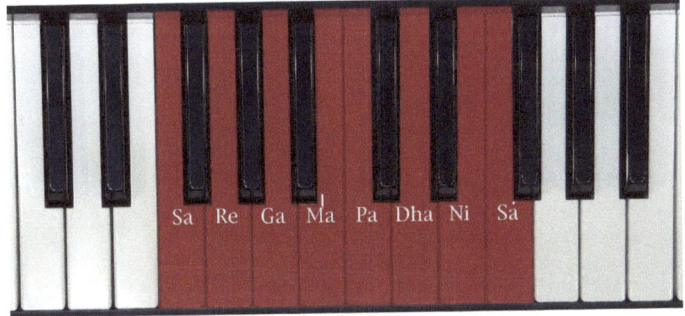

## Khammaj

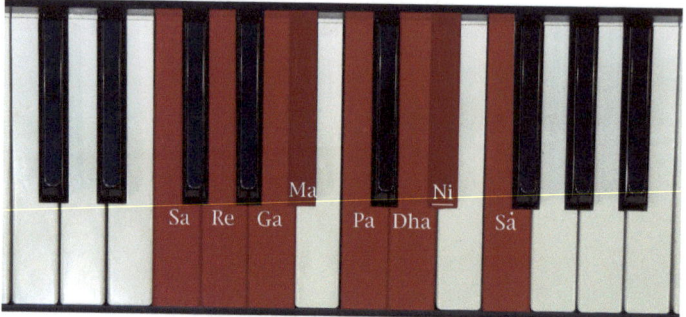

## Kafi

## Asawari

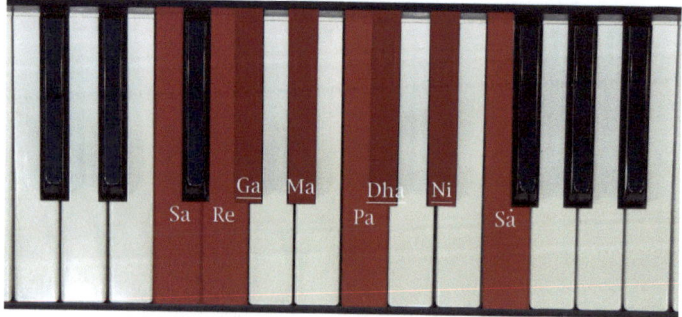

## Bhairav

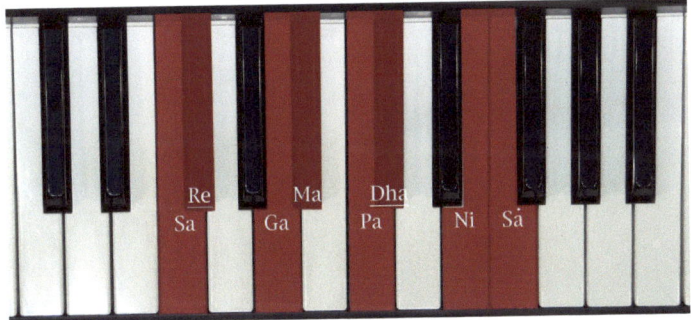

## Bhairavi

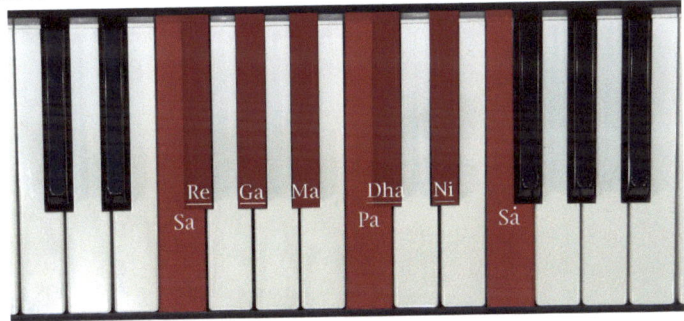

## Purvi

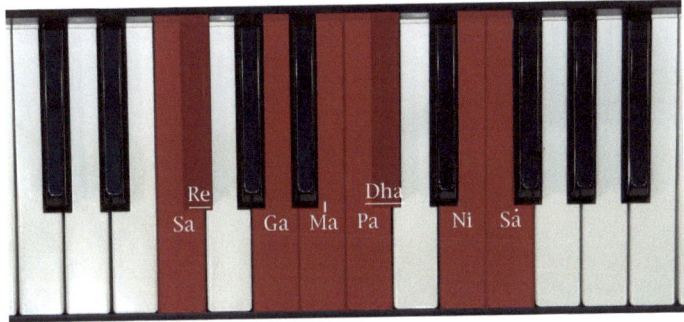

## Marwa

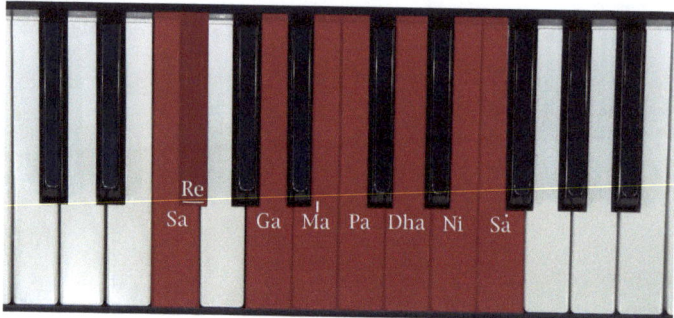

## Todi

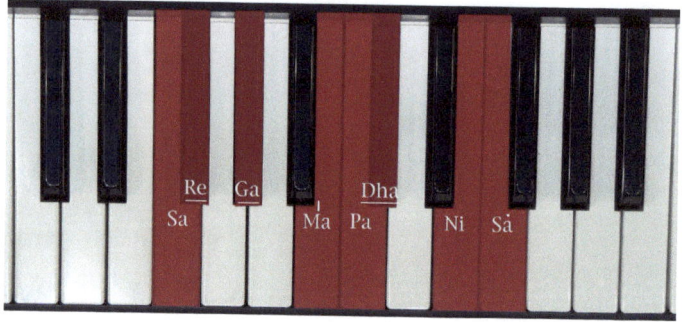

# APPENDIX 7
# COMMON THATS IN THE KEY OF F#

Bilawal

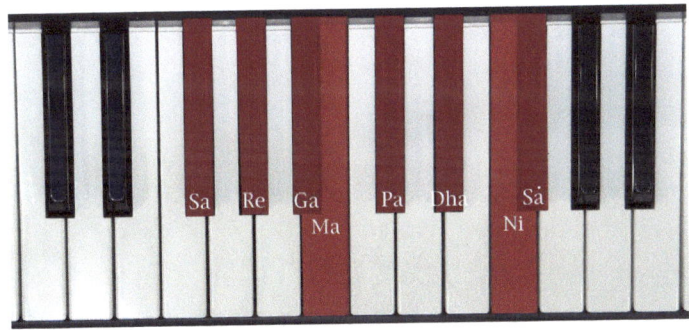

Kalyan

## Khammaj

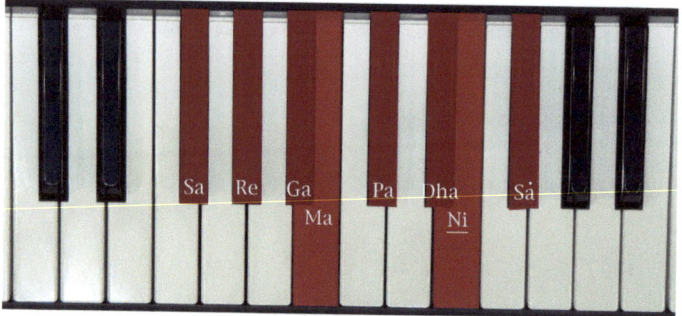

## Kafi

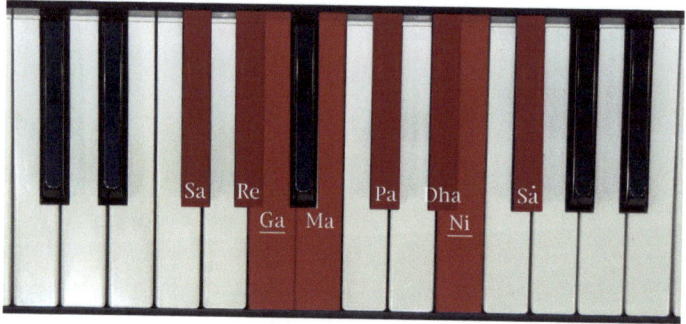

## Asawari

## Bhairav

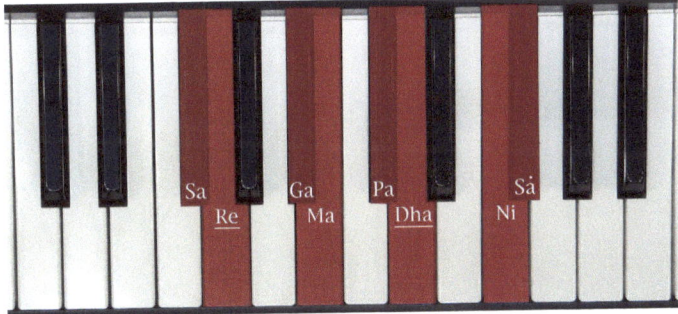

## Bhairavi

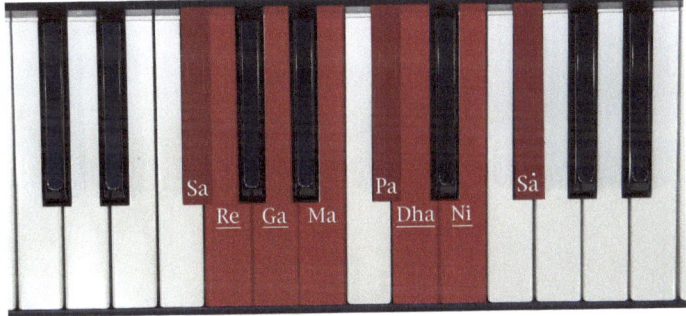

## Purvi

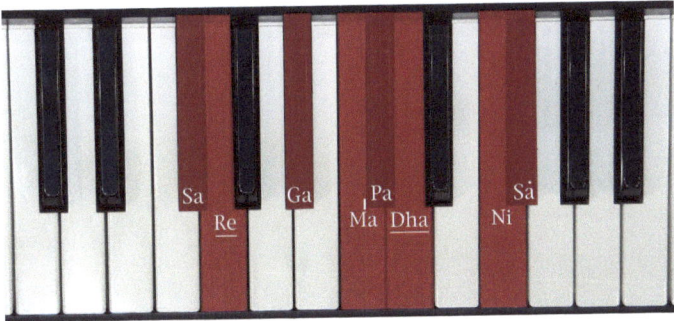

## Marwa

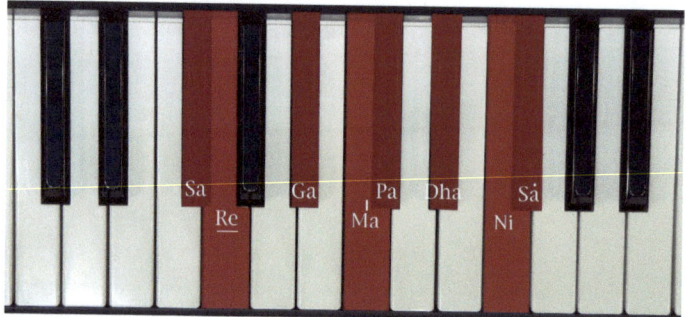

## Todi

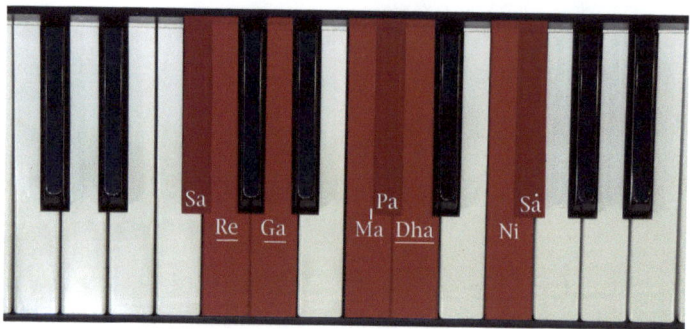

# APPENDIX 8
# COMMON THATS IN THE KEY OF G

Bilawal

Kalyan

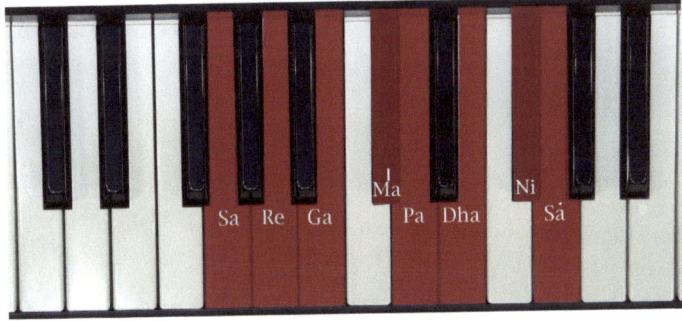

## Khammaj

## Kafi

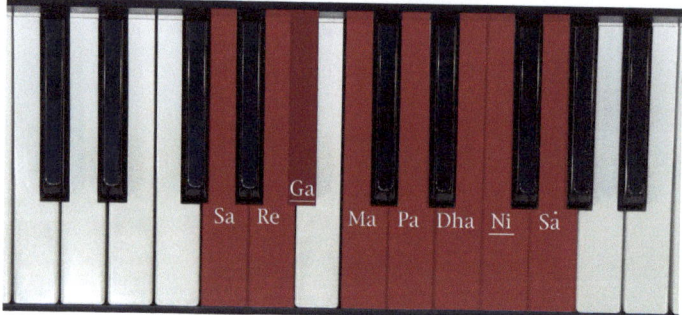

## Asawari

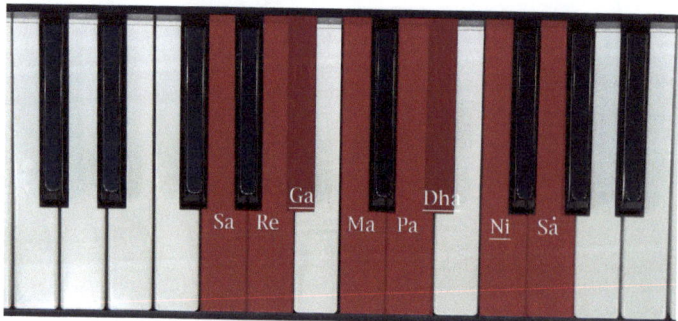

## Bhairav

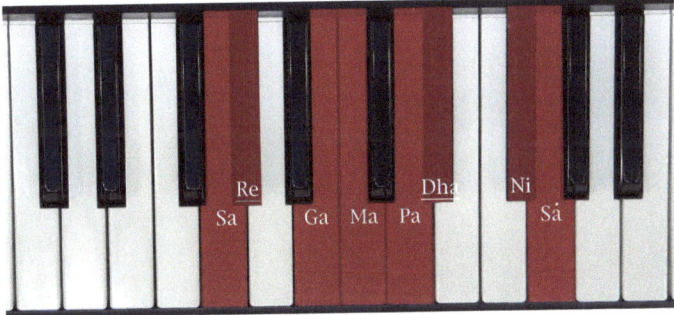

## Bhairavi

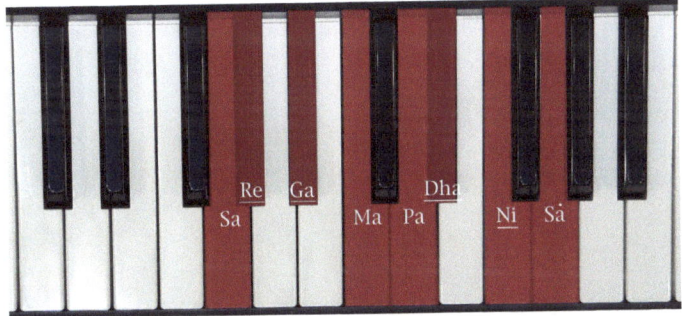

## Purvi

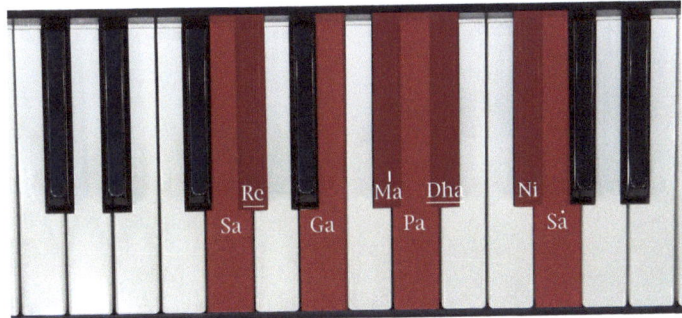

## Marwa

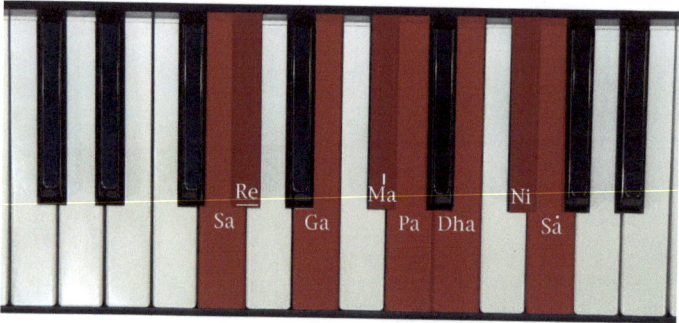

## Todi

# APPENDIX 9
# COMMON THATS IN THE KEY OF G#

Bilawal

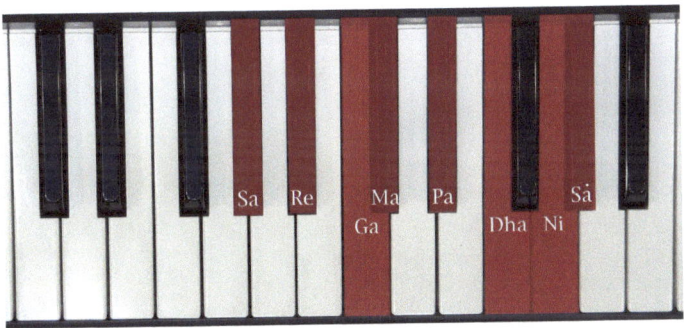

Kalyan

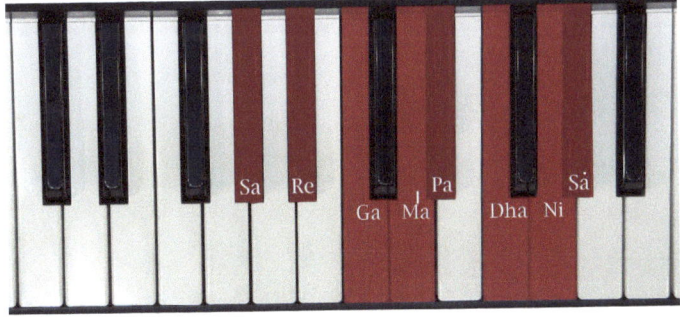

## Khammaj

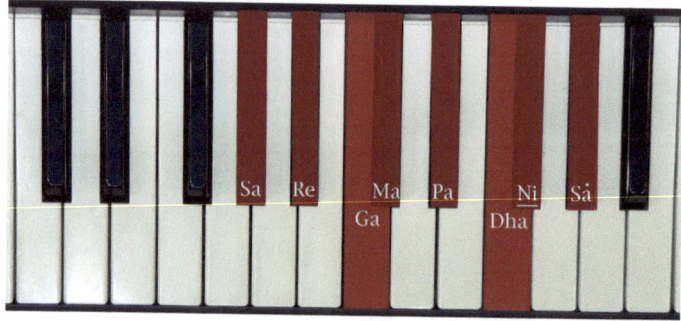

## Kafi

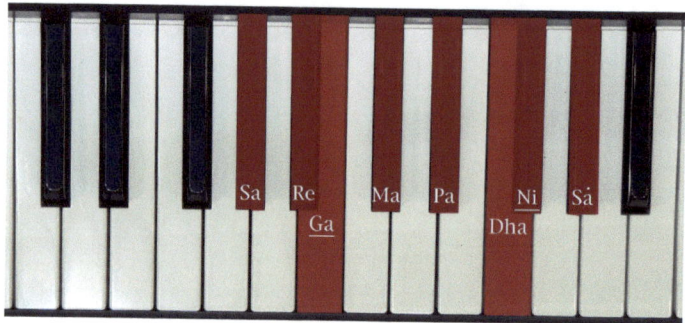

## Asawari

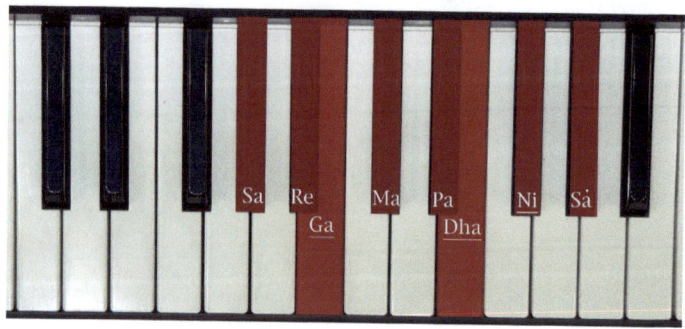

## Bhairav

## Bhairavi

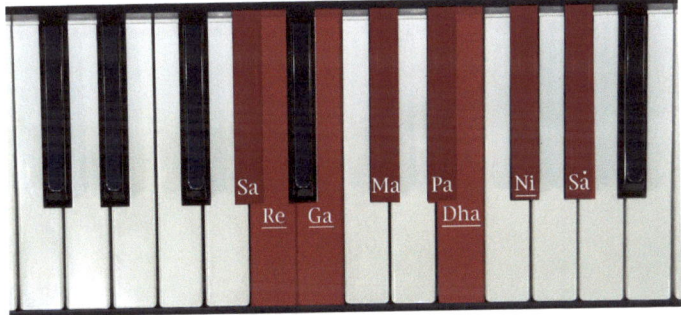

## Purvi

**Marwa**

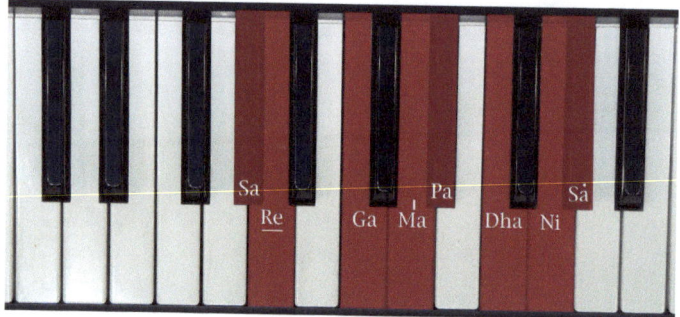

**Todi**

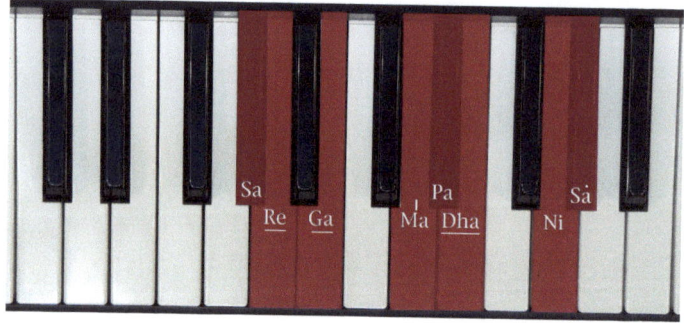

# APPENDIX 10
# COMMON THATS IN THE KEY OF A

Bilawal

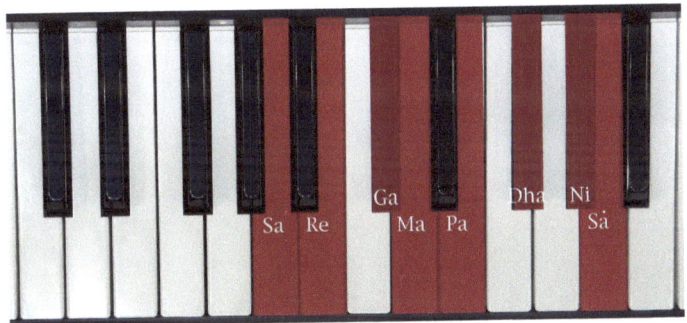

Kalyan

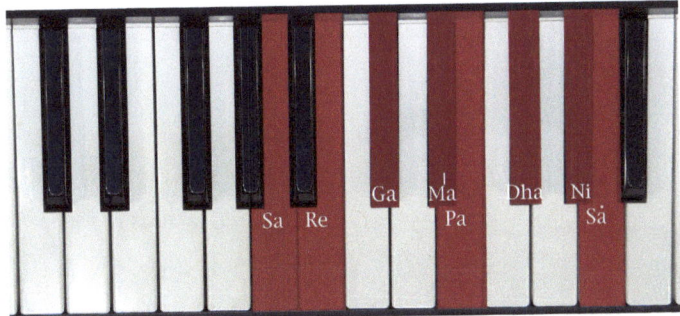

## Khammaj

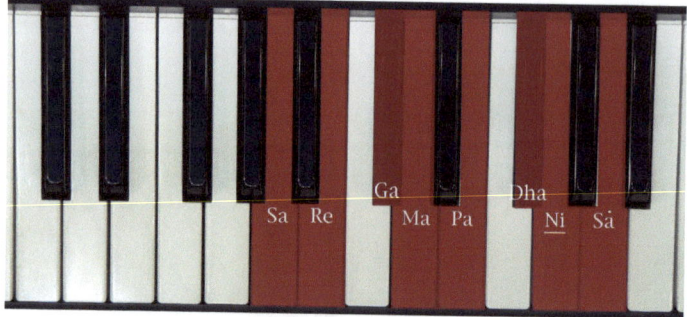

## Kafi

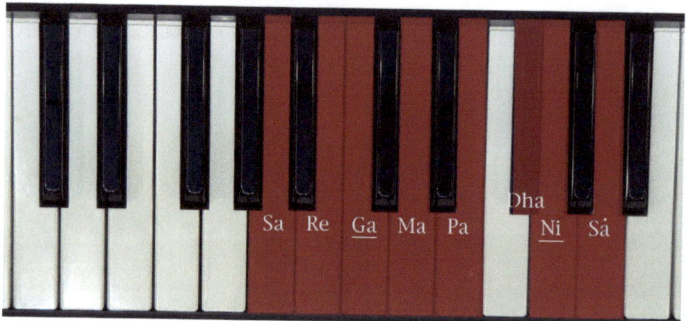

## Asawari

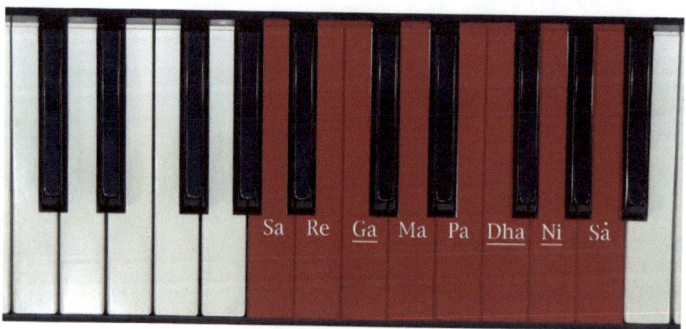

## Bhairav

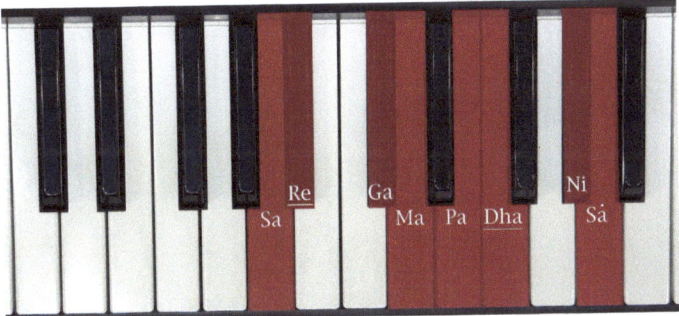

## Bhairavi

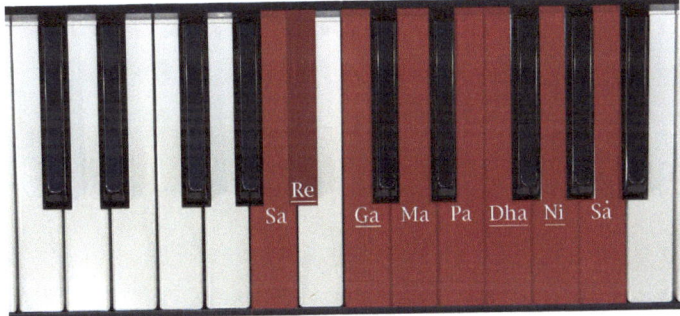

## Purvi

## Marwa

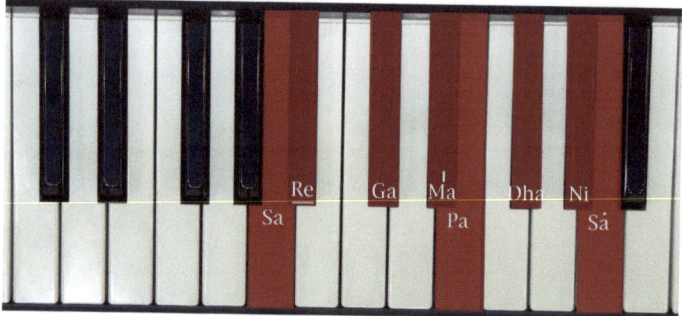

## Todi

# APPENDIX 11
# COMMON THATS IN THE KEY OF A#

Bilawal

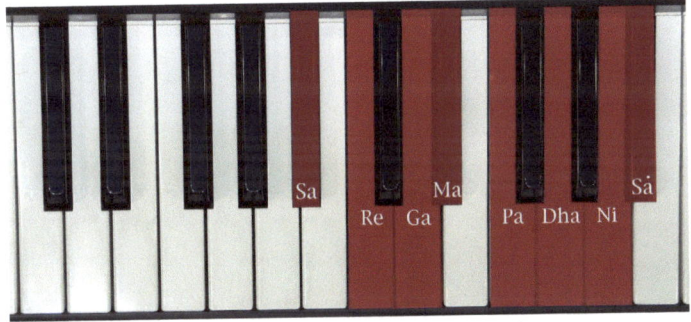

Kalyan

## Khammaj

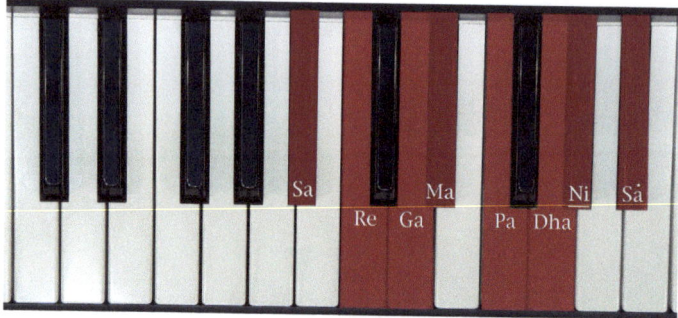

## Kafi

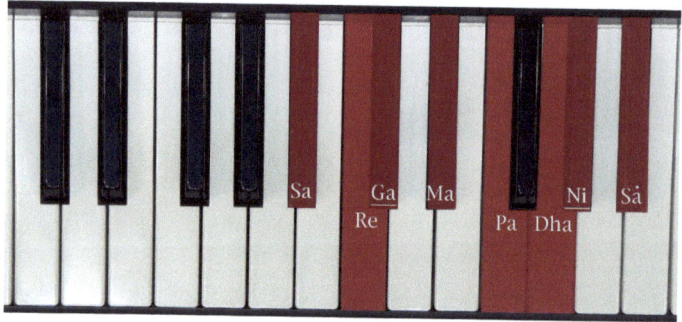

## Asawari

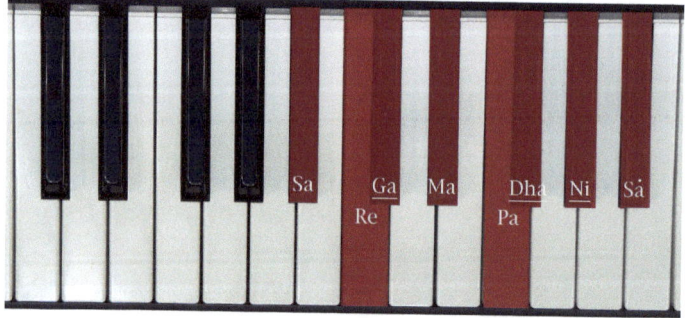

## Bhairav

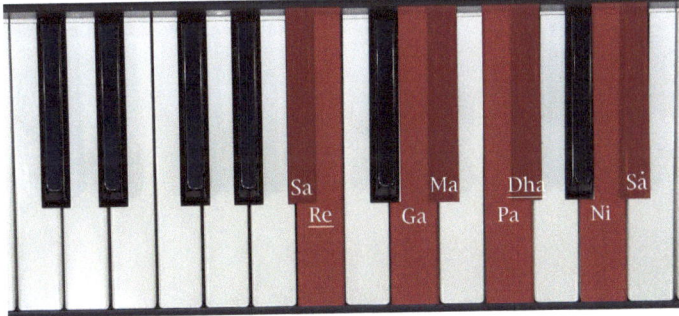

## Bhairavi

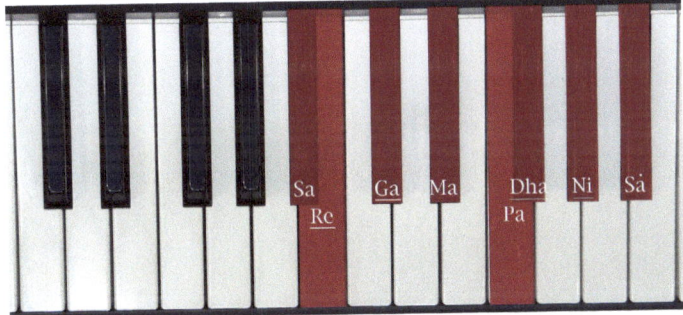

## Purvi

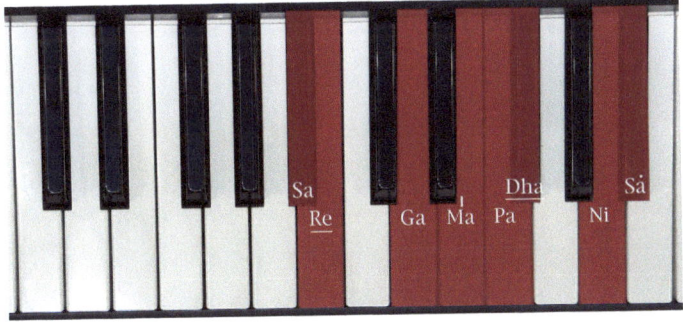

## Marwa

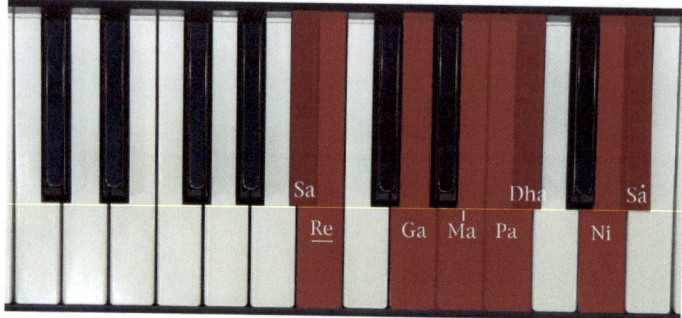

## Todi

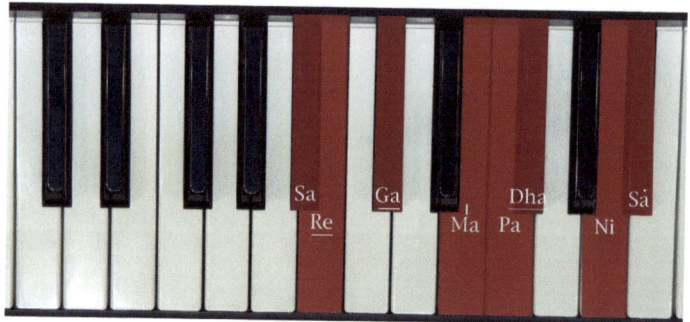

# APPENDIX 12
# COMMON THATS IN THE KEY OF B

Bilawal

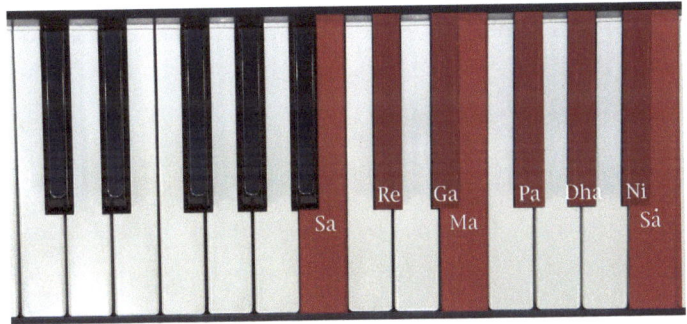

Kalyan

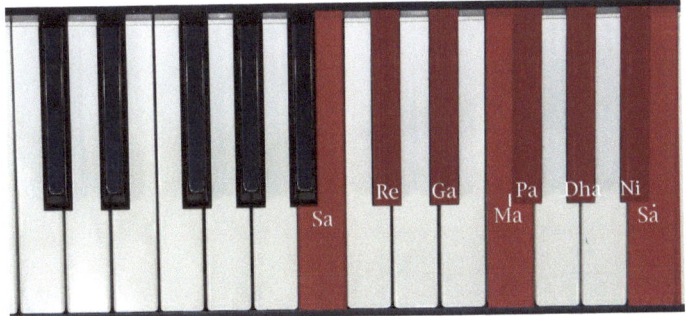

## Khammaj

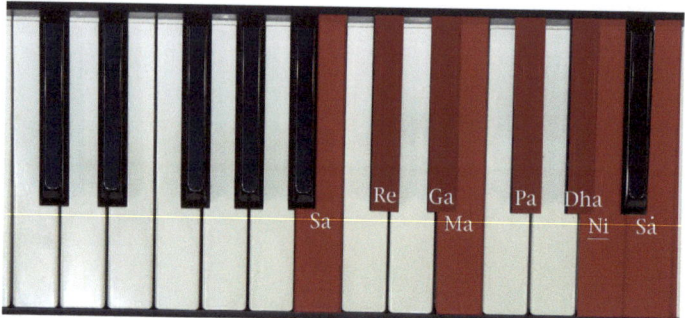

## Kafi

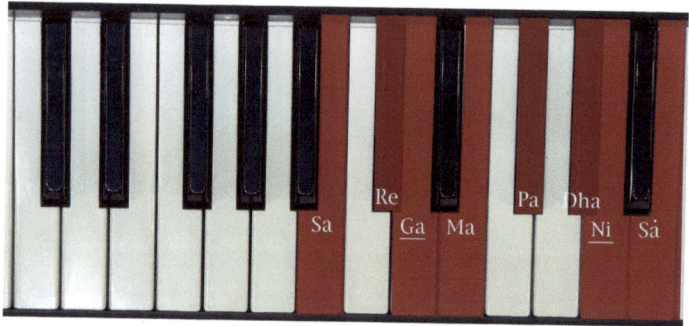

## Asawari

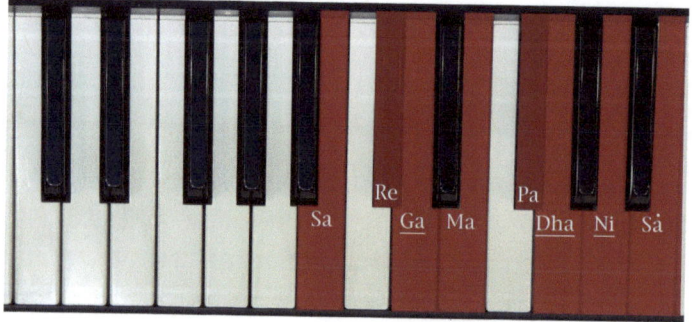

## Bhairav

## Bhairavi

## Purvi

**Marwa**

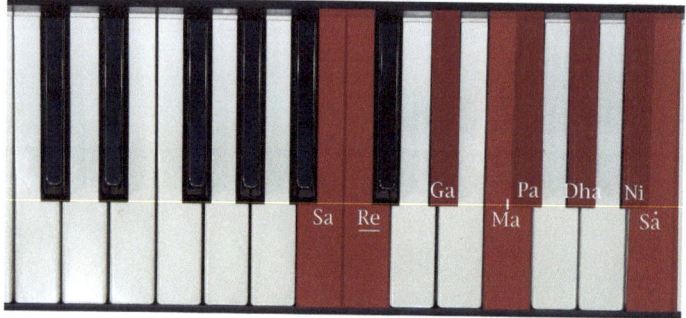

**Todi**

# APPENDIX 13
# SAMPLE QUESTIONS

Sample Questions (Difficulty Level 1)

# INDIAN MUSIC

1) Which country does NOT border India?
   ( ) Nepal
   ( ) Pakistan
   (X) Afghanistan
   ( ) Bangladesh

2) How many systems of classical music are there in India?
   ( ) One
   (X) Two
   ( ) Three
   ( ) Four

3) Which statement is true?
   ( ) Arabic is the most common language for Indian classical music.
   (X) Brij Bhasha is commonly used for classical North Indian Songs.
   ( ) Mandarin is commonly used in North Indian Songs.
   ( ) Pashtu is commonly used for North Indian Songs.

4) Ravi Shankar was famous for playing the ...
   ( ) Piano
   ( ) Tabla
   ( ) Flute
   (X) Sitar

5) Carnatic Sangeet is...
   ( ) ...the North Indian system of classical music.
   (X) ...the South Indian system of classical music.
   ( ) ...a style of folk music.
   ( ) ...a style of chicken curry.

6) Rag is...
   ( ) ...the Indian system of rhythm.
   ( ) ...an Indian dance form.
   ( ) ...a style of Indian theatre.
   (X) ...the Indian system of melody.

7) Tal is...
   (X) ...the Indian system of rhythm
   ( ) ...an Indian dance form
   ( ) ...a style of Indian theatre
   ( ) ...the Indian system of melody

8) Which statement is true?
   ( ) India has no folk music.
   ( ) India has a folk music which represents a single Indian culture.
   (X) India has many folk musics which represent a variety of Indian cultures.
   ( ) India had a folk music, but it was banned in the Emergency of the 1970s.

9) The word "sangeet" means?
   ( ) Instrumental music
   ( ) Vocal music
   ( ) Dance
   (X) All of the above

10) Songs in Carnatic music are performed...
    (X) ...In a variety of languages
    ( ) ...entirely in Sanskrit
    ( ) ...Brij Bhasha (an old dialect of Hindi)
    ( ) ...entirely in Tamil

Sample Questions (Difficulty Level 1)

# MUSIC OF PAKISTAN

1) Which country does NOT border Pakistan?
   (X) Nepal
   ( ) India
   ( ) Afghanistan
   ( ) China

2) How many systems of classical music are there in Pakistan?
   (X) One
   ( ) Two
   ( ) Three
   ( ) Four

3) Tal is...
   ( ) ...the Pakistani system of melody.
   ( ) ...a dance form.
   (X) ...the Pakistani system of rhythm.
   ( ) ...a style of theatre.

4) Rag is...
   (X) ...the Pakistani system of melody
   ( ) ...a dance form
   ( ) ...the Pakistani system of rhythm
   ( ) ...a style of theatre

5) Which statement is true?
   ( ) Pakistan has no folk music.
   ( ) Pakistan has a folk music which represents a single culture.
   (X) Pakistan has many folk musics which represent a variety of Pakistani cultures.
   ( ) Pakistan shares the same folk music with most of China.

6) The most common language used in Pakistani music is:
   (X) Urdu
   ( ) Hindi
   ( ) Farsi
   ( ) Arabic

7) The traditional music of Pakistan is...
   ( ) ...most similar to the music of Turkey
   (X) ...most similar to the music of India
   ( ) ...most similar to the music of Greece
   ( ) ...most similar to the music of China

8) Ghazal is...
   ( ) ...performed primarily in Arabic
   ( ) ...performed primarily in Farsi
   ( ) ...performed primarily in Punjabi
   (X) ...performed primarily in Urdu

9) Which statement is FALSE?
   ( ) The ghazal is much more popular than the classical music.
   ( ) The ghazal places more emphasis on the words than the classical music.
   (X) The ghazal is primarily oriented towards mundane daily matters.
   ( ) The ghazal uses daily matters as a metaphor for lofty spiritual conditions.

10) Which statement is FALSE
   ( ) The sitar is used in Pakistani music.
   ( ) The rabab is used in Pakistani music.
   ( ) The tabla is used in Pakistani music.
   (X) The mridangam is used in Pakistani music.

Sample Questions (Difficulty Level 1)

# MUSIC OF BANGLADESH

1) Which country does NOT border Bangladesh?
   ( ) Nepal
   ( ) India
   ( ) Bhutan
   (X) China

2) The traditional music of Bangladesh is...
   ( ) ...most similar to the music of Turkey
   ( ) ... most similar to the music of Greece
   (X) ... most similar to the music of India
   ( ) ... most similar to the music of China

3) Tal is...
   ( ) ...the Bangladeshi system of melody
   ( ) ... a dance form
   (X) ... the Bangladeshi system of rhythm
   ( ) ... a style of theatre

4) Rag is...
   (X) ...the Bangladeshi system of melody
   ( ) ... a dance form
   ( ) ... the Bangladeshi system of rhythm
   ( ) ... a style of theatre

5) The most common language used in Bangladeshi music is:
   ( ) Urdu
   ( ) Hindi
   ( ) Farsi
   (X) Bengali

6) Baul Sangeet is...
   (X) ...a very popular form of music in Bangladesh.
   ( ) ....a classical form of music in Bangladesh.
   ( ) All of the above
   ( ) None of the above

7) One of these instruments is NOT used in the music of Bangladesh
   ( ) Sitar
   (X) Nadaswaram
   ( ) Tabla
   ( ) Khol

8) Rabindra Sangeet is a popular musical form that...
   ( ) ...is peculiar to Bangladesh
   (X) ...is common to both India and Bangladesh
   ( ) ...is popular throughout Bangladesh, India, and Pakistan
   ( ) ...is popular throughout Bangladesh, India, Pakistan, and Afghanistan

9) Keyboard instruments are...
   ( ) ...purely Western instruments and are not found in the music of Bangladesh.
   (X) ...Western in origin, but have been used in the music of this region for a very long time.
   ( ) ...very popular in Bangladesh, but were only introduced in the last 50 years.
   ( ) ...were invented in the Bengal, and from there spread to Europe.

10) The Bangladeshi dotara is...
    ( ) A transverse flute made of bamboo.
    ( ) A large drum.
    ( ) A double reeded folk oboe.
    (X) A simple rabab-like lute made with skin and strings.

Sample Questions (Difficulty Level 2)

# MUSIC AND INSTRUMENTS

1) The sitar ...
   - ( ) ... has a bridge located on a membrane similar to a Western Banjo
   - ( ) ... was only introduced into India from Iran about the turn of the 20th century
   - (X) ...is popular throughout India, Pakistan, Nepal, and Bangladesh.
   - ( ) All of the above.

2) Tabla...
   - (X) ... means "drum" in Arabic
   - ( ) ... means "drum" in Sanskrit
   - ( ) ... got its name from the Portuguese word for "table"
   - ( ) ... is Persian and means "made of wood"

3) Which of the following statements are true?
   - ( ) The rag is based upon a musical mode.
   - ( ) This musical mode is known as "that".
   - ( ) The rag is traditionally ascribed to a time of the day or a season.
   - (X) All of the above.

4) Carnatic Music...
   - ( ) ...differs from Hindustani Sangeet in nomenclature.
   - ( ) ...differs from Hindustani Sangeet in performance style.
   - ( ) ...has fundamental similarities to Hindustani Sangeet.
   - (X) All of the above

5) The saptak...
   - ( ) ...is composed of 5 notes.
   - ( ) ...is composed of 6 notes.
   - (X) ...is composed of 7 notes.
   - ( ) All of the above

6) Jati is...
   - (X) ...the number of notes in a rag.
   - ( ) ...the important notes of a rag.
   - ( ) ...the ascending structure.
   - ( ) ...the descending structure.

7) Avartan is...
   - ( ) ...the beat.
   - ( ) ...the measure (bar).
   - ( ) ...the rhythmic syllable.
   - (X) ...the rhythmic cycle.

8) Bol is ...
   - ( ) ...the beat.
   - ( ) ...the measure (bar).
   - (X) ...the rhythmic syllable.
   - ( ) ...the rhythmic cycle.

9) The matra is ...
   - (X) ...the beat.
   - ( ) ...the measure (bar).
   - ( ) ...the rhythmic syllable.
   - ( ) ...the rhythmic cycle.

10) Tanpura...
    - ( ) ...plays full melodies.
    - ( ) ...provides a rhythmic accompaniment.
    - (X) ...provides a musical drone.
    - ( ) None of the above

Sample Questions (Difficulty Level 3)

# MUSIC (TAL)

1) How many matras does Tintal Have?
   ( ) Three
   ( ) Four
   ( ) Eight
   (X) Sixteen

2) How many vibhags does Dadra Tal have?
   ( ) One
   (X) Two
   ( ) Three
   ( ) Six

3) When timekeeping, a clap of the hand is called?
   ( ) Matra
   (X) Tali
   ( ) Khali
   ( ) Avartan

4) When timekeeping, a wave of the hand is called?
   ( ) Matra
   ( ) Tali
   (X) Khali
   ( ) Avartan

5) The term "Tintal" literally means...
   ( ) ..."One clap".
   ( ) ..."Two claps".
   (X) ..."Three claps".
   ( ) ..."Sixteen claps".

6) How many matras are in Ektal?
   ( ) One
   ( ) Two
   ( ) Ten
   (X) None of the above

7) How many vibhags are in Ektal?
   (X) Four
   ( ) Five
   ( ) Six
   ( ) Twelve

8) What is unique about Rupak Tal?
   (X) The sam is designated with a Khali.
   ( ) It is the only tal that has seven matras.
   ( ) It is the only tal which is asymmetric.
   ( ) None of the above

9) Most of the folk/lighter music is performed in ...
   ( ) ...Tintal.
   ( ) ...Tivra Tal.
   ( ) ...Ektal.
   (X) ...Kaherava.

10) The first beat of the cycle is known as...
    ( ) "matra".
    (X) "sam".
    ( ) "avartan".
    ( ) "bol".

Sample Questions (Difficulty Level 3)

# MUSIC (RAG)

1) A rag is partly defined by ...
   ( ) ...the That.
   ( ) ...the ascending structure.
   (X) All of the above
   ( ) None of the above

2) "Shuddha Swar Saptak" is...
   (X) ...a natural scale.
   ( ) ...a harmonic minor.
   ( ) ...the time of the day in which a rag is supposed to be performed.
   ( ) None of the above.

3) Bilawal That is...
   ( ) ...the natural scale according to the Bhatkhande system.
   ( ) ...the same as the Ionian mode.
   ( ) ...the Western natural scale.
   (X) all of the above

4) Khammaj That uses...
   ( ) ...an augmented fourth (Tivra Ma).
   ( ) ...a minor third (Komal Ga).
   (X) ...a minor seventh (Komal Ni).
   ( ) ...a minor sixth (Komal Dha).

5) The Difference between Rag Khammaj and Khammaj That is...
   ( ) Khammaj That uses only a Komal Ni, While Rag Khammaj uses both Nis.
   ( ) Rag Khammaj skips the 2nd (Re) in the ascending structure.
   (X) All of the Above
   ( ) None of the Above

6) Arohana refers to ...
   (X) ...the ascending structure of the rag.
   ( ) ...the descending structure of the rag.
   ( ) ...a particular "catch" phrase.
   ( ) ...the important note of the rag.

7) Avarohana refers to ...
   ( ) ...the ascending structure of the rag.
   (X) ...the descending structure of the rag.
   ( ) ...a particular "catch" phrase.
   ( ) ...the important note of the rag.

8) Pakard refers to ...
   ( ) ...the ascending structure of the rag.
   ( ) ...the descending structure of the rag.
   (X) ...a particular "catch" phrase.
   ( ) ...the important note of the rag.

9) Purvi That uses...
   ( ) ...all natural (shuddha) notes.
   (X) ...Sa, Komal Re, Ga, Tivra Ma, Pa, Komal Dha, Ni, Sa.
   ( ) ...is the same as Arabic Minor.
   ( ) ...Sa, Re, Ga, Tivra Ma, Pa, Dha, Ni, Sa.

10) Komal Pancham ...
   ( ) ...is not acknowledged in the contemporary music of South Asia.
   ( ) ...corresponds to the diminished 5th in Western music.
   ( ) ...sounds very similar to the Devil's Interval.
   (X) All of the above.

# GLOSSARY

**aakar** (आकार) – To sing without words and only use the vowel "A" (as in father).
**abhang** (अभंग) – Marathi devotional song.
**abhay** (अभय) – Fearless.
**abhog** (अभोग) – Derived from the word "*bhuj*" which means "to fulfil". The tertiary theme of a *dhrupad*.
**abhyas** (अभ्यास) – Practice – See *riyaz*.
**achala** (अचल) – Immovable notes (i.e., Sa and Pa).
**adachartal** (आड़ाचारताल) – See *Adachautal*.
**adachautal** (आड़ाचौताल) – A common 14 beat tal.
**addha tal** (अड्ढा ताल) – A tal of 16 beats.
**adha** (आध) – Half.
**adi lay** (आड़ी लय) – In a four unit time, one plays six units (i.e., 1 1/2 time or *tisra jati*).
**adi rag** (आदि राग) – The primordial *rag*, said to be *Bhairav* (*Mayamalavagaula*) in some mythology.
**adi tal** (आदिताल) – A south Indian *tal* of 8 beats similar to both *Tintal* and *Kaherava*.
**agra** (आगरा) – A city south of Delhi 2) A vocal *gharana* of the same place.
**ahat nad** (आहत नाद) – Lit. "struck sound". The physical vibrations which compose sound.
**ahir bhairav** (अहिर भैरव) – A common *rag*.
**ajrada** (अजराड़ा) – A village near Meerat.
**ajrada baj** (अजराड़ा बाज) – A style of *tabla* playing originally from Ajrada.
**akshar** (अक्षर) – A character or letter of the alphabet. A syllable.
**alakh** (अलख) – A lock of hair, a curl.
**alankar** (अलन्कार) – An ornamental phrase.
**alap** (आलाप) – A rhythmless exposition of the *rag*.
**alapini karuna** (आलापिनी करुणा) – The 14th *shruti* (microtone).

**alhaiya bilaval** (अल्हैय बिलावल) - A common *rag* similar to the Western natural scale.

**amad** (आमद) - A *kathak* piece used to make an entry onto the stage. A *tabla* or *pakhawaj* composition used for such an entry.

**anagat (grah)** (अनागत) - The process of ending a composition before the *sam*.

**anagat tihai** (अनागत तिहाई) - A *tihai* which ends before the *sam*.

**anahat nad** (अनाहत नाद) - "Un-struck sound". A metaphysical resonance which pervades the entire universe.

**anand bhairav** (आनंद भैरव) - A *rag*.

**anavarat** (अनवरत) - Always, continuously.

**andolan** (आंदोलन) - A slow vibrato.

**ang** (अंग) - (Lit. "limb" or "section") A measure or *vibhag*.

**angushtana** (अंगुश्ताना) - *Tabla tukadas* which concentrate on the fingers.

**ansh** (अंश) - The starting note of a *murchana*.

**antara** (अन्तरा) - The secondary theme of a classical song.

**anudrut** (अणुद्रुत) - See *ati drut*.

**anupam** (अनुपम) - Unequaled, incomparable, most excellent.

**anuvadi** (अणुवादी) - The notes of the *rag* other than the *vadi* and *samavadi*.

**apne** (अपने) - One's own.

**ardhya tal** (अर्ध्य ताल) - An obscure *tal* of 27 beats.

**arjun tal** (अर्जुन ताल) - An obscure *pakhawaj tal* of 20 beats.

**aroh** (आरोह) - The ascending structure of the *rag*.

**arohana** (आरोहन) - see *aroh*.

**asavari** (आसावरी) - 1) A *that*. 2) A common *rag*.

**ashta** (अष्ट) - Eight.

**ashta-jam** (अष्ट चाम) - 24 hours a day.

**ashtapadi** (अष्टपदी) - A lyrical form made famous by Jaidev in his *Gita Govinda*. It acquired its meaning because of its eight-line format.

**ashuddh** (अशुद्ध) - Incorrectly performed music.

**ati drut** (अति द्रुत) - Ultra-fast tempo.

**ati tar saptak** (अति तार सप्तक) - Two octaves above the middle register.

**ati vilambit** (अति विलंबित) - Ultra-slow tempo.

**atit (grah)** (अतीत) - The process of ending a tihai after the *sam*.

**avanaddh** (अवनद्ध) - A membranous percussive instrument (e.g., *tabla, dholak, mridang,* etc.).

**avaroh** (अवरोह) - 1) The descending structure of a *rag*. 2) The second half of a *lom-vilom* gat.

**avarohana** (अवरोहन) - See *avaroh*.

**avartan** (आवर्तन) - A cycle.

**ave** (आवे) – Come.

**avrati** (आव्रती) – See *avartan*.

**baat** (बात) – 1) Words, talk. 2) A matter for discussion, an affair, an event, an incident.

**bada kheyal** (बड़ा खयाल) – The slow portion of the *kheyal*.

**badal** (बदल) – Change.

**bageshri** (बागेश्री) – A common *rag*.

**bahar** (बहार) – A common *rag*.

**baiju bavra** (बैजू बावरा) – A famous musician of the 16th century.

**baj** (बाज) – A style of instrument playing.

**baj ka tar** (बाज का तार) – Main playing string on *sarod, sitar,* or *sarangi*.

**bakhan** (बखान) – Description, praise.

**bala** (बला) – Pressure, stress, strength.

**banarasi baj** (बनारसी बाज) – A style of *tabla* playing originating in Benares, often considers synonymous with *purbi baj*.

**band** (बन्द) – Lit "closed". Non-resonant strokes such as *Te, Ka, Kat, Tak*, etc.

**bande** (बंदे) – A prisoner

**bandish** (बंदिश) – A composition or fixed musical piece.

**banmali** (बनमाली) – A forester.

**bansuri** (बांसुरी) – A bamboo flute.

**banti** (बँटी) – Another name for *kaida*.

**barva** (बरवा) – A rare *rag*.

**basant** (बसंत) – A common *rag*, generally associated with spring.

**basi** (बसी) – Dwell, reside.

**baurane** (बौराने) – Those who are confused, mad, or insane.

**bayan** (बायाँ) – The large metal left hand drum of the *tabla* pair.

**bedamdar tihai** (बेदमदार तिहाई) – A *tihai* in which each section is not separated by a pause.

**beenkar** (बीनकार) – *Gharana* that has tradition of playing the *bin* (*rudra vina*).

**beguni** (बेगुणी) – Unskilled, unvirtuous, untrained.

**benares** (बेनारस) – 1) A city in north India. 2) A *tabla gharana* from that city (see Banarasi baj).

**besura** (बेसुर) – Out of tune.

**betal** (बेताल) – Out of rhythm.

**bhagavan** (भगवान) – God, Supreme being, Vishnu, prosperous, glorious.

**bhai** (भाई) – Lit. "brother". A masculine form of address indicating familiarity.

**bhairav** (भैरव) – 1) A *that*. 2) A common morning *rag* associated with Siva.

**bhairavi** (भैरवी) – 1) A *that*. 2) A common *rag* generally played at the end of performances.
**bhaj** (भज) – Pray.
**bhajan** (भजन) – A Hindu religious song, prayer, worship.
**bhala** (भला) – Good, well, trim, gentle, noble, excellent.
**bhalo** (भलो) – Good, well, gentile.
**bharan** (भरन) – A filler. Something used to fill up a certain number of beats.
**bhari** (भरी) – Lit. "full", clapped, see "*tali*".
**bhatiyar** (भटियार) – A common *rag*.
**bhatkat** (भटकत) – Mislead, deceive.
**bhatkhande** (भातखन्दे) – See Vishnu Narayan Bhatkhande.
**bhatkhande paddhati** (भातखन्दे पद्धति) – The theoretical and notational system developed by Bhatkhande.
**bhayanak** (भयानक) – The emotion of fear. One of the nine principal emotions (*nava ras*).
**bhed** (भेद) – 1) Secret. 2) Difference.
**bhendi bazar gharana** (भेंड़ी बज़र घराना) – *Bhendi bazaar* is a place in Bombay (Mumbai). Some consider this to be a *gharana*, some do not. Its antiquity cannot be traced back further than the turn of the 20th century.
**bhimpalasi** (भिमपलासी) – A common *rag*.
**bhola** (भोला) – Simple, innocent.
**bhupal todi** (भूपाल तोड़ी) – A *rag*.
**bhupali** (भूपाली) – A common *rag* of five notes, similar to the Western pentatonic scale.
**bhushan** (भूषण) – An ornament, an embellishment, jewel.
**biadi lay** (बिआड़ी लय) – In a four-unit time, one plays seven units per beat.
**bihag** (बिहाग) – A common *rag*.
**bihagada** (बिहागड़ा) – A *rag*.
**bilaskhani todi** (बिलासखानी तोड़ी) – A *rag*, attributed to Bilas Khan.
**bilawal** (बिलावल) –1) A *that*. 2) A common *rag*. 3) The natural scale.
**bin** (बीन) – 1) A *rudra vina*. 2) Without.
**binat** (बीनत) – Entreaty, an earnest request.
**bol** (बोल) – 1) The mnemonic syllables of *tabla, pakhawaj, sitar*, or *sarod*. 2) Referring to words (e.g., *bol-tan, bol-paran*, etc.).
**bol alap** (बोल अलाप) – *Alap* which uses the words of the song.
**bol bant** (बोल बांट) – Division of the lyrics in the *dhrupad* style.
**bol paran** (बोल परण) – A type of *tabla* or *pakhawaj* composition whose syllables are actually words.

**bol tan** (बोल तान) – A *tan* based upon the words of the song.
**brahma** (ब्रह्म) – The supreme creator (God).
**brahma-chhabi** (ब्रह्म छबि) – Beauty of the eternal spirit.
**brindavani sarang** (बृन्दावनी सारंग) – A common *rag*, reminiscent of the land of Krishna.
**carnatic sangeet** (कर्नाटिक संगीत) – See *Carnatic sangeet*.
**chachar tal** (चाचर ताल) – See *Dipchandi*.
**chai** (छई) – Reflection, image, shadow.
**chaiti** (चैती) – A folk song from Uttar Pradesh, concerning the month of *Chait* (March or April).
**chakradar** (चक्रदार) – A *tihai* in which each phrase is a *tihai* in itself.
**chal** (चल) – Literally "move", a note which is movable, (i.e., *Re, Ga, Ma, Dha*, or *Ni*).
**chala** (चाला) – See *chalan*.
**chalan** (चलन) – 1) A *tabla* composition. Some consider this to be similar to *peshkar* while some consider it to be similar to *laggi* or *ladi*. 2) The manner in which the *rag* progresses.
**champak tal** (चंपक ताल) – See *adachautal*.
**chanchar** (चाँचर) – See *diphandi*.
**chandovati madhya** (छंदोवती मध्य) – The first *shruti*.
**chandra** (चंद्र) – Moon.
**chang** (चँग) – A musical instrument in which the musical portion is enclosed in a frame. In Persian and Urdu it is a harp; in common Hindi it is a large tambourine (*daf*). Sometimes, it is a jew's harp (*murchang*).
**chant** (चाँट) – See *chat*.
**charan** (चरण) – 1) The feet, usually of the guru, saint, or other great personality. 2) A bard, common in Rajasthan.
**chart** (चार्ट) – See *chat*.
**chartal** (चारताल) – See *chautal*.
**chat** (चाट) – Kinar, the outer section of the *tabla* skin.
**chati** (चाटी) – *Kinar*, same as *chat*.
**chatur** (चतुर) – Expert, wise.
**chatur pandit** (चतुर पंडित) – *Nom de plume* of Vishnu Narayan Bhatkhande.
**chaturai** (चतुराई) – Ingenuity, wisdom, tact.
**chaturstra jati** (चतुरस्र जाती) – Any rhythm composed of 2, 4, 8, 16, 32, etc. beats.
**chaugun** (चौगुन) – A *layakari* of 4:1. (i.e., quadruple time.)

**chaupalli** (चौपल्ली) - 1) A *tabla* composition, the same as *tipalli* except with four sections. 2) A *tabla* composition revolving around a quadruple repetition of a single bol (e.g., ... धा धा धा धा ...).

**chautal** (चौताल) - An old 12-beat *pakhawaj tal*.

**chaya** (छाय) - Resemblance of one *rag* found in another.

**chayanat** (छायानट) - A common *rag*.

**chikari** (चिकारी) - The drone strings on a *sitar* or *sarod*.

**chinh** (चिन्ह) - Notational elements.

**chiz** (चीज़) - A classical composition. See *bandish*.

**choti savari tal** (चोटी सवारी ताल) - A *tal*, considered by most to be synonymous to *pancham savari*.

**chutta** (छुट्टा) - The cushioned rings which support the *tabla*.

**da** (ड) - A *tabla bol*.

**da** (द) - A *tabla bol* of *pakhawaj* origin.

**dadra** (दाद्रा) - A very light style of singing, very similar to thumri.

**dadra tal** (दाद्रा ताल) - A common six beat *tal* used in light and semi-classical music.

**daf** (डफ़) - A large tambourine.

**dafli** (डफ़ली) - A small tambourine.

**dagga** (डग्गा) - The large metal left hand drum of the *tabla* pair.

**damaru** (डमरू) - An hour-glass shaped drum associated with Shiva.

**damdar tihai** (दमदार तिहाई) - A *tihai* in which each section is separated by a pause.

**dan** (दान) - Assurance of protection, safety, or amnesty.

**daras** (दरस) - Seeing, sight.

**darbari** (दरबारी) also called *darburi kanada* (दरबारी कान्हड़ा) - A common *rag* ascribed to Tansen.

**dayak** (दायक) - Bestower, giver.

**dayan** (दायाँ) - The small wooden right hand drum of the *tabla* pair.

**dayavati karuna** (दयावती करुण) - The second *shruti* (microtone).

**dee** (दी) - A *tabla bol* of *pakhawaj* origin.

**dekhiye** (देखिए) - Look (polite form).

**dekho** (देखो) - Look.

**delhi** - See Dilli.

**desh** (देश) - 1) Country, land, people 2) A common *rag*.

**deshi** (दैशी) - An old rag.

**deshkar** (देशकार) - A *rag* similar to *Bhupali*.

**devan** (देवन) - Gods.

**dha** (ध) - 1) An uncommon bol of *tabla*. 2) *Dhaivat*.

**dhaa** (धा) – A fundamental bol of both *tabla* and *pakhawaj*.
**dhaivat** (धैवत) – The sixth note of the scale.
**dhamar tal** (धमार ताल) – See *dhammar (tal)*.
**dhammar** (धम्मार) – 1) An old style of singing, similar to *dhrupud*, generally associated with the spring season. 2) A 14-*matra tal* associated with that style of singing.
**dhanashri** (धनाश्री) – A *rag*.
**dheen** (धीं) – A fundamental *tabla bol*.
**dhi** (धि) – A fundamental *tabla bol*.
**dhin** (धिं) – A fundamental *tabla bol*.
**dholak** (ढोलक) – A crude folk drum characterized by a cylindrical wooden shell covered with skin on both sides.
**dhrupad** (ध्रुपद) – Old classical style of singing.
**dhruvapad** (ध्रुवपद) – See *dhrupad*.
**dhumali tal** (धुमाली ताल) – A variation of *kaherava tal*.
**dhyan** (ध्यान) – Concentration.
**dhyavat** (ध्यावत) – Chanting.
**di** (दि) – A *tabla bol* of *pakhawaj* origin.
**dikhan** (दीखन) – To look, to appear, to see.
**dilli** (दिल्ली) – The present capitol of India.
**dilli baj** (दिल्ली बाज) – A style of playing *tabla*, originally from Delhi, characterized by extensive use of the middle finger, and the striking of *Naa* on the extreme rim of the *dayan*.
**dilruba** (दिलरूबा) – A bowed instrument with frets like a *sitar*, but a body like a *sarangi*.
**din** (दिं) – A *tabla bol*.
**din** (दिन) – Day.
**dipak** (दीपक) – A rare rag associated with fire.
**dipchani tal** (दीपचंदी ताल) – A common 14-beat *tal*.
**diya-sikha** (दीय सिखा) – The flame of a lamp.
**doha** (दोहा) – A couplet in Hindi poetry.
**dohatthu** (दोहत्थु) – A *tabla* composition where both hands are played on the same drum.
**dotar** (दोतार) – A simple two stringed lute.
**drut** (द्रुत) – Fast tempo.
**dugdugi** (डुगडुगी) – A *damaru*.
**duggi** (डुग्गी) – An extremely small kettle drum.
**duggan** (दुगुन) – A *layakari* of 2:1 (i.e., double time).
**dupalli** (दुपल्ली) – A type of *gat* where a phrase repeats twice.

**durga** (दुर्गा) - A common *rag*, similar to the Western pentatonic scale.
**dval** (ड्राल) - The *tasma* or lacing of the *tabla*.
**ek** (एक) - One, a, an, single.
**ekaki vadan** (एकाकी वादन) - Instrumental solo.
**ekgun** (एकगुन) - A *layakari* of 1:1 (i.e., single time).
**ekhatthi** (एकहत्थी) - See *ekhatthu*.
**ekhatthu** (एकहत्थु) - A *tabla* or *pakhawaj* composition which can be played with a single hand.
**ektal** (एकताल) - A common *tal* of 12 beats.
**ektali** (एकताली) - See *iktali*.
**ektar** (एकतार) - A simple one stringed lute.
**farmaishi paran** (फरमाइशी परण) - Any *tabla paran* which is used for a *farmaish* (encore).
**farodast tal** (फरोदस्त ताल) - An old and obscure *tal* of 7 or 14 beats.
**farukhabad** (फरुखाबाद) - 1) A place in north India. 2) The *tabla gharana* from this place.
**firat** (फिरत) - Wandering, returning, going around, something rejected or returned.
**fuljhadi** (फुलझड़ी) - (lit. a type of fireworks, a sparkler), a type of *tabla gat* characterized by sudden changes in the overall speed.
**ga** (ग) - 1) *Gandhar*. 2) A common *tabla bol*.
**gagan** (गगन) - Sky.
**gahe** (गहे) - To hold
**gai** (गई) - Gone, done, happened.
**gajara** (गजरा) - The braid of the *tabla pudi*. (Lit. a small string of flowers in a women's hair.)
**gamak** (गमक) - A fast ornamentation of the note.
**gandhar** - (गंधार) - The third note of the scale.
**gandharva** (गांधर्व) - The celestial beings.
**gandharva veda** (गांधर्व वेद) - The science of classical music.
**ganesh** (गणेश) - The elephant headed god who removes obstacles.
**gara** (गारा) - A common *rag*.
**gat** (गत) - 1) A fixed composition for instrumental styles; similar to sthai. 2) A compositional type common in the purbi style of *tabla* playing.
**gat kaida** (गत कायदा) - A *tabla gat* which is performed in a strict *kaida* format.
**gatani** (गतनी) - Past.
**gatta** (गट्टा) - The wooden dowels in the lacing of *tabla*.
**gaud malhar** (गौड़ मल्हार) - A common *rag*.
**gaud sarang** (गौड़ सारंग) - A common *rag*.

**gaur** (गौर) – A rare *rag*.
**gauri** (गौरी) – A *rag*.
**gavat** (गावत) – Singing, praising.
**gave** (गावे) – Sing.
**gayan** (गायान) – Vocal music, one of the three aspects of *sangeet*.
**gaz** (गज़) – Bow of *sarangi*, violin, *dilruba*, or *esraj*.
**ge** (गे) – A *tabla bol* for the left hand.
**gee** (गी) – A *tabla bol* for the left hand.
**geet** (गीत) – Any song.
**gha** (ध) – A basic *tabla bol* of the left hand.
**ghan** (घन) – 1) A non-membranous percussion instrument (e.g., bells, *manjira*, *jal tarang*, etc.) 2. Great.
**ghar** (घर) – A house.
**gharana** (घराना) – A particular subtradition or "school" (lit. "house".)
**ghata** (घटा) – A gathering of clouds.
**ghazal** (ग़ज़ल) – A musical style of poetic recitation.
**ghe** (घे) – A *tabla bol* for the left hand.
**ghee** (घी) – A *tabla bol* for the left hand.
**ghi** (घि) – A *tabla bol* for the left hand.
**gin** (घिं)– A *tabla bol* for me left hand.
**gi** (गि) – A *tabla bol* for the left hand.
**gin** (गीं) – A *tabla bol* for the left hand.
**gnyan** (ज्ञान) – Wisdom, understanding, a visceral sense about something.
**gopal nayak** (गोपाल नायक) – A great musician and contemporary of Amir Khusru.
**grah** (ग्रह) – (Literally "house"). 1) The method of handling *sam*. There are four types: *sam*, *visham*, *atit* and *anagat*. 2) The starting note of the *rag* (i.e., Sa).
**gujari todi** (गुर्जरी तोड़ी) – A common *rag*, similar to *Miyan ki Todi* except there is no *Pa*.
**gun** (गुण) – Quality, attainment.
**gunijan** (गुणिजन) – Experts, virtuous and talented people.
**guniyan** (गुणियन) – Same as *gunyan*.
**gunkali** (गुणकली) – A *rag*.
**gunkari** (गुणकरी) – A *rag*.
**guru** (गुरु) – A teacher.
**guru bahin** (गुरु बहिन) – Female fellow disciples of the guru.
**guru bhai** (गुरू भाई) – Male fellow disciples of the guru.
**guru-mukha-vidhya** (गुरू मुख विद्य) – Knowledge which must be learned directly from the guru.

**guru-shishya-parampara** (गुरू शिष्य परम्परा) - The lineage of teacher to disciple.
**gwalior** (ग्वालियर) - 1) A place in northern India. 2) The *gharana* from this place.
**hamir** (हमीर) - A common *rag* similar to *Kedar*.
**hamsadhwani** (हंसध्वनि) - A common *rag*, originally from the South, but today found in the North.
**har** (हर) - Every.
**hari** (हरि) - Brown, yellow, Vishnu, Indra, Shiva, Krishna, Ram, name of mountain.
**haridas swami** (हरिदास स्वामी) - A saint of old who was said to be the guru of Tansen (circa late 15th or early 16th century).
**harmonium** (हार्मोनियम) - A small hand pumped reed organ, originally of European origin, but today common throughout the Indo-Pakistan subcontinent.
**hathodi** (हथोड़ी) - The small hammer used to tune the *tabla*.
**haveli sangeet** (हवेली संगीत) - A *Vaishnava* devotional song usually performed in a *dhrupad* style.
**he** (है) - Is.
**hem kalyan** (हेम कल्यान) - A *rag*.
**hi** (ही) - Only, solely, none other.
**hindol** (हिण्डोल) - A common *rag*.
**hindustani sangeet** (हिन्दुस्तानी संगीत) - North Indian classical music.
**ho** (हो) - To be, exists, become.
**hoga** (होगा) - Happen.
**hriday** (हृदय) - Heart.
**indri** (ईंडरी) - The cloth and fibre ring cushions upon which the *tabla* rests. (see chutta).
**jab** (जब) - When, at whatever time.
**jag** (जाग) - A sacrifice.
**jagat** (जगत) - World.
**jaipur** (जयपुर) - 1) A city in Northern India. 2) The vocal *gharana* from Jaipur.
**jait kalyan** (जैत कल्याण) - A *rag*.
**jaitshri** (जैतश्री) - A *rag*.
**jaldhar kedar** (जलधर केदार) - A rare rag.
**jaltarang** (जलतरंग) - A set of bowls tuned with water, hit with small wooden sticks.

**jam** (जाम) - A period of 3 hours.
**jana** (जाना) - To go.
**janat** (जानत) - Knowing.
**jap** (जप) - The muttering of a *mantra* or prayer.
**jati** (जाति) - 1) A class of rhythm. 2) The number of notes present in a *rag*. 3) An ancient modal form of singing.
**jaunpuri** (जौनपुरी) - A common *rag*.
**jayjayvanti** (जयजयवन्ती) - A common *rag*.
**jhala** (झाला) - A very fast instrumental style based upon the constant droning of the *chicari* strings.
**jhaptal** (झपताल) - A common tal of 10 beats.
**jhinjhoti** (झिंझोटी) - A common *rag*.
**jhumra tal** (झूमरा ताल) - A *tal* of 14 beats, used primarily in *kheyal*.
**jit** (जित) - Victory.
**jiya** (जिया) - Life, heart, soul.
**jo** (जो) - Who, which, that.
**jod** (जोड) - A rhythmic style of free improvisation.
**jog** (जोग) - 1) A common *rag*. 2) Fit for, on account for, capable.
**jogia** (जोगिया) - A common *rag*.
**jori** (जोड़ी) - The *tabla* pair.
**jugalbandhi** (जुगलबंधी) - Duet between two similar instruments or vocalists.
**ka** (क) - A *tabla bol* of the left hand.
**kabir** (कबीर) - A famous saint-musician of the 15th century.
**kafi** (काफी) - 1) A *that*. 2) A common *rag*.
**kahat** (कहत) - Say.
**kahe** (काहे) - Why? What for? With what aim?
**kaherava tal** (कहरवा ताल) - A common 8-beat *tal*.
**kaida** (कायदा) - A highly formalized approach to a *tabla* solo.
**kaida peshkar** (कायदा पेशकार) - A *tabla peshkar* whose variations adhere strictly to the *kaida* format.
**kaida rela** (कायदा रेला) - A *tabla rela* performed in a strict *kaida* format.
**kaise** (कैसे) - How? Like what?
**kal** (काल) - The entire concept of time and musical timing.
**kala** (कला) - Art.
**kalingada** (कालिंगड़ा) - A *rag*.
**kalyani** (कल्याणी) - 1) A musical mode (*mela*) of the the South which corresponds to the north Indian *Kalyan that*. 2) A South Indian *rag* similar to *Kalyan*, 3) Auspicious, beautiful, happy.

**kamali paran** (कमाली परण) - A *paran* which is constructed in a highly unusual yet fascinating manner.
**kamod** (कामोद) - A common *rag*.
**kanth** (कंठ) - Throat.
**kar** (कर) - 1) To do, or perform. 2) Duty. 3) Hand.
**karat** (करत) - The distance to which a gunshot can reach.
**karnatic sangeet** (कर्नाटक संगीत) - See *carnatic sangeet*.
**karo** (करो) - Do.
**kasht-tarang** (काष्टतरंग) - A wooden xylophone.
**kat** (कत्) - A *tabla bol*.
**kathak** (कथक) - A common north Indian style of classical dance.
**kawali** (कव्वाली) - See *qawwali*.
**kawali tal** (कव्वाली ताल) - A tal of 8 beats similar to *kaherava*.
**kdan** (क्डां) or (क्डान्) - A powerful *bol* of both *pakhawaj* and *tabla*.
**ke** (के) - 1) A *tabla bol* of the left hand. 2) The inflected form of का which is used before substantives in the plural number (i.e., plural usage of "of" or "of the").
**kedar** (केदार) - A common *rag*.
**kerva tal** (केरवा ताल) - See *kaherava*, a common 8-beat *tal*.
**keshav** (केशव) - An epithet of Krishna.
**khali** (खाली) - Literally "empty", a measure which is defined by a wave. (opposite of *bhari* or *tali*).
**khambavati** (खंबावती) - A *rag*.
**khammaj** (खमाज) - 1) A common *rag*. 2) A *that*, characterized by a flattened 7th.
**khand jati** (खण्ड जाती) - Any rhythm based upon 2 1/2, 5, 10, etc. beats.
**khat** (खत) - A *rag*.
**khayal** (खयाल) - See *kheyal*.
**khemta tal** (खेमटा ताल) - A fairly common yet amorphous *tal* variously described as 6 or 12 beats.
**kheyal** (खयाल) - The most prominent style of classical vocal today.
**khol** (खोल) - A folk drum of northeast India.
**khula** (खुला) - Lit. "open". Resonant *tabla* strokes such as *Ga*, *Thun*, etc.
**khyal** (खयाल) - See *kheyal*.
**ki** (कि) or (की) - A *tabla bol* of the left hand.
**ki** (की) - The feminine form of "of".
**kinar** (किनार) - Lit. "edge". The *tabla chat*.
**kirana** (किराना) - 1) A small town in Northern India. 2) A *gharana* (subtradition) of *kheyal*.

**kirtan** (कीर्तन) – A group devotional song.
**ko** (को) – "Who", "which", the case termination of the accusative and dative in Hindi.
**komal** (कोमल) – A note which is flat. When applied to *Ma*, it means the natural fourth.
**krishna** (कृष्ण) – An incarnation of lord Vishnu.
**krodha ayata** (क्रोधा आयता) – The sixth *shruti* (microtone).
**kshiti mrudu** (क्षिति मृदु) – The 11th *shruti* (microtone).
**kshobhini madhya** (क्षोभिणी मध्य) – The 19th *shruti* (microtone).
**kuadi lay** (कुआड़ी लय) – In a four-unit time, one plays five units.
**kuch** (कुछ) – Some, somewhat, a little.
**kumudvati ugra** (कुमुद्वती उग्रा) – The 21st *shruti* (microtone).
**kundal** (कुण्डल) – The small ring at the bottom side of both *tabla*, used for the lacing.
**kunj-ban** (कुंज-बन) – A crane-like bird.
**kuri** (कूड़ी) – The shell of the *bayan*.
**ladi** (लड़ी) – A *tabla* composition similar to *laggi*.
**ladi kaida** (लड़ी कायदा) – A *tabla kaida* created by having a *ladi* follow a strict *kaida* format.
**laggi** (लग्गी) – A fast lively style of *tabla* playing, similar to *rela*, used in light styles of playing, particularly with *bhajans, thumris, ghazal*, etc.
**laggi kaida** (लग्गी कायदा) – A *laggi* constructed upon a strict *kaida* structure.
**lahara** (लहरा) – A simple, repetitive melody used to accompany *tabla* solos and *kathak* dance, sometimes referred to as *naghma*.
**lakadi** (लकड़ी) – Lit. wood. The wooden shell of the *tabla*.
**lakhnowi baj** (लखनवी बाज) – The style of *tabla* playing originating from Lucknow.
**lakshan geet** (लक्षण गीत) – A style of singing where the lyrics are a description of the *rag*.
**lakshmi** (लक्ष्मी) – Goddess of wealth.
**lalit** (ललित) – A common *rag*.
**lalit-pancham** (ललितपंचम) – A rare north Indian *rag*.
**lalkila paran** (लालकिला परण) – A *tabla* composition, specifically a *dohatthu* which is inspired from *nagada*.
**lasya** (लास्य) – A feminine interpretation of dance.
**lav** (लव) – Maidan, the *sur*, the part of the *tabla's* playing surface between the *chat* (*kinar*) and the *syahi*.

**lay** (लय) – Tempo.
**layakari** (लयकारी) – The relationship between the performed pulse of a composition and the theoretical beat.
**log** (लोग) – People.
**logan** (लोगन) – People.
**lom-vilom** (लोम-विलोम) – A novel *tabla* structure which is composed of two parts. The first part being a mirror image of the second. Therefore, the composition is the same whether it is read backwards or forwards.
**lucknow** (लखनऊ) – 1) A city in northern India. 2) The *gharana* from this area.
**mad** (मद) – Help, support.
**madanti karuna** (मदंती करुण) – The 15th *shruti* (microtone).
**madhur** (मधुर) – Sweet.
**madhuvanti** (मधुवंती) – A common *rag*.
**madhya lay** (मध्य लय) – Medium tempo.
**madhya saptak** (मध्य सप्तक) – The middle octave.
**madhyam** (मध्यम) – 1) The fourth note of the scale. 2) Middle, between.
**madhyamad sarang** (मध्यमाद सारंग) – A *rag*.
**maha** (महा) – Great, large, very, most.
**maha tal** (महा ताल) – A non-standard name for *Tintal*.
**mahaadi lay** (महाआड़ी) – Double tempo of *adi lay*.
**mahabiadi lay** (महाबिआड़ी लय) – Double tempo of *biadi lay*.
**mahakuadi lay** (महाकुआड़ी) – Double tempo of *kuadi lay*.
**mai** (मई) – Filled.
**makta** (मक्ता) – Last line of a *ghazal's* couplet.
**malgunji** (मालगुंजी) – A *rag*.
**maligaura** (मालीगौरा) – A rare *rag*.
**malkauns** (मालकौंस) – A common *rag*.
**malkosh** (मालकोश) – See *malkauns*.
**malshri** (मालश्री) – A rare *rag*.
**man** (मन) – The heart, soul, or mind.
**mand** (मांड) – A common *rag*.
**manda mrudu** (मंदा मृदु) – The 22nd *shruti* (microtone).
**mandra saptak** (मन्द्र सप्तक) – The lower octave.
**mane** (माने) – Meaning, purport.
**manjira** (मँजीरा) – Small cymbals.

**mansingh tomar** (मानसिंह तोमार) - A king who was famous for his devotion to music (1486-1518).

**margi sangeet** (मर्गी संगीत) - Literally a "path". A music which is based upon a spiritual path, as opposed to a music which is for mere sensual enjoyment.

**marjani madhya** (मार्जनी मध्या) - The 10th *shruti* (microtone).

**marubihag** (मारूबिहाग) - A common *rag*.

**marwa** (मारवा) - 1) A common *rag*. 2) A *that*.

**masitkhani gat** (मसीतखानी गत) - A type of slow *gat* played on *sitar* or *sarod*.

**matla** (मत्ला) - The first verse of a *ghazal*.

**matra** (मात्रा) - The beat.

**matt tal** (मत्त ताल) - An obscure *pakhawaj tal* of 9 or 18 beats.

**me** (में) - In, within.

**meend** (मीन्ड) - A slow glissando.

**megh malhar** (मेघ मल्हार) - A *rag*.

**meghranjani** (मेघरंजनी) - A rag.

**mela** (मेला) - 1) Assemblage, gathering of people, fair, congregation. 2) A musical mode, or *that* of the south Indian system.

**mira malhar** (मीरा मल्हार) - A rare *rag*.

**mira** (मीरा) - A famous devotee and composer of *bhajans* (1559-1620).

**mirasi** (मीरासी) - 1) A caste of musicians. 2) A prostitute.

**mishra jati** (मिश्र जाति) - Any rhythm based upon 1 3/4, 3 1/2, 7, 14, etc. beats.

**mishra rag** (मिश्र राग) - A *rag* which is performed in such a way as to mix unrelated *rags*.

**miyan ki malhar** (मियां की मल्हार) - A common *rag*.

**miyan ki sarang** (मियां की सारंग) - A common *rag*.

**mizrab** (मिज़राब) - A plectrum for *sitar* or *vina* which is worn on the lingers.

**mo** (मो) - Me, myself.

**mohani** (मोहनि) - Charming.

**mohar** (मोहर) - 1) Face. 2) A gold coin.

**mohara** (मोहरा) - A *tabla* piece. A short structure, similar to *mukhada*, which ends on *sam*.

**mridang** (मृदंग) or (मृदङ्.) - Any two headed barrel shaped drum of the *pakhawaj* variety.

**mridangam** (मृदङ्.म) or (मृदंगम) - A south Indian *mridang*.

**mrigamad** (मृगमद) - Musk.

**mudra** (मुद्र) - (literally a "stamp") The hand signals which represent certain actions or things, used extensively in dance.

**mukhada** (मुखड़ा) – A very small phrase or composition ending on *sam*. The important section of a *kheyal*.

**multani** (मुलतानी) – A common *rag*,

**murat** (मूरत) – An idol.

**murchana** (मूर्च्छना) – 1) The process of modal progression (i.e., creating a new scale by taking the old one and shifting the tonic to another note). 2 An exercise based upon sequentially shifting a pattern up and down the scale.

**murchang** (मुरचंग) – A jew's harp.

**na** (ना) or (न) – 1) A fundamental *tabla bol*. 2) "No", "not", the negation of something.

**nad** (नाद) – Sound.

**nadaswaram** (नादस्वरम) – A very large double reed instrument of south India similar to an oboe.

**nagada** (नगाड़ा) – A pair of kettle drums played with sticks.

**naggada** (नग्गाड़ा) – See *nagada*.

**nagma** (नग्मा) – 1) A bandish, or piece of music. 2) A repeating melody used for *tabla* solos.

**nahak** (नाहक) – Improperly, unjustly, in a useless manner.

**nahin** (नहीं) – No, not.

**nai** (नई) – New.

**nam** (नाम) – Name.

**namaskari paran** (नामस्कारी परण) – An unusual *tabla* piece which incorporates a *namaskar* into the structure, usually into the *tihai*.

**nand** (नंद) – A common *rag*.

**nar** (नर) – Man, *men*.

**narad** (नारद) – See *Narada*

**narada** (नारद) – 1) A famous sage, son of Vishvamitra, who is responsible for the introduction of music and dance to the world. 2) A troublemaker.

**naradamuni** (नारदमुनी) – See narada.

**narayan** (नारायनण) – Vishnu, God.

**nari** (नारी) – Woman.

**nartan** (नर्तन) – Dance and mime. One of the aspects of *sangeet*.

**nat** (नट) – A *rag*.

**nat bilawal** (नट बिलावल) – A *rag*.

**navaras** (नवरस) – The nine principal emotions which underly all art forms.

**nilakanth** (नीलकंठ) –1) A bluejay 2) shiva.

**nishad** (निषाद) – The 7th note of the scale.

**nohakka** (नवहक्का) – A type of *tihai* in which the *bol* "dhaa" comes nine times.

**nom-tom** (नोम-तोम) – A style of singing found in *dhrupad*, *dhammar* and a few styles of *kheyal*.
**nrtya** (नृतय) or (नृत्य) – Dance.
**nyare** (न्यारे) – Unique, queer, idiosyncratic, distinctive.
**nyas** (न्यास) – Resting notes of a *rag*.
**om** (ॐ) – *Nad brahma*, the primordial sound.
**padhati** (पद्धति) – A school or theoretical system.
**padmanabh** (पद्मनाभ) – An epithet of lord Vishnu.
**pahadi** (पहाड़ी) – A common *rag*.
**pakad** (पकड़) – The characteristic movement of a *rag*.
**pakhawaj** (पखावज) – A barrel shaped drum with playing heads on both sides.
**palta** (पलटा) or (पल्टा) – A passage of a *tabla kaida*.
**paluskar** (पलुस्कर) – See Vishnu Digambar Paluskar.
**panang** (पनंग) – Snake.
**pancham** (पंचम) – The 5th note of the scale.
**pancham savari tal** (पंचम सवारी ताल) – A rare *tal* of 15 beats.
**par** (पर) – On, on top.
**paraj** (परज) – A *rag*.
**parameshwar** (परमेश्वर) – The Almighty, the supreme being.
**parampara** (परम्परा) – A lineage, or continuum (e.g., *guru-shishya-parampara*)
**parampurush** (परमपुरुष) – Lord Vishnu.
**paran** (परण) or (परन) – A type of composition on *tabla* or *pakhawaj*.
**parayan** (पारायन) – End, completion.
**parda** (परदा) – (Literally "curtain") The fret of *sitar*, *vina*, or similar instrument.
**parvati** (पार्वती) – The goddess Durga, wife of Shiva.
**pashtu** (पश्तो) – 1) Pertaining to the language or culture of the Patthan people of Pakistan and Afghanistan. 2) A *tal*. Some consider this to be mere *prakar* of *Rupak tal*, while others consider this to be a distinctly separate 7 beat *tal*.
**patadip** (पटदीप) – A common *rag*.
**patiyala** (पटियाला) – 1) A place in the Punjab. 2) A vocal *gharana* from Patiyala.
**peshkar** (पेशकार) – A *tabla* composition. An introductory movement similar to *kaida* but with a different system of permutation.
**peshkar kaida** (पेशकार कायदा) – A *tabla kaida* produced by having a *peshkar* follow a strict *kaida* format.
**pilu** (पीलू) – A common *rag*.

**pital** (पीतल) - Lit. "brass", the brass shell of the *bayan*.
**prabhand** (प्रबंध) - 1) A totally fixed composition. 2) A fixed composition formerly used in the ancient dramas.
**prabhat** (प्रभात) - A *rag*.
**prahar** (प्रहार) or (प्रहर) - 1) A period of three hours. 2) The time that a *rag* should be rendered.
**prakar** (प्रकार) - Different varieties of *tabla theka*.
**prasarini ayata** (प्रसारिणी आयता) - The eighth *shruti* (microtone).
**prastar** (प्रस्तार) - 1) Permutation upon the note, used in the creation of *tans* and the elaboration of the *rag*. 2) An approach to *tabla*. Permutations upon a *kaida* or given theme.
**pratap** (प्रताप) - Dignity, glory, splendour, majesty.
**pratham** (प्रथम) - First, beginning.
**pritit mrudu** (प्रीति मृदु) - The ninth *shruti* (microtone).
**pudi** (पुड़ी) - A *tabla* head.
**punjab** (पंजाब) - 1) An area along the border between India and Pakistan. 2) The *tabla gharana* from this area.
**punjabi** (पंजाबी) - (Lit. from Punjab) A 16-beat *tal* similar to *Tintal*.
**purbi** (पूरबी) - (Lit. "Eastern") The style of *tabla* playing in the Farukhabad, Lucknow, and Benares traditions.
**puriya** (पूरिय) - A *rag*.
**puriyadhanashri** (पूर्यधनाश्री) - A common *rag*.
**purvang** (पूर्वङ्ग.) - The lower tetrachord.
**purvi** (पूर्वी) - A common *rag*.
**putriya** (पुतरिया) - Pertaining to a son.
**qawwali** (क़व्वालि) - An Islamic devotional song.
**ra** (इ) - A *tabla bol*.
**ra** (र) - A *tabla bol*.
**raas** (रास) - A folk dance common in Gujarat.
**raat** (रात) - Night.
**rabab** (रबाब) - An instrument found in Northern India, Pakistan, and Afghanistan.
**rag** (राग) - The Indian musical modes.
**ragi** (रागी) - A *shabad* singer in a *Sikh gudwar*.
**ragmala** (रागमाला) - A musical piece based upon a string of several rags.
**rahat** (रहत) - Continuing, lasting.
**rain** (रैन) - Night.
**rakhle** (राखले) - Saviour, protector.
**rakta madhya** (रक्ता मध्या) - The 12th *shruti* (microtone).

**ram** (राम) – Lord Ram, Ram Chandra, son of Dasaradha.
**raman** (रमन) – Cupid, husband, handsome.
**ramkali** (रामकली) – A *rag*.
**rampur** (रामपुर) – 1) A place in Northern India. 2) The *gharana* from Rampur which is an offshoot of the Gwalior *gharana*.
**ramya madhya** (रम्या मध्या) – The 17th *shruti* (microtone).
**rang** (रंग) – Colour.
**rangan** (रंगन) – Colours.
**rangila gharana** (रंगीला घराना) – The Agra *gharana*.
**ranjani madhya** (रंजनी मध्या) – The third *shruti* (microtone).
**ras** (रस) – The essence or emotion of a *rag*.
**rassi** (रस्सी) – The rope lacing on the *dholak*.
**ratika mrudu** (रतिका मृदु) – The fourth *shruti* (microtone).
**raudri dipta** (रौद्री दीप्ता) – The fifth *shruti* (microtone).
**ravindra sangeet** (रविन्द्र संगीत) – A semi-classical style of music popular in Bengal. This style was created by Rabindranath Tagore.
**razakhani gat** (राज़ाखानी गत) – A type of fast instrumental *gat*.
**re** (रे) – 1) The second note of the Indian scale. 2) A vocative.
**rekhab** (रेखब) – *Rishabh*.
**rela** (रेला) – A very fast manipulation of small *tabla* structures.
**ri** (री) – A *tabla bol*.
**ridhi** (रिध्दी) – Prosperity, good fortune.
**rijhave** (रिझावे) – Happiness.
**rijhit** (रीझत) – Pleasure.
**rishabha** (ऋषभ) – The 2nd note of the scale.
**riyaz** (रियाज़) – Practice.
**rohini ayat** (रोहिणी आयता) – The 16th *shruti* (microtone).
**rudra vina** (रुद्र वीण) – A very ancient instrument made of bamboo and gourds (i.e., *been*).
**rupak tal** (रूपक ताल) – A common 7 beat *tal* with uncommon variations of 5, 6, 9, or 11 beats.
**Sa** (सा) – Similar, equal.
**sab** (सब) – All, whole, every, entire.
**sabko** (सबको) – Everybody, whole.
**sada** (सदा) – Constantly, always, continually.
**sadhana** (साधना) – A lifestyle of practice and devotion to music.
**sahayak** (सहायक) – A helper, supporter, a friend.
**sakal** (सकल) – All, whole, entire, every.
**sakhi** (सखि) – Friend.

**sam** (सम) - The first beat of a cycle.
**samajh** (समझ) - To know, to understand, to realize, to comprehend.
**samavadi** (संवादी) - The second-most important note of a *rag*.
**samay** (समय) - Time.
**sampurna jati** (संपूर्ण जाति) - A *rag* which contains all seven notes.
**sanchari** (संचारी) - The quaternary theme.
**sandipani ayata** (संदीपनी आयता) - The 13th *shruti* (microtone).
**sangati** (संगति) - Accompaniment.
**sangeet** (संगीत)or (सङ्गीत) - Music and dance.
**sankadik** (सनकादिक) - The sons of Brahma and so forth.
**sankirna jati** (संकीर्ण जाति) - A rhythm of 4 1/2, 9, 18, etc. beats.
**santur** (सन्तूर) - A hammered dulcimer.
**saptak** (सप्तक) - The gamut or scale. (i.e, *Sa, Re, Ga, Ma, Pa Dha,* and *Ni*)
**sarangi** (सारंगी) - A fretless bowed instrument with numerous strings.
**saras** (सरस) - Beautiful, attractive, charming, passionate.
**sarasvati** (सरस्वती) - Hindu goddess of music, arts, and learning.
**sargam** (सरगम) - The syllables of the scale (i.e., *Sa, Re, Ga, Ma, Pa,* etc.)
**sarod** (सरोद) - A classical stringed instrument derived from *rabab*.
**sath** (साथ) - A class of compositions found in the *pakhawaj* styles.
**sath sangat** (साथ संगत) - A style of playing where the *tabla* follows the main artist in a beat-for-beat fashion.
**shadaj** (षड्ज) - The base note of the scale.
**shadav** (षाड़व) - A *rag* with only six notes.
**shai** (शाई) - Vernacular of *syahi*. (see *syahi*)
**shakti** (शक्ति) - Energy, force, power.
**shankar** (शंकर) - Lord Shiva.
**shankara** (शंकरा) - A common *rag*.
**shankh** (शङ्ख) - A conch shell horn.
**shastriya sangeet** (शास्त्रीय संगीत) - Classical music.
**shehnai** (शहनाई) - An Indian oboe.
**shishya** (शिष्य) - A student, or disciple.
**shiva** (शिव) - The Hindu god of destruction, movement, rhythm, dance, sexuality, etc.
**shri** (श्री) - 1) A common *rag*. 2) Lakshmi, wife of Vishnu, Saraswati. 3) A lotus. 4) Sandalwood.
**sri kalyan** (श्री कल्यान) - A *rag*.
**shruti** (श्रुति) - Lit. "to be heard." 1) The drone. 2) A microtone. 3) The key. 4. Holy scriptures.

**shuddha** (शुद्ध) – 1) A note which is natural. 2) A *rag* which is performed in its fundamental style.
**shuddha kalyan** (शुद्ध कल्यान) – A rag similar to *Bilawal*.
**shuddha sarang** (शुद्ध सारंग) – A common *rag*.
**shukla bilawal** (शुक्ल बिलावल) – A *rag*.
**shultal** (शूलताल) – See *soolfak tal*.
**shyam** (श्याम) – (Literally "the dark one") Au epithet of Krishna.
**sidha** (सीधा) – The small wooden right hand drum of the *tabla*.
**sidhi** (सिध्दी) – Success, fulfilment, accomplishment.
**sindura** (सिंदूरा) – A *rag*.
**sit** (सित) – White, clear, shining, bright.
**sitar** (सितार) – A common long necked, fretted instrument.
**sitarkhani** (सितारखानी) – A 16-beat *tal*, which according to some is the same as *Addha Tintal*, and according to others is the same as *Punjabi*.
**soch** (सोच) – Think, meditation, consideration.
**sohani** (सोहनि or सोहनी) – Beautiful. 2) A common *rag*.
**sool tal** (सूल ताल) – See *Soolfak tal*.
**soolfak tal** (सूलफाक ताल) – An old *pakhawaj tal* of 10 beats.
**sorath** (सीरठ) – A *rag*.
**sthai** (स्थायी) – The primary theme of a classical song.
**stuti** (स्तुति) – (lit. prayer, praise of God) 1) A *bol paran*.
**sudha** (सुध) – See *shuddha*.
**suha** (सूह) – A *rag*.
**sujan** (सुजान) – Intelligent, wise, clever, learned, polite.
**sul tal** (सूल ताल) – See *Soolfak tal*.
**sumat** (सुमत) – Concord.
**sumiran** (सुमीरन) – Recollect.
**sundar** (सुंदर) – Beautiful, handsome.
**sur** (सुर) – 1) The pitch, note, melody (see *swar*). 2) The key (see *shruri*).
**sur** (सूर) – Sun.
**sur malhar** (सूर मल्हार) – A *rag*.
**surat** (सूरत) – Face.
**surbahar** (सुरबहार) – A bass sitar.
**surdas** (सुरदास) – A musician saint who composed many *bhajans* (1535-1640).
**surmandal** (सुरमंडल) – A small harp used to provide the drone.
**sushir** (सुषिर) – A musical instrument characterized by blowing air (flute, *shehnai*, harmonium, etc.)
**svarlipi** (स्वरलिपि) – Musical notation.

**swar** (स्वर) – A musical note.
**syahi** (स्याही) – The black application on the heads of the *tabla*.
**ta** (ट) – Fundamental *tabla bol*.
**ta** (ता) – Fundamental *tabla bol* of the right hand.
**taan** (तान) – Along run or trill. A fast elaboration on the *rag*.
**tab** (तब) – Then, at that time, afterwards.
**tabla** (तबला) – 1) The pair of Indian hand drums. 2) The right hand drum of the pair 3) The Arabic word for any drum.
**tabla tarang** (तबला तरंग) – A musical instrument composed of numerous wooden *tabla* tuned to different pitches.
**tahe** (ताहे) – Until, for the sake of, toward, nearby.
**taj** (तज) – Omit.
**tal** (ताल) – 1) The Indian system of rhythm. 2) A particular rhythmic cycle (e.g., *Tintal, Rupak tal,* etc.) 3) The palm of the hand.
**tal-lipi** (ताल लिपी) – Percussion notation.
**tal paddhati** (ताल पद्धति) – A theoretical framework of rhythm.
**tal-vadhya-kachari** (ताल-वाद्य कचहरी) – A percussion ensemble.
**taleem** (तालीम) – Formal training.
**tali** (ताली) – A measure which is clapped.
**tamboura** (तंबूरा) – See *tanpura*.
**tan** (तन) – The body, skin.
**tandava** (ताण्डव) – An energetic, masculine dance style reminiscent of Shiva.
**tanpura** (तानपूरा) – A long necked, stringed instrument that provides the drone.
**tansen** (तानसेन) – A famous musician of the court of Akbar (circa late 16th century).
**tap** (तप) – Devotion, worship.
**tappa** (टप्पा) – A Punjabi style of semi-classical singing.
**tar saptak** (तार सप्तक) – The higher octave.
**tar shehnai** (तार शहनाई) – An instrument similar to *esraj*.
**tar** (तार) – 1) String of musical instrument. 2) A stringed instrument of Afghanistan.
**tarana** (तराना) – A style of singing, originally of Persian origin, today characterized by meaningless syllables.
**tarasay** (तरसाय) – To long for, to strongly desire.
**tasma** (तस्मा) – The rawhide lacing of the *tabla*.
**tat** (तत्) – 1) A *tabla bol*. 2) A plucked string instrument (e.g., *sitar, sarod,* etc.)
**te** (टे) – A *tabla bol*.

**te** (ते) – A *tabla bol*.
**teharo** (तेहारो) – Your, yours.
**tej** (तेज) – See *tez*.
**ten** (तें) – They, those people.
**tere** (तेरे) – Yours.
**tevra tal** (तेवरा ताल) – See *Tivra tal*.
**tez** (तेज़) – Sharp, keen pointed, swift, intelligent.
**thanh** (ठाँह) – 1) *Vilambit* 2) Single time.
**that** (थाट) – A musical mode.
**theka** (ठेका) – The fundamental rhythmic pattern.
**thu** (थु) or (थू) – A *tabla bol*.
**thumri** (ठुमरी) – A semiclassical style of singing.
**thun** (थुं) or (थूं) – A *tabla bol*.
**ti** (ति) or (ती) – Fundamental *tabla bol*.
**tigun** (तिगुन) – A *layakari* of 3:1 (i.e., triple time.)
**tihai** (तिहाई) – A cadenza composed of three identical sections.
**tilak kamod** (तिलक कामोद) – A common *rag*.
**tilang** (तिलंग) – A common rag.
**tilwara tal** (तिलवाड़ा ताल) – A 16 beat *tal* similar to *Tintal*.
**tin** (तिं) – Fundamental *tabla bol*.
**tintal** (तीनताल) – A very common tal of 16 beats.
**tipalli** (तिपल्ली) – Type of *tabla* tihai where each phrase is in a different tempo.
**tisra jati** (तीसरा जाति) – Triplets. (See *tryastra jati*)
**tisra** (तीसरा) – Third.
**tisri tali** (तीसरी ताली) – Third clap.
**tit** (तित) – At that place, there.
**tivra** (तीव्रा) or (तीवरा) – A note which is in the upper position. (e.g., the augmented 4th)
**tivra dipta** (तीव्रा दीप्ता) – The 20th *shruti* (microtone).
**tivra tal** (तीव्रा ताल) – An old *pakhawaj tal* of 7 beats.
**tiya** (तीया) – See *tihai*.
**to** (तो) – Then, so, in case that, thy, thine.
**toda** (तोड़ा) – A *tabla tukada*.
**todi** (तोड़ी) – 1) A *that*. 2) A common *rag*.
**top** (तोप) – (Lit, cannon) A loud *paran* which characterizes thunder, battles, or similar moods played on the *tabla*.
**tra** (त्र) or (तृ) – A *tabla bol* of the right hand.
**tripalli** (त्रिपल्ली) – See *tipalli*.

**triputa tal** (त्रिपुट ताल) – An obscure *tal* of 8, 9, 11, or 13 beats.
**trital** (त्रिताल) – *Tintal*, a common 16 beat *tal*.
**tryastra jati** (त्र्यस्र जाति) – Any rhythm composed of 3, 6, 12, etc. beats.
**tu** (तू) – You, normally familiar or even abusive except when referring to God.
**tu** (तु) or (तू) – A tabla bol.
**tukada** (टुकड़ा) – A small *tabla* composition containing a small body and a *tihai*, very similar to *paran*.
**tun** (तुं) or (तूं) – A *tabla bol*.
**uddhare** (उद्धारे) – Redemption, rescue, renovation.
**ugra dipta** (उग्रा दीप्ता) – The 18th *shruti* (microtone).
**ustad** (उस्ताद) – A learned man, a master.
**uthan** (उठान) – A *tabla* piece, commonly used in dance and *tabla* solos.
**uttarang** (उत्तरङ्ग.) – The upper tetrachord.
**vadan** (वादन) – Instrumental music. One of the aspects of *sangeet*.
**vadi** (वादी) – 1) The key note of a *rag*. 2) A spokesman.
**vajrika dipta** (वज्रिका दीप्ता) – The seventh *shruti* (microtone).
**vakra** (वक्र) – Anything which is twisted, convoluted, or oblique.
**vamadev** (वामदेव) – The name of a *Vedic* sage.
**vashisht** (वशिष्ट) – A saint.
**vasudev** (वासुदेव) – An epithet of lord Krishna.
**ve** (वे) – They.
**veda** (वेद) – Ancient Hindu religious text (circa 1500–900 B.C.E.)
**vibhag** (विभाग) – The measure or "bar".
**vibhas** (विभास) – A common *rag*.
**vidh** (विध) – Creation, arrangement.
**vidwan** (विद्वान) – Any learned person.
**vijay** (विजय) – Victory.
**vikari** (विकारी) – See *chal*.
**vikrat** (विकृत) – See *chal*.
**vilambit** (विलंबित) or (विलम्बित) – Slow tempo.
**vina** (वीणा) – 1) Any stringed instrument. 2) The *saraswati vina* of south India.
**vishad** (विशद) – Elaborate.
**visham** (grah) (विषम) – The process of hiding or de-emphasizing the *sam*.
**vishnu digambar paddhati** (विष्णु दिगम्बर पद्धति) – A theoretical and notational system developed by Vishnu Digambar Paluskar.
**vishnu digambar paluskar** (विष्णु दिगम्बर पलुस्कर) – A famous Indian musicologist/musician.

**vishnu** (विष्णु) – The preserver (i.e., God).
**vishnu narayan bhatkhande** (विष्णु नारायन भातखण्डे) – A famous Indian musicologist (1860-1936).
**vitat** (वितत) – A bowed, string instrument (e.g.,. violin, *dilruba, sarangi*, etc.)
**yah** (यह) – This.
**yaman** (यमन) – A common Indian *rag*.
**yamuna** (यमुना) – The river Jamuna.
**zilaf** (ज़िलाफ़) – A common *rag*.

# BIBLIOGRAPHY

## INDIAN MUSIC

Adesh, H.S.
1993 *Sargam*. Trinadad: Jeewan Jyoti Ptakashan.
1993 *Shadaj*. Trinadad: Jeewan Jyoti Prakashan.

Agarwal, Viney K.
1975 *Traditions and Trends in Indian Music*. Meerat: Rastogi Publications.

Bhatkhande, Vishnu Narayan
1934 *A Short History of the Music of Upper India*. Bombay, India. (reprinted in 1974 by Indian Musicological Society, Baroda).
1985 *Hindustani Sangeet Paddhati, Kramik Pustak Malika, Vol. 1*. Hathras, India: Sangeet Karyalaya.
1985 *Hindustani Sangeet Paddhati, Kramik Pustak Malika, Vol. 3*. Hathras, India: Sangeet Karyalaya.
1985 *Hindustani Sangeet Paddhati, Kramik Pustak Malika, Vol. 4*. Hathras India: Sangeet Karyalaya.
1989 *Hindustani Sangeet Paddhati, Kramik Pustak Malika, Vol. 2*. Hathras, India: Sangeet Karyalaya.

Bor, Joep
1987 "The Voice of Sarangi: An Illustrated History of Bowing in India". *Quarterly Journal for the National Centre for the Performing Arts*; Vol. XV and XVI Nos. 3, 4, & 1; Sept, Dec, & March 87; Bombay, NCPA.

Chaturvedi, Balmukund
1989 *Sur Sagar*. Shri Gopal Pustakalay: Mathura.

Courtney, D.R
1977 "Harmonium: Controversial Instrument", *Pallavi*. Hyderabad: India Vol. 1, No 3, April 20, 1977: pp. 13.
1980 *Introduction to Tabla*. Hyderabad, India Anand Power Press.
1985 "Tabla Making in the Deccan", *Percussive Notes*. Urbana Ill: Percussive Arts Society. Vol. 23, No 2, January 1985: pp. 33-34.
1987 "Tata and his Kamakshi Veena", *Experimental Musical Instruments*. Nicasio CA: EMI. Vol. 3, No 4 December 1987: pp. 5-9.
1988 "Rag: Hindustani vs. Carnatic", *Svar Gnyan*. Houston: Sur Sangeet Services. April 1988: pp. 3.
1988 "Time Theory of Ragas", *Svar Gnyan*. Houston: Sur Sangeet Services. June 1988.
1988 "Rag Yaman", *Svar Gnyan*. Houston: Sur Sangeet Services. August, 1988: pp. 3
1988 "That and Mela", *Svar Gnyan*. Houston: Sur Sangeet Services. September, 1988: pp. 3-4
1988 "The Tabla Puddi", *Experimental Musical Instruments*. Nicasio, CA: EMI. Vol. 4, No 4, December 1988: pp. 12-16.
1990 "North Indian Ragas", *Experimental Musical Instruments*. Nicasio, CA: EMI. Vol. 6, No 2, August 1990: pp. 15- 16.
1992 "New Approaches to Tabla Instruction", *Percussive Notes*. Lawton OK: Percussive Arts Society. Vol. 30, No 4, April 1992: pp. 27-29.
1993 "Mrdangam et Tabla: un Contraste", *Percussions: Cahier Bimensiel d'Etudes et d'Informations sur les Arts de la Percussion*. Chailly-en-Biere, France; Vol. 28, March/April 1993; pp 11-14.
1994 "An Introduction to Tabla", *Modern Drummer*. Mt. Morris, IL: MD Publications. October 1993; Vol. 17, #10:pp. 38-84.
1994 "The Cadenza in North Indian Tabla", *Percussive Notes*. Lawton, OK: Percussive Arts Society. August 1994; Vol 32. No 4: pp. 54-64.
1994 *Fundamentals of Tabla*. Houston: Sur Sangeet Services. Houston TX.

Devangan, Tulsiram
1984 *Thumri-Gayaki*. Hathras: Sangeet Karyalaya.

Dhavan, Devakinandan
1970 "Pad". *Bhakti Sangeet Ank.* (edited by Lakshminarayan Garg). Hathras, India: Sangeet Karyalaya.

Garg, Prabhulal (Editor)
1977 *Sangeet Sagar.* Hathras: Sangeet Karyalya.

Garg, Lakshminarayan
1973   *Bal Sangeet Shiksha, Vol. 2*. Hathras, India: Sangeet Karyalaya.
1984   *Hamare Sangeet-Ratna*. Hathras, India: Sangeet Press.

Jairazbhoy, N. A.
1971   *The Rags of North Indian Music*. Middletown CT: Wesleyan University Press.

Kripalvanand, Swami
1972   "Purush Rag, Stri Rag Aur Putra Rag", *Rag-Ragini Ank*. Hathras: Sangeet Karyalaya; pp. 7-51.

Kulshreshth, Jagdish Sahay
1983   *Sangeet Kishor*. Hathras, India: Sangeet Karyalaya.

Mital, Prabhudayal
1960   *Sangeet Samrat: Tansen: Jivani aur Rachanaen*. Mathura, India: Sahitya Samsthan.

Neuman, Daniel M.
1980   *The Life of Music in North India*. Detroit: Wayne State University Press,

Rangacharya, Adya
1966   *Introduction to Bharata's Natya-Sastra*. Bombay, India Popular Prakashan.

Rao, B. Subba
1980   *Raganidhi: A Comparative Study of Hindustani and Karnatak Ragas, Vol. 1*. Madras, India: The Music Academy.
1982   *Raganidhi: A Comparative Study of Hindustani and Karnatak Ragas, Vol. 2*. Madras India: The Music Academy.
1984   *Raganidhi: A Comparative Study of Hindustani and Karnatak Ragas, Vol. 3*. Madras, India: The Music Academy.
1985   *Raganidhi: A Comparative Study of Hindustani and Karnatak Ragas, Vol. 4*. Madras, India: The Music Academy.

Shankar, Ravi
1968   *Ravi Shankar: My Music, My Life*. New Delhi, India: Vikas Publishing House Pvt. Ltd.

Singh, Lal Bahadur
1977   *Rag Yaman, Tintal, Sangeet Sagar.* Hathras, India: Sangeet Karyalaya.

Stewart, Rebecca Marie
1974   *The Tabla in Perspective.* Ph.D. Dissertation, University of California (UMI: Ann Arbor).


## GENERAL MUSIC

Courtney, David R.
1990   "The Value of Musical Training", *Informensa.* Houston: Gulf Coast Mensa. Vol. 23, No 9, September 1990 pp. 35.
1991   "Introduction to MIDI", *Syntax,* Tomball: CHUG Inc., Tomball: Dec./Jan 1991: pp. 11-13.
1991   "MIDI Protocol", *Syntax.* Tomball: CHUG Inc. Dec./Jan 1991: pp. 14-19.

Diagram Visual Information Ltd.
1976   *Musical Instruments of the World.* New York: Facts on File Publications.

Randel, Don Michael
1978   *Harvard Concise Dictionary of Music.* Cambridge Mass: Belknap Press of Harvard University Press.


## INDIAN DANCE

Courtney, David R.
1988   "*Kathak Maestro Pt. Anju Babu*", Indo-American News. Houston. Sat, Aug. 20 1988: pp. 13.

Shrivastava, Harish Chandra
1973   *Kathak Nritya Parichay.* Allahabad: Sangeet Sadan Prakashan.

# LANGUAGE

Kapoor, R.K.
no date *Kamal's Advanced Illustrated Oxford Dictionary of Hindi-English.* Delhi, India: Verma Book Depot.

Barz, R.K.
1977 *An Introduction to Hindi and Urdu.* Canberra, Australia: Australian National University Press.

Fallon, S.W
1984 *A New Hindustani-English Dictionary: With Illustrations from Hindustani Literature and Folklore.* Allahabad: Bharti Bhandar.

Ganathe, N.S.R.
1981 *Learn Urdu in 30 Days.* Madras: Balaji Publications.

Greaves, Edwin
1983 *Hindi Grammar.* New Delhi: Asian Educational Services.

Nathani, Sultan
1992 *Urdu for Pleasure.* Bombay: Emms Art Printers.

Srinivasachary, K.
1983 *Learn Sanskrit in 30 Days.* Madras: Balaji Publications.

Van Olphen, H.H.
1992 *Hindi Pravesikaa-Beginners Hindi: Writing and Conversation.* Austin: University of Texas.

# MISC.

Allami, Abu I-Fazl
Circa 1590 *Ain-i Akbari.* (Translated by H. Blockmann). Delhi: New Taj Office.

Carterette, Edward C.K. Vaughn, and N Jairazbhoy
1989 "Perceptual, Acoustical, and Musical Aspects of the Tambura Drone". *Music Perception*. Winter 1989, Vol. 7 No 2, 75-108. Berkeley: University of Califomia Press.

Courtney, David R.
1989 "Timbre: Psycho-Acoustic Considerations", *Svar Gnyan*. Houston: Sur Sangeet Services. September 1989 p. 3.
1994 "Freemasonry in India", *The North Carolina Mason*. Raleigh, NC: Grand Lodge of AF&AM of N. Carolina: Jan/Feb: 1994; Vol. CXIX No 1: pp. 6.
1994 "Electronic Aids in Indian Music Education", *Technological Directions in Music Education*. San Antonio: Institute for Music Research, University of San Antonio: 1994; pp. 32-40.
1988 "Alla Rakha", *Svar Gnyan*. Houston: Sur Sangeet Services. October, 1988: pp. 2.
1991 "Tuning the Tabla: A Psychoacoustic Perspective", *Percussive Notes*. Urbana Ill: Percussive Arts Society Vol. 29, No 3, February 1991: pp. 59-61.
1991 "The Application of the C=64 to Indian Music: A Review". *Syntax*: Tomball. June/July 1991: pp. 8-9.
1992 "Bridges: An Indian Perspective", *Experimental Musical Instruments*. Nicasio, CA: EMI Vol. 7, No 5, April 1992: pp8-11.
1993 "Repair and Maintenance of Tabla", *Percussive Notes*. Lawton OK: Percussive Arts Society, October 1993; Vol. 31, No 7: pp29-36.

Mallory, J.P.
1989 *In Search of the Indo-Europeans; Language Archeology and Myth*. London: Thames and Hudson Ltd.

Mukri, Naseem
1990 *Junoon*. Bombay: Intel Communications.

Mishra, Balaram
1979 *Konark*. Bhubaneshwar. Bibarani Prakashani.

# INDEX

abhog, 61
achalla swar, 8
aeolian mode, 10
aesthetics (of rag), 16
alap (instrumental), 54
alap (vocal), 60
amir khusru, 3, 63
antara, 61
arabic script, 73
arabic, 69
arohana, 13
asawari (rag), 134-144
asawari that, 10, 131-134, 212, 216, 220, 224, 228, 232, 236, 240, 244, 248, 252, 256
audav jati, 13
avanaddh, 47-53
avarohana, 13
avartan, 20
bansuri, 31-32
bengali, 76
bhairav that, 11
bhairav that, 145-148, 213, 217, 221, 225, 229, 233, 237, 241, 245, 249, 253, 257
bhairav (rag), 148-157, 162-172
bhairavi that, 11, 159-162, 213, 217, 221, 225, 229, 233, 237, 241, 245, 249, 253, 257
bhajan ka theka, 24
bhajan, 63-64, 69-70
bhakti movement, 69
bhatkhande, 3
bilawal (rag), 82-87

bilawal that, 10, 79-82, 211, 215, 219, 223, 227, 231, 235, 239, 243, 247, 251, 255
bin, 34
bol, 20
brihaddeshi, 3
brijbhasha, 69-70
cabas, 29
carnatic sangeet, 4
chautal, 25
dadra (song), 63, 70
dadra tal, 24, 65
daf, 52
dance, 55
devanagari, 71-72
dhaivat, 8
dhammar (singing), 62
dholak, 50
dholki, 51
dhrupad, 61-62, 101-103
dhun, 64
dilruba, 46
dorian mode, 10
dotar, 41
dynamics, 54
ektal, 23
ektar, 42-43
esraj, 45
film song, 65
fipple flute, 31
gandhar, 8
gandharva, 2
gat, 55
geet, 65

gender (hindustani), 75
ghali, 70
ghan - see non-membranous percussive
ghatam, 29
ghazal, 65, 70
ghunghuru, 30
gotuvadyam, 39
grammar (hindustani), 74
harmonium, 34-35
hindi script - see devanagari
hindi, 69, 71
hindustani (language), 68
hindustani sangeet (introduction), 4
indo-european theory, 2, 68
instrumental styles, 54-55
ionian mode, 10
jal tarang, 28
jati, 13
jhala, 55
jhaptal, 22
jor, 54
kafi (rag), 118-129
kafi that, 10, 115-118, 212, 216, 220, 224, 228, 232, 236, 240, 244, 248, 252, 256
kaherava tal, 24, 65
kalyan rag, 92-103
kalyan that, 11, 89-92, 211, 215, 219, 223, 227, 231, 235, 239, 243, 247, 251, 255
kanjira, 53
kartal, 31
kash tarang, 28
khali, 20
khammaj (rag), 108-113
khammaj that, 10, 105-108, 212, 216, 220, 224, 228, 232, 236, 240, 244, 248, 256
kheyal, 62, 70
khol, 50-51
kirtan, 64

komal, 8
lakshan-geet, 61
laya (tempo), 20
lydian mode, 11
madhya saptak, 12
madhyam, 8
mandra saptak, 12
manjira, 29
marwa (rag), 188-194
marwa that, 11, 185-187, 214, 218, 222, 226, 230, 234, 238, 242, 246, 250, 254, 258
matanga, 3
matra, 20
mian-ki-todi, 198-205
mixolydian mode, 10
mode, 10, 13
modes (7 ancient), 2
modulation - see murchana
mridangam, 49-50
murchang, 29
mythology, 2
nadaswaram, 36
nagada, 51
natya shastra, 3
nishadh, 8
nomtom, 60
octave, 12
ornamentation, 16
pakad, 14
pakhawaj, 48-49
paluskar, 3
pancham, 8
persia (influence over music), 3
persian script, 73
persian (language), 69
phrygian mode, 11
plucked stringed instruments, 37
proto-indo-european, 68
pungi, 34
punjabi, 76
purvi (rag), 176-182

purvi that, 11, 173-176, 213, 217,
    221, 225, 229, 233, 237, 241,
    245, 249, 253, 257
qawwali, 64
rabab, 38
rabindra sangeet, 76
rag (introduction), 13
rag (times), 14
ragmala (old taxonomy of rags), 15
ravi shankar, 37
rishabh, 8
rudra vina, 39
rupak tal, 22, 65
sam, 20, 95
samavadi, 14
samay - see rag (times)
sampurna jati, 13
samveda, 2
sanchari, 61
sangeet (definition), 1
sangeet ratnakar, 3
sanskrit, 2, 63, 68-69
santur, 42
saptak, 12
sarangi, 44
saringda, 47
sarod, 39
see non-membranous percussive, 28
shabad, 64
shadaj, 8
shadav jati, 13
shankh, 35-36
sharangdev, 3
shehnai, 33
shuddha swar, 9-10
sitar, 37
sthai, 60
surbahar, 39
surmandal, 43
sushir, 31
swar, 8
swarmalika, 60

tabla tarang, 50
tabla, 47-48
tali, 20
tambura - see tanpura
tanpura, 40
tansen, 3
tappa, 64
tar saptak, 12
tarana, 62-63
tat - see plucked stringed
    instruments
tavil, 52
test questions, 261-272
that, 10-11
theka, 20-21
thumri, 63
tihai, 100
tintal, 21
tivra, 8
todi that, 11, 195-198, 214, 218,
    222, 226, 230, 234, 238, 242,
    246, 250, 254, 258
turkish 69
urdu (script), 73-74
urdu calligraphy, 74-75
urdu, 69-71
vadi, 14
venu, 32
vibhag, 20
vichitra vina, 40
vina, 38
vitat, 43-47

# AUTHORS

**DAVID COURTNEY** is the primary author of this work.

He has been performing on the *tabla* since 1972. He first studied *pakhawaj* (an ancient barrel shaped drum) under the famous Zakir Hussain at the Ali Akbar College of Music. He then moved to India and spent a number of years learning *tabla* under the late Ustad Shaik Dawood Khan of Hyderabad. He is also well versed in *dilruba*, and *esraj*. For these instruments, he received his initial training under Sayed-ur-Rahman of Hyderabad and later under Pdt. Atma Ram Sharma. He has also received training in *santur* under the late Hasaan Mohd., and *sarangi* under Mohd. Aslam Khan. He has performed extensively on stage, TV, disk, and radio, in India, Europe and the United States. He has accompanied many great musicians including Ashish Khan, Lakshmi Shankar, and Pandit Jasraj.

He is well versed in the academic side of music. During the 80s he received great acclaim in academic circles for his pioneering work in the application of computers to Indian music. This work is found in his dissertation *A Low Cost System for the Computerization of North Indian Classical Music*. He is the author of numerous books and articles on the subject of Indian music including: *Introduction to Tabla*, *Learning the Tabla*, *Fundamentals of Tabla*, *Advanced Theory of Tabla*, *Manufacture and Repair of Tabla*, *Learning the Sitar*, and *Focus on the Kaidas of Tabla*. His articles have appeared in "Modern Drummer" and "Percussive Notes". Along with his wife Chandra, he was given an award of recognition for outstanding contributions to the arts by the American Telugu Association. In 2009, he and his wife were designated as "Cultural Jewels of India" by the Indian Cultural Centre of Houston. He has also released his memoir, *An American in Hyderabad: Life in India in the 1970s*.

He is also active in progressive politics. He twice ran for the position of Texas State Senate, and served one term as the Treasurer for the Texas State Green Party.

**CHANDRAKANTHA COURTNEY** is coauthor of this book and sang on most of the recordings in the companion CDs.

She was born in Macchalipatnam on Feb 2, 1954. She began to sing professionally as a child. She was a regular contributor to Balala Karyakramam in All

India Radio, Vijaywada, and was attached to Suvartha Vani, Bhavana Kala Samiti, Rasana Samaikhya. In 1971, she enrolled in the Govt. College of Music and Dance (Vijaywada) and trained under J.V. Subba Rao until 1975 when she moved to Hyderabad. She then became an artist with AIR (Hyderabad) and Swara Tharangini. When the TV station was established she then became a regular artist in Doordarshan (Hyderabad). In 1977 she was an artist in the Om International troupe which toured South Africa, Malaysia, Singapore, and Mauritius. In 1978, she married David Courtney, who brought her to the United States in 1980. She has been teaching Indian classical vocal in the Houston area since this time.

In 1990, she became a board member of the Texas Institute for Indian Studies. In 1994 she was awarded the "Artist of the Year" by Asian Women Magazine. It was in 1995, that she gave a number of programs in Germany under the sponsorship of the Deutsch Indische Geselschaft. Subsequently she has given numerous performances in Germany and the UK under the sponsorship of a variety of organizations. In 1996 she was given (along with her husband) the "Award of Excellence" for her artistic contributions in the field of music by the American Telugu Association. Along with her husband, she was designated as a "Cultural Jewel of India" by the Indian Cultural Centre" of Houston.

Her activities are not limited to traditional Indian music. She is also the female vocalist with the band "Vani". This is a band which specializes in a genre of fusion called "Raga Rock".

It is impossible to enumerate 40 years of her professional career. She is a teacher, performer, and active promoter of Indian culture. She has traveled all over India working hard to maintain the cultural traditions. She regularly performs in elementary, middle, and senior high schools, and many universities to propagate Indian culture. She has performed on countless cassettes, disks, TV, radio programs, and CDs.

# OTHER BOOKS BY DAVID COURTNEY

**An American in Hyderabad: Life in India in the 1970s**

What was India like before globalisation, call centres, and Bollywood? This author moved to India in 1976 and lived there for a number of years. This book describes what it was like to live, study and marry there.

**Fundamentals of Tabla**

This is a book about the South Asian pair of hand drums known as tabla. This is the first volume of the series, "The Complete Reference for Tabla". It covers basic technique, exercises, and notation. There is a special emphasis on the compositional forms known as Theka and Prakar.

**Focus on the Kaidas of Tabla**

This is the fourth volume of the series, "The Complete Reference for Tabla". This entire book is devoted to the compositional form known as the Kaida. Kaida is the most important approach to theme-and-variation for the tabla.

### Learning the Sitar

The sitar has been popular since the 1960s. Since that time it has always had a considerable mystique among musicians. It also has an undeserved reputation for being difficult to play. This book/CD set cuts though the mystique and misapprehensions and presents the material in a simple fashion that is easily understood.

### Learning the Tabla - Volume 1

The tabla, a hand drum which originated in India, has become very popular throughout the world. This method covers everything you need to know to learn to play the tabla, including the history and parts of the tabla, tuning and maintenance, positioning, basic exercises, and numerous techniques and patterns.

### Learning the Tabla - Volume 2

The Indian tabla is a difficult pair of hand drums, but by no means should it be considered inaccessible. For those who have gone through the introductory Learning the Tabla, this book/ CD set is an ideal next step. It contains much new material which is appropriate for an intermediate level student.

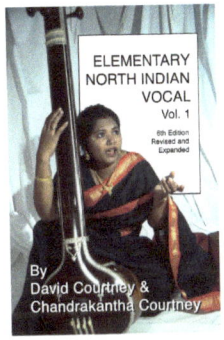

### ELEMENTARY NORTH INDIAN VOCAL: VOL. 1

This is the first volume of a comprehensive instructional set for Hindustani vocal. It covers the basic history, approach, instruments, and 10 thats along with their corresponding rags. There are also a set of optional companion disks.

www.ingramcontent.com/pod-product-compliance
Lightning Source LLC
Chambersburg PA
CBHW042054290426
44111CB00001B/3